CLARENDON ANCIENT HISTORY SERIES

The aim of the CLARENDON ANCIENT HISTORY SERIES is to provide authoritative translations, introductions, and commentaries to a wide range of Greek and Latin texts studied by ancient historians. The books will be of interest to scholars, graduate students, and advanced undergraduates.

Marcus Tullius Cicero

Speeches on Behalf of Marcus Fonteius and Marcus Aemilius Scaurus

Translated with Introduction and Commentary by

ANDREW R. DYCK

OXFORD
UNIVERSITY PRESS

OXFORD
UNIVERSITY PRESS

Great Clarendon Street, Oxford, OX2 6DP,
United Kingdom

Oxford University Press is a department of the University of Oxford.
It furthers the University's objective of excellence in research, scholarship,
and education by publishing worldwide. Oxford is a registered trade mark of
Oxford University Press in the UK and in certain other countries

First Edition published in 2012

Impression: 1

British Library Cataloguing in Publication Data
Data available

Library of Congress Cataloging in Publication Data
Data available

ISBN 978-0-19-959006-3 (HB)
978-0-19-959005-6 (PB)

Printed in Great Britain
on acid-free paper by
MPG Books Group, Bodmin and King's Lynn

For Janis

Preface

On Behalf of M. Fonteius and *On Behalf of M. Scaurus* comprise early and late Ciceronian pleadings before the extortion court (*quaestio de repetundis*) and provide examples of his art of character-drawing and character defamation as well as his ability to stir powerful emotions. Anglophone readers have, however, not been well served by available texts and exegesis. Perhaps because of their fragmentary state of preservation the two speeches were not included in the survey by MacKendrick 1995 or the sets of speeches translated by Berry 2000 and Zetzel 2009. N. H. Watts's 1931 Loeb edition with facing English translation is available but is less than fully satisfactory. In the defence of Scaurus Watts has made Beier's conjectural supplements seem more authoritative than they are by inserting them (albeit italicized) into the Latin text and including an English version in square brackets; nowadays editors banish them from the text. Moreover, Watts is unreliable on some aspects of background and interpretation, confusing, for example, the discoverers of the Ambrosian and Turin palimpsests (p. 264) and raising the claim that the P. Crassus whose suicide is mentioned at *Scaur.* 1 is the son of the triumvir even though he was still alive when the speech was delivered (p. 270nc). Watts likewise has a shaky grip on legal procedure, remarking apropos of the defence of Fonteius 'for some reason the case was adjourned for a second hearing' (p. 307) as if this were an oddity and not standard procedure in extortion trials of the time. For interpretation of the ethnic stereotypes in both speeches readers can find some help in Vasaly 1993: ch. 6, but for detailed exegesis they have had to have recourse to older publications in foreign languages, namely for *Font.* Clemente 1974 and for *Scaur.* Gaumitz 1879. A new English translation and commentary on these speeches is thus overdue.

It is a pleasure to thank those who have encouraged and forwarded this project. The series editors, in particular Susan Treggiari and Miriam Griffin, as well as the Press's reader, Andrew Lintott, have contributed many suggestions that have improved the MS throughout; Robert A. Kaster was so kind as to allow maps from his *Speech on Behalf of Publius Sestius* to be adapted for use in the present volume; and Hilary O'Shea and her staff at OUP have been unfailingly helpful at every stage. My greatest debt is indicated in the dedication. I bear sole responsibility for any remaining errors.

A.R.D.

Los Angeles, California

Contents

List of Maps

Abbreviations

CAH	*The Cambridge Ancient History*. 2nd edn. 14 vols. Cambridge, 1984–2005
CIL	*Corpus inscriptionum Latinarum*. 17 vols. Berlin, 1863–
ESAR	T. Frank (ed.), *An Economic Survey of Ancient Rome*. 5 vols. + index vol. Baltimore, 1933–40
FGrH	F. Jacoby (ed. and comm.), *Die Fragmente der griechischen Historiker*. Berlin and Leiden, 1923–
gram.	*Grammaticae Romanae fragmenta*, ed. H. Funaioli. Vol. 1. Leipzig, 1907
ILS	H. Dessau (ed.), *Inscriptiones Latinae selectae*. Berlin, 1892–1916
LIMC	*Lexicon Iconographicum Mythologiae Classicae*. 18 vols. Zurich, 1981–99
LTUR	E. M. Steinby (ed.), *Lexicon Topographicum Urbis Romae*. 6 vols. Rome, 1993–2000
MRR	T. R. S. Broughton, *Magistrates of the Roman Republic*. 3 vols. New York 1951–Atlanta, 1986
OCD	S. Hornblower and A. Spawforth (eds.), *The Oxford Classical Dictionary*. 3rd edn. Oxford and New York, 1996
OLD	*Oxford Latin Dictionary*. Oxford 1968
orat.	*Oratorum Romanorum Fragmenta*, ed. H. Malcovati. 4th ed. Turin, 1976
RE	G. Wissowa and W. Kroll (eds.), *Paulys Realencyclopädie der classischen Altertumswissenschaft*. 34 vols. in 68 + index and 15 supplements. Stuttgart, 1893–1980
RLM	K. Halm (ed.), *Rhetores Latini Minores*. Leipzig, 1863
RRC	M. H. Crawford, *Roman Republican Coinage*. 2 vols. Cambridge, 1974
RS	M. H. Crawford (ed.), *Roman Statutes*. 2 vols. London, 1996
TLL	*Thesaurus Linguae Latinae*. Leipzig, 1900–
TLRR	M. C. Alexander, *Trials of the Late Roman Republic, 149 BC to 50 BC*. Toronto, 1990

General Introduction

1. THE EXTORTION COURT (*QUAESTIO DE REPETUNDIS*): FUNCTION AND HISTORY[1]

The third-century military encounters with Carthage led Rome to acquire her first overseas territories: much of Sicily by the end of the First Punic War (264–41), Sardinia in 227, and Spain established as two provinces in 197 in the aftermath of the Second Punic War (218–202). Though in each case Rome put an administration in place headed by a promagistrate, she was slow to develop a formal system for bringing corrupt provincial governors to book. Thus when in 172 Spanish envoys went to the senate to complain that their people had been plundered and humiliated by several previous governors, a special tribunal was empanelled consisting of five assessors (*recuperatores*) of senatorial rank presided over by the praetor who had been allotted Spain as a province (*MRR* 1, 416). An impressive group of advocates (*patroni*) were found to represent the plaintiffs: M. Porcius Cato, L. Aemilius Paullus, P. Cornelius Scipio Nasica, and C. Sulpicius Gallus. One of the defendants, M. Titinius (pr. 178), was acquitted; the other two, P. Furius Philus (pr. 174) and M. Matienus (pr. 173), went into voluntary exile after the first adjournment of the trial.[2]

In 149 an extraordinary court was proposed to consider charges of misconduct levelled against Ser. Sulpicius Galba in connection with his governorship of Lusitania the previous year; the proposal failed (*TLRR* 1). Perhaps moved in part by that failure, L. Calpurnius Piso Frugi as tribune of the plebs that year carried the first law regulating

[1] The approach taken here has been much influenced by Lintott 1981; dates throughout are BC unless otherwise indicated.

[2] Livy 43.2; for this and other such cases prior to 149 cf. Lintott 1981, 164–72.

extortion.[3] The *lex Calpurnia* established the first standing court (*quaestio perpetua*) at Rome. This court was established, according to C., 'for the sake of the allies' (*Ver.* 2.2.15, 3.127 and 218, 5.126; similarly *Div. Caec.* 17–18). By this enactment the senate recognized that misconduct by public officials in the provinces was an ongoing problem that should be dealt with in a regular forum, rather than on an *ad hoc* basis, as in the past. The procedure was modelled on that of private lawsuits seeking recovery of property or funds (*res* or *pecunias repetere*); hence the name *quaestio de repetundis*, literally 'the court about (funds) to be recovered'. The *lex Calpurnia* called for simple restitution without any additional penalty. The court was to consist of a panel of assessors (*recuperatores*) presided over by the praetor charged with handling disputes between Romans and foreigners (*praetor peregrinus*). The proceedings took the form of a *legis actio sacramento* ('suit by oath') according to which both parties asserted a claim under oath and the court determined which was correct (*iustum*).[4] This form of litigation was otherwise open only to Roman citizens, so it has been questioned whether Piso's law, in fact, benefited Rome's allies;[5] possibly some sort of legal fiction enabled an advocate (*patronus*) to swear on behalf of the allied plaintiff(s); otherwise one would have to assume that the allies still had to obtain authorization from the senate, as the Spaniards had in 172.[6] A *lex Iunia* is known to have intervened between the *lex Calpurnia* and the Gracchan extortion law, but its date and the nature of its modifications of Piso's law remain unclear.[7]

A law recorded on a tablet discovered in Urbino, sometimes called the 'lex Bembina' after Giovanni Bembo, the Venetian merchant and statesman (1473–1545) who was its first owner,[8] evidently represents the next stage of legislation on extortion. On the other side of the tablet is an agrarian law that seems to be identical with the third law

[3] Riggsby 1999*a*, 127, chooses to emphasize that there was no 'immediate triggering event' for Piso's law; while it is true that Galba's murder of some Lusitani and sale of others into slavery would not have fallen within the scope of the *lex Calpurnia*, the situation highlighted the absence of a regular procedure for handling provincials' complaints.

[4] Cf. Rotondi 1912, 292; Berger 1953 s.v. *legis actio sacramento*.

[5] Cf. Richardson 1987.

[6] Cf. Lintott 1992, 15.

[7] It is referred to at lines 23, 74 and (by restoration) 81 of the Urbino law.

[8] On him cf. Ventura and Moretti 1966; the law is also known as the 'lex Acilia' after its presumed sponsor, M'. Acilius Glabrio; see below.

discussed at Appian, *BC* 1.4.27; it is to be dated to 111. The text of the extortion law contains engraving errors at the bottom and was probably turned to the wall and never posted publicly; it will thus be older than the agrarian law.

There now seems to be consensus that the Urbino law represents the Gracchan reform of the extortion process and is likely to be the law carried by the *popularis* tribune M'. Acilius Glabrio to which C. twice refers (*Ver.* 1.51 and 2.1.26). It shows a fundamental rethinking of the whole problem, perhaps spurred by dissatisfaction on the part of the allies, since not a single conviction of a provincial governor in a public extortion trial is attested from 149 to 123.[9] The law removes a conflict of interest that must have been felt by senatorial jurors who might themselves one day face such a court, leverages state power to provide incentives to the prosecutor, and adds a punitive element as a deterrent. The prosecution begins with the laying of information against an individual (*nominis delatio*) before a praetor. The plaintiff can request certain advocates (*patroni*) or reject unsuitable ones. Rewards are made available for the successful prosecutor, such as citizenship (in the case of a non-citizen) or exemption from military service. Though the prosecutor could call as many as forty-eight witnesses and provide documentary evidence to the court, there is no indication that an onsite investigation in the province was available. The trial was divided into two parts, the determination of guilt or innocence (*in iure*) and, in the event of a guilty verdict, the assessment of damages (*litis aestimatio*); the punitive element consists in the exaction of a double penalty, rather than simple restitution, and exclusion from future participation as a juror in this court. The jury was to be non-senatorial (presumably equestrian, though this provision is not preserved) and to consist of fifty members. The compulsory adjournment after the first proceeding (*comperendinatio*), provision for recovery from the final recipient of the money (*quo ea pecunia pervenerit*),[10] and a contest among alternative prosecutors (*divinatio*) are not yet found.[11]

[9] Three acquittals are attested: *TLRR* 8, 9, and 23; in one case the trial was interrupted when the defendant was convicted in a family court presided over by his father and committed suicide (*TLRR* 7).

[10] See below.

[11] For text and commentary cf. Lintott 1992, 73 ff.; *RS* 65 ff.

Riding a tide of reaction against the preceding consulship of the *popularis* C. Marius, Q. Servilius Caepio was elected consul for 106. Called the 'patron of the senate' (V. Max. 6.9.13), he restored senators to the jury panels, probably as one component of mixed juries (Livy's epitomators represented by Cassiod. *chron.* under 106 and Obseq.), rather than as the sole jurors (so Tac. *An.* 12.60).[12] A further innovation of the *lex Servilia Caepionis* is likely to have been the limitation on the allies' choice of prosecutor by the process of *divinatio* in which several prospective prosecutors argued their claims before a jury.[13]

Very different in tendency was the *lex Servilia Glauciae* carried by C. Servilius Glaucia (tr. pl. 101, pr. 100), an associate of the revolutionary L. Appuleius Saturninus. Glaucia's law, probably carried either in 104 or 100,[14] rescinded a provision of Caepio by restoring the juries to the equites. Glaucia's law also provided for the first time for recovery from the final recipient of the money (*quo ea pecunia pervenerit*).[15] A procedural innovation of Glaucia's law was to divide the trial into two sessions (*actiones*) separated by the compulsory adjournment (*comperendinatio* (*Ver.* 2.1.26)), a provision that may in practice have restricted the use of repetition (*ampliatio*) of a pleading when the jury found the case to have been insufficiently clarified. Formal inquiry by the prosecutor in the affected province (*inquisitio*) is known to have been instituted by the time of the mutual prosecutions of Scaurus and Caepio *c.*92/91 (cf. *TLRR* 96 and 97); this feature, too, is likely to have been added by Glaucia since it is a sharpening of prosecutorial power.

The laws so far discussed provide remedies for Roman allies who complained of misconduct by Roman officials and, beginning with the *lex Acilia*, a criminal penalty for misconduct. Another approach to governance was to provide directives as to permissible conduct. As praetor in Sardinia, Cato the Elder gave an example by curtailing allies' expenditures for the maintenance of the governor and his staff

[12] Cf. Balsdon 1938, 102 ff.

[13] Cf. Lintott 1981, 188.

[14] It has been argued that Glaucia's law may have dated from an earlier tribunate, in 104, because C. Fimbria (cos. 104) was tried by equestrian jurors (*Font.* 26); but the evidence is also compatible with Fimbria's having been prosecuted after a praetorship (prior to 106) under the *lex Acilia*; cf. Lintott 1981, 189 with literature; *TLRR* 61.

[15] *Rab. Post.* 8; the provision was also incorporated into the *lex Cornelia* and *lex Iulia* (see below); C. Rabirius Postumus was alleged to have violated this; cf. *TLRR* 305; Klodt 1992, 52–9; Siani-Davies 2001, 90–1; Alexander 2002, 111–16.

(Livy 32.27.4), and his conduct was evidently the model for the legislation carried *c.*101 by his great-grandson, also named M. Cato, that limited a governor's impositions on the allies (and also his power of intervening in a province not assigned to him).[16] This law, which may have been coordinated with Caepio's as part of the same legislative programme, is the precursor of the elaborate rules for gubernatorial conduct embodied in the *lex Iulia* (59).

Sulla restored senatorial juries to all the standing courts (*quaestiones perpetuae*), including that for extortion, presumably in a separate *lex Cornelia* governing each.[17] He retained the competition among prospective prosecutors (*divinatio*), the prosecutor's onsite investigation in the province (*inquisitio*), the compulsory adjournment (*comperendinatio*), and the possibility of demanding restitution from the final recipient (*quo ea pecunia pervenerit*). The evidence also suggests that under the Sullan extortion law the charge could rise to a capital level (though it did not need to do) and could include the taking of bribes by a juror.[18] A *lex Aurelia* of 70 modified Sulla's provisions by revising the jury rolls of all the standing courts, the extortion court included, in such a way that they henceforth consist in equal parts of three groups, the senators, the equites, and the *tribuni aerarii*, a group with the same property qualification as the equites.[19] Fonteius was tried under the *lex Cornelia* so modified (cf. 36n.).

Julius Caesar's consular law of 59 represents the final stage of Republican legislation on extortion. The *lex Iulia* continues and adds detail to restrictions on governors' conduct of office initiated in the *lex Porcia* and further elaborated in the *lex Cornelia de maiestate*:[20] the governor could not enter another province or an allied kingdom without senatorial permission; was restricted in his requisitions of grain, money, and other commodities; had to respect privileges and immunities that the senate had granted to individuals or groups; and had to deposit copies of his accounts in two cities in the

[16] There appears to be a reference to this law at col. III lines 4–5 of the Cnidos inscription published by Hassall *et al.* 1974, 202, as well as in the Antonian law about the citizens of Termessus (*RS* p. 334, ll. 16–17).

[17] For his extortion law cf. Rotondi 1912, 360.

[18] Cf. the detailed argument from *Clu.* 115–16 at Lintott 1981, 198–201; it is possible that Caepio was the first to include these provisions; for the taking of bribes cf. also *Dig.* 48.11.7 (*lex Iulia*).

[19] Rotondi 1912, 369; Berger 1953 s.v. *tribuni aerarii*.

[20] On this cf. Rotondi 1912, 360; *Dig.* 48.11.

province and with the urban quaestor at Rome upon his return. There were likewise new procedural rules: the maximum number of witnesses to be called by the prosecution was raised to 120 (from 48), the number of assistants who could accompany the prosecutor to the province was restricted and documentary evidence gathered was to be deposited with the praetor and sealed with the jurors' seals. Brutality (*saevitia*) was probably proscribed in some form, though the provision is not directly attested.[21] Scaurus' trial was conducted under this law.

In 4 BC the *senatusconsultum Calvisianum* added an alternative, expedited procedure for provincials seeking only simple restitution without criminal penalties. It harked back to the procedure used to deal with the Spaniards' complaints in 171: the injured party or parties would apply directly to the senate, which would appoint a board of five senatorial assessors (*recuperatores*) with instructions to complete the process within thirty days.[22]

With the *senatusconsultum Calvisianum* granting the allies a tool for redressing their grievances, the Romans returned to their original aim in dealing with extortion by officials in the provinces. In the interim the extortion court had become a football in the political struggle between the equites and the senate and a vehicle for imposing strict standards of conduct on provincial governors; these developments had entailed some marginalization of the provincials even though their complaints continued to form the starting point for litigation.

2. A NOTE ON THE TRANSLATIONS

Effective rhetoric in a Roman court of the first century BC is very different from that of an anglophone court of the twenty-first century. One can move all the words across the linguistic divide but yet lose the effect. C. plays the Latin language as a virtuoso does an instrument, with supreme mastery of all its various registers and resources; no translator can begin to approximate the many shadings

[21] It was an item in the prosecution of Scaurus (cf. F 7n) and in extortion trials under the Empire; cf. Lintott 1981, 205; Henderson 1951, 74–5; Riggsby 1999*a*, 125.

[22] Cf. Lintott 1981, 206 with literature.

and subtleties, the coordinated effects of diction, figures of speech, word order, and rhythm. I have tried to approximate the sense in a fairly standard mid-Atlantic English and produce a version that can be read on its own, not merely a crib for readers of the Latin text. But the commentary must be consulted about the special qualities of the Latin since they are often difficult or impossible to represent in English.

On Behalf of Marcus Fonteius

INTRODUCTION

1. The Romans and Transalpine Gaul

Gaul beyond the Alps was an area primarily of Celtic settlement with some Ligurians and Iberians in the south and German inroads in the north-east. Besides the fertile soil of the river valleys, the resources included copper and silver, which were mined from early times. Finds show a population distributed in fortified villages, usually numbering in the hundreds, with peasants cultivating nearby fields and artisans plying crafts. The southern littoral enjoys a mild climate where olive trees and other Mediterranean vegetation flourish and so proved attractive to Greek colonists who settled at Massilia (modern Marseilles), a Greek colony founded from Phocis *c.*600, and later to Romans as well. Roman traders were active in southern Gaul from the fourth century BC on, as finds of pottery and, to a lesser extent, coin-hoards show.[1]

Rome's earliest relations in the region were with Massilia, which during the Hannibalic War supplied the Romans with both intelligence and naval assistance.[2] Rome's early interventions in the region were in support of this ally. Thus in 154 Rome sent troops to protect Massilia's colonies Antipolis and Nicaea against encroachment by two Ligurian tribes, the Deciates and Oxybii, and to avenge an attack on the Roman envoy Flaminius; upon their defeat the consul Q. Opimius handed over a portion of their territory to Massilia.[3] Similarly, in 125 an attack of the Salluvii on Massiliote territory triggered the dispatch of Roman troops under the consul M. Fulvius

[1] Clemente 1974, 112–14.

[2] For early intelligence cf. Livy 21.18.1 and 20.8; in general Rivet 1988, 37.

[3] Cf. Rivet 1988, ch. 2.

Flaccus, who in 123 celebrated a triumph over the Salluvii, other Ligurians, and the Vocontii. The following year saw further military action, this time involving the consul C. Sextius Calvinus, who in due course triumphed over the Salluvii and Vocontii and established the first permanent Roman outpost, the fort at Aquae Sextiae (modern Aix-en-Provence).[4] Further hostilities with the Arverni and Allobroges followed in 122–1 and culminated in great victories by Cn. Domitius Ahenobarbus at Vindalium and Q. Fabius Maximus at the confluence of the Isar (modern Isère) and the Rhodanus (modern Rhône); cf. 12n. The former built the Via Domitia, still the major thoroughfare between Narbo and the Pyrenees in C.'s day (18). In the following period the Romans tended to view the Transalpina as an export market for wine (indicated by finds of Italian amphorae) and a communications link valuable for the defence of Spain.[5]

More substantial Roman involvement followed when in 118 L. Licinius Crassus carried in the teeth of the nobles' opposition a law for establishing the first Roman colony north of the Alps at Narbo Martius; the plan will have been implemented within the next several years. Other Romans followed in the colonists' wake to serve their needs and to exploit emerging business opportunities. Such an immigrant was C. Quinctius, the brother of Cicero's client P. Quinctius, who owned in partnership with another Roman, Sextus Naevius, a well-managed cattle-farm in Gaul (*Quinct.* 12). Gradually the infrastructure developed as described by C.: 'so many businessmen, settlers, publicans, farmers, cattle-breeders' (12). Large-scale urbanization followed only from the Augustan period onward.[6]

In 90 yet another rising of the Salluvii had to be put down by C. Coelius Caldus.[7] Perhaps around this time Transalpine Gaul was first organized as a Roman province. The first known governor is one L. Manlius, who campaigned unsuccessfully in Aquitania and Spain.[8] M. Aemilius Lepidus (cos. 78) was assigned both Gauls in 78 but revolted, marched on Rome, was defeated, and died in Sardinia.[9] Fonteius is the next governor known to us by name.[10]

[4] Ibid. 39–40.
[5] Cf. Clemente 1974, 21–71; Badian 1966, 904.
[6] Cf. sketch by C. Goudineau, *CAH* x. 471–87; detailed study by Christol 2010: 41 ff.
[7] Livy per. 73; cf. Badian 1964, 93–6.
[8] 'Apparently 78' according to Brunt 1971, 464.
[9] *MRR ii.* 89; Badian 1966, 910–11; Labruna 1976.
[10] Brunt 1971, 465, conjectures that Mam. Aemilius (cos. 77) succeeded to the governorship of both Gauls abandoned by Lepidus.

2. Fonteius' Career to 74

The Fonteii were a plebeian family of Tusculum. The earliest known member was a M. Fonteius (pr. 166; *MRR* i. 437). If he was praetor in 75 (see below), our M. Fonteius will have been born by 115. The defendant's father, whose praenomen is not attested, was killed by an angry mob in Asculum as a legate of the praetor Q. Servilius in late 91 or early 90, the immediate cause of the Social War (ibid. ii. 20, and 23; Thomasson 1991, 108, 90). C.'s words at 41 ('unbroken series of praetorships') imply that his father and grandfather also attained that office. His sister, a Vestal Virgin by 91/90, and his mother were both still living at the date of the trial: 46–7 with n; the relation to a Manius Fonteius, moneyer (*triumvir monetalis*) in 85 (*RRC* no. 353), and the legate C. Fonteius (18) is unclear.[11] C.'s client was moneyer before 87[12] and urban quaestor probably in 84 (*MRR* ii. 60; see further 2n.). His financial dealings in both offices gave rise to charges at the trial; cf. 5n. Though C.'s defence of his client's conduct as moneyer is lost in the lacuna at the beginning of the speech, enough survives to show that he was accused as quaestor of skimming a profit on repayments of Rome's public debt at a quarter of the face value as provided for by the Valerian Law of 86; cf. pp. 35–6. He was legate in Spain in 83 (6 with n.); he served as legate in Macedonia at a time of Thracian incursions, i.e. probably in 77–76 under the governorship of Ap. Claudius Pulcher (cos. 79), who is known to have battled the Thracians; see 44n. If so and if his tenure of Gaul was 74–72 (see below), the praetorship of 75 would be indicated (*MRR ii.* 97 with query; *MRR* iii. 93).

3. Fonteius' Governorship of Gaul

At issue in the trial was Fonteius' governorship of Gaul, which was of three years' duration (32). The onset has been placed in every year from 77 to 74.[13] The onset of his tenure must, however, have been

[11] Since Manius was the son of a Gaius, perhaps he and the legate were brothers; in that case they will have been cousins of the defendant; cf. Schneider 1876, 2 and 18n.

[12] So with a query *RRC* no. 347.

[13] Coskun 2006, 356 n. 6, cites the relevant literature, to which may be added Brennan 2000, 509–11, arguing for 77–75.

after the fall of 77 when, on his way to Spain, Pompey put down a revolt of the Sallyes and stripped them of territory (14). Again, during Fonteius' tenure Pompey's troops wintered in Gaul (16); this occurred twice, in 77–76 and 74–73. Perhaps the best clue is the reference to the Romans' waging of war 'in the whole world' (13), which seems to glance at the war with Mithridates, active again beginning in 74. If he was legate in Macedonia 77–76 (see above), then praetor in Rome in 75, the governorship can be plausibly set in 74–72. The late dating of the governorship also seems most plausible because it yields the shortest interval between it and the trial (see the next section).

The prosecution's major complaint against Fonteius appears to have been that during his tenure of office he allowed his province to fall massively into debt (11) (and that he siphoned some of the money for himself). In spite of C.'s obfuscation (ibid.), the debtors will have been for the most part the Gauls, who were subject to exactions in specie, kind, and cavalry; these must have steeply risen to support the war effort in neighbouring Spain and also, after 74, in Asia (13, quoted above); the fact that the Romans resident in Gaul supported Fonteius (15) shows that they largely benefited (e.g. as money-lenders) rather than suffered under his regime. Certainly the war that Pompey waged in Spain against the Marian rebel Q. Sertorius (pr. 83) was the major event in this part of the world between 77 and 71.[14] On his way to Spain Pompey cleared away resistance and did the essential work of reorganizing Transalpina;[15] Fonteius was left to mop up, execute any unfinished business in the province, and assist Pompey's efforts in Spain by supplying cavalry, food, and money (*Font.* 12–13); hence the improvement of the road system proved to be an urgent need (ibid. 17–18).[16]

The Gauls' subsidiary complaints are as follows: (1) in administering the roadwork, including the major thoroughfare, the Via Domitia, Fonteius accepted bribes to secure exemptions or to certify shoddy work (17–18); (2) he devised at Rome a new duty on wine, presumably involving kickbacks paid to himself (see on 19 and p. 12); (3) he waged war on the Vocontii (20); (4) he distributed winter quarters unfairly

[14] Cf. the narrative by Seager, *CAH* ix. 215–23.

[15] *Font.* 14; Ebel 1975.

[16] It has been suggested, in view of other appointments in the region around this time, that Fonteius may have been 'Pompey's man'; cf. 11n.

(ibid.). C. responds to (1) with a simple denial that bribes were accepted and a claim that some work was denied certification, but the assertions are short on proof; these arguments are combined with an attempt to fob off responsibility on to the legates in charge, C. Annius Bellienus and C. Fonteius (though this would not free the governor of responsibility; cf. 18n.). C.'s responses to the other charges are either incomplete (2) or not preserved at all ((3) and (4)).

4. The Prosecution

The prosecution was conducted by two men, M. Fabius and M. Plaetorius Cestianus. Fabius is known only from C.'s brief reference to him as the junior prosecutor (*subscriptor*) in this case (36);[17] the family had ties of patronage to the Allobroges going back to their conquest by Q. Fabius Maximus (cos. 121). In the passage that alludes to Fabius, C. also mentions Plaetorius, for whom the Gauls are said to be 'new clients'; possibly Fabius won the young man's collaboration. C. speaks of Plaetorius, possibly ironically, as a friend (36); ties of friendship did in any case not deter C. from launching a scurrilous joke at the expense of his late mother (F 13). Plaetorius appears to have served as quaestor by the date of the trial (cf. 1n.). His further career included curule aedile (67?), presidency of the homicide court (*quaestio inter sicarios*) (66), the praetorship (64?) and a promagistracy in Macedonia (63–62; all dates as in *MRR* ii. 601); by December 51 he had suffered some misfortune: C. speaks, perhaps metaphorically, of 'Plaetorius' fire' (*Att.* 5.20(113).8); he is not heard of again.

Fonteius was prosecuted after the Aurelian Law (70) enlarged the jury pool to include equites and *tribuni aerarii* (another citizen group meeting a property qualification) as well as senators (cf. p. 5 and 36n.). The trial is usually dated to 69 on the assumption that the prosecutors would have wanted to proceed as quickly as possible. Coskun 2006, 358–61, is keen to accommodate the trial in 70. But though the Aurelian Law was promulgated before the date scheduled for the beginning of the second session of Verres' trial (*c.*20 September: *Ver.* 2.5.177–8), it is not clear when it was passed or how quickly a new list of jurors could be drawn up. There was also need for Indutiomarus and other witnesses to travel from Gaul for the

[17] Cf. Münzer, *RE* s.v. Fabius 26.

occasion. Nor is the absence from the extant remains of the name of Metellus Pius, who was also fighting in Spain at this time, decisive, even though M. Caecilius Metellus was president of the extortion court in 69; C. may have mentioned the presiding officer's relative in a passage now lost.

If on balance 69 still appears to be the likeliest date for the trial and 74–72 for Fonteius' governorship, the question arises why, if the Gauls were as outraged as C. suggests (cf. 15 with n.), they interposed so long an interval. One suspects that Verres' case[18] as well as the reorganization of the juries so as to break the senatorial monopoly must have given the Gauls hope that they could redress their grievances by litigation, rather than war (though the latter remained an option: 33). It is not excluded, however, that enemies of Fonteius (alluded to by C. at 20) might have wanted to use the trial to block his further career; it has also been suggested that opponents of Pompey might have sought to take advantage of the trial to embarrass him.[19]

5. Cicero's Defence

In some ways C.'s approach looks like a fairly standard defence on charges of extortion. He interprets the case as a whole as an attempt to intimidate Roman governors and make them hesitate to take strong action in the state interest (17). He makes much of the contrast in witnesses (Gauls for the prosecution, Roman citizens and allies for the defence) and the lack of any Roman evidence against his client (4, 14–16, 45–6). He gives the jurors many reasons to distrust the prosecution's Gallic witnesses, from their foreign dress and manners (33) to their impiety towards the gods (and therefore likely perjury) (30–1). Their arrogant talk of war, far from intimidating Romans, should make them want to emulate their ancestors' conquests (36). At the same time C. wants Fonteius to be seen as the loyal servant of Rome's empire in conquering territories and providing money, supplies, and cavalry for the war effort in other theatres (12–13); his military prowess makes him a valuable citizen who should not be discarded at a time when such qualities are rare (42–3). Finally his

[18] Alluded to by C. in the exordium (Jul. Vict. *RLM* p. 400) and no doubt also by the prosecution; see ad loc.

[19] So Ward 1968, 803–5; cf., however, Gruen 1971, 12–13, pointing to the absence of known personal ties between Fonteius and Pompey.

client's family has an honourable record; he points to an unbroken string of praetorships, the death of his father at the hands of a mob in Asculum, the trigger for the Social War, and the service of his client's sister as a Vestal Virgin interceding with the gods on behalf of the Roman people (41, 46–9).

6. The Outcome

Though the extant remains of C.'s defence speech do not really deal adequately with any of the prosecution's charges (though the picture might be different if we had the full speech), it may have struck a chord with the jury nonetheless. In the stirring of emotions C. was an acknowledged master; hence Hortensius ceded him last place in their joint pleadings (cf. *Brut.* 190; *Orat.* 130). In this case he is unlikely to have misread the jurors' susceptibility to resentment of the Gallic witnesses and their behaviour and to patriotic appeals based upon Fonteius' martial prowess and his sister's service as a Vestal Virgin.[20] In addition to these general considerations, there is a potentially relevant passage from a letter dated a little after 23 November 68 in which C. reports the sale of a property in Naples for HS 130,000 to one M. Fonteius (*Att.* 1.6(2).1). This appears to be a house Atticus himself was thinking of purchasing.[21] This looks, then, like a desirable property. On the assumption that the purchaser was C.'s client, the transaction has been interpreted as indication that Fonteius was convicted and is settling into Neapolitan exile.[22] But as an exile he would have to reside in a place outside Roman sovereignty.[23] If the purchaser was C.'s client, he was evidently acquitted.[24] The possibility may also be worth

[20] Cf. North 2000, 363: 'It is hard to believe that the *Pro Fonteio* could have failed to succeed'; similarly Stroh 2008, 30. As Riggsby 1999a, 150, observes, the harm in extortion cases 'is more remote (from the Roman point of view) and so is more easily turned aside by appeals to other values'. Indeed, in Flaccus' case C. is said to have procured acquittal by means of a *bon mot* (Macr. *Sat.* 2.1.13).

[21] Cf. C.'s words: 'I wanted you to know this in case the fact had a bearing on your plans'.

[22] So Schneider 1876, 33–4.

[23] Cf. Kelly 2006, 54–5 and *passim.*

[24] Cf. *TLRR* no. 186 n. 4 with the additional suggestion that, if the property belonged to C., the transaction might have been the reward for a successful defence; C. refers to the house as belonging to one Rabirius (*domus Rabiriana*), however.

raising that the Fonteius (without praenomen) for whose sake C. hurried to Rome in July 54 (*Att.* 4.15(90).6) was our defendant.[25]

7. The Surviving Text

The text of C.'s defence of Fonteius is preserved in two manuscripts, both housed in the Vatican Library: sections 1–6 were discovered on a single palimpsest leaf (Vat. Pal. lat. 24, fr, 9), written in fifth-century uncial and first published in 1820 (P);[26] sections 11 to the end are preserved in Vatican Arch. S. Pietro H. 25 (V), which was written in Northern Italy, perhaps in the second quarter of the ninth century. This manuscript also includes portions of *Against Piso* and *On Behalf of Flaccus* (the latter is run together with and under the same title as our speech); all three speeches are mutilated as a result of the loss of quires I and III–VI, which has been called 'the biggest disaster that can be seen to have occurred in the medieval transmission of Cicero's speeches'.[27] Before its mutilation V was, however, excerpted in the ninth century by Sedulius Scotus; his florilegium came into the possession of Nicholas of Cues (fourteenth century) and is preserved in Cues, Nikolaus Hospitalbibliothek 52, folios 246–73 (twelfth century).[28] Some of the excerpts correspond to matter still extant in V, but nine of them must have appeared on quires now lost; in the text printed here these are included among the fragments with the numeration in Cues's collection indicated after the fragment number. Traditionally the fragments attested in literary sources have been numbered 7–10, i.e. have been placed between the palimpsest material and V's text; but this gives a false notion of the sequence of arguments; in this edition these are instead included with the other fragments[29] at the back of the continuous text.

[25] Broughton, *MRR* ii. 221, posits an otherwise unknown Fonteius as praetor urbanus this year presiding over the Ludi Apollinares; this is possible, but Cicero's statement that he went to see the games (*veni spectatum*) is not necessarily related to his hastening to Rome 'for Fonteius' sake' (*Fontei causa*).

[26] Niebuhr 1820; cf. Lowe 1934, no. 76.

[27] R. H. Rouse and M. D. Reeve in Reynolds 1983, 73.

[28] Cf. in general ibid. 56–7, 73–4; for another possible use of V in the 9th cent. prior to mutilation cf. 6n.

[29] So already Garuti 1967.

TRANSLATION

I. Remains from the Vatican Palimpsest

1 . . . ought he to have . . . or did he discharge the debt in the way that all others have done? My defence of M. Fonteius and my contention is that after the Valerian law was carried . . . in your . . . quaestorship down to that of T. Crispinus no one discharged debts differently. I claim that my client followed the authority of all his predecessors and that all his successors followed his authority. *2* What do you accuse (him of), what fault do you find? When he finds Fonteius failing in his duty regarding the 3/4 and 1/4 account books begun by Hirtuleius, I cannot judge whether he is in error himself or wishes to lead you into error. I ask you, M. Plaetorius, whether our case could find favour with you if, in the matter in which you accuse M. Fonteius, he has as his authority that Hirtuleius on whom you bestow particular praise: on the point on which you praise Hirtuleius Fonteius is found to have done the same. You find fault with the type of discharge of debt; the public account books prove that Hirtuleius discharged the same way. You praise him on the grounds that he introduced the account books providing for a 3/4 reduction; Fonteius introduced the same and for the same type of money. For lest you perhaps be unaware and suppose that those account books pertain to a different type of old debt, they were introduced for a single cause and in a single type. For when . . . publicans who . . . Africa, who [had contracted for] the transit-dues of Aquileia . . .

3 . . . quickly . . . No one, no one, I say, will be found to claim that he gave a single sesterce to M. Fonteius during his quaestorship or that he removed a single coin from the money that was credited to the treasury; no indication of any theft by my client will be found in the account books, no trace of loss or reduction (of money) will be found in those accounts. And yet we see the men accused in this type of tribunal first criticized by witnesses; for it is difficult for the man who has given money to a magistrate not to be either induced to speak by hatred or compelled by regard for obligation. Then again if witnesses have been deterred by favour, the account books at any rate remain uncorrupted and sound. Assume that all of them were on the friendliest terms with Fonteius, that so large a number of utterly unknown and unconnected persons spared his life, took thought for his reputation; nonetheless the fact itself and the nature of records and composition of the account books has the effect that any falsification of credits and debits or removal by stealth or inconsistency comes to light. They recorded the receipt of all monies from the Roman people; if they either paid or gave to others equally large amounts right away so that what was credited to the Roman people was paid out to someone, nothing can at any rate have been removed. But if they took something home, from their strongbox, from . . .

4 As heaven is my witness! No witness is found in a matter of 23 million sesterces! Of how many men? More than six hundred. In what lands was the business transacted? In that place, that one, I say, which you see. Was the money given irregularly? On the contrary, no sesterce was moved without copious documentation. What then is that accusation, which could more easily ascend the Alps than the few steps of the treasury, which defends the treasury of the Ruteni more diligently than that of the Roman people, which prefers to use witnesses unknown than known, foreign than domestic and thinks that it confirms the charge more clearly by the unbridled greed of barbarians than the documents of our own people? *5* An account has been rendered of two magistracies, each of which has been involved in handling and managing very large amounts of money, the triumvirate and the quaestorship, in such a way, jurors, that in matters that were transacted in full view, had bearing on many persons, were concluded by public and private account books, no indication of theft, no suspicion of any crime is discovered. *6* The Spanish legateship followed when the state was in a most disorderly condition, when with the arrival in Italy of Lucius Sulla's very large army the citizens contended by violence, not by courts and laws; and in this desperate state of the commonwealth what manner of . . .

II. Remains preserved in the Vatican MS and its copies

11 . . . that under his praetorship Gaul was crushed by debt. By whom do they allege that such great sums of money were borrowed to pay creditors? By Gauls? Absolutely not. By whom, then? By Roman citizens who conducted business in Gaul. Why do we not hear their words? Why are none of their account books produced? I am going on the offensive and press the accuser, jurors; I am going on the offensive, I say, and demand witnesses. In this case I am using more effort and trouble in calling for witnesses than other defenders do in refuting them. I say this boldly, jurors; I do not affirm it rashly. Gaul is replete with businessmen, full of Roman citizens. No Gaul conducts any business without a Roman citizen; in Gaul no sesterce stirs without the account books of Roman citizens. *12* See to what lengths I am going, jurors, how far I am departing from my customary caution and diligence. Let one set of account books be produced in which there is any trace to indicate money given to M. Fonteius; let them produce a single witness from the number of so many businessmen, settlers, publicans, farmers, cattle-breeders; I shall concede that he has been rightly accused. By the immortal gods! What kind of case is this, what kind of defence?

M. Fonteius had charge of the province of Gaul, which consists of the types of people and of communities which, to leave aside ancient history, in part fought bitter and protracted wars with the Roman people within living memory, in part have just now been subjected by our commanders, just now subdued in war, just now branded with disgrace in triumphs and monuments, just now been stripped by the senate of lands and cities, which in part joined combat with M. Fonteius himself and through copious sweat and labour on his part have fallen under the rule and sway of the Roman people. *13* There is in the same province Narbo Martius, a colony of our citizens, a look-out post and bulwark of the Roman people, planted and thrust in the way of those very tribes. There is likewise the city of Massilia, about which I previously spoke, consisting of the bravest and most loyal allies who have offset the perils of the Gallic wars with the Roman people's troops and rewards. There is besides a very large number of Roman citizens and equites, most honourable men.

M. Fonteius had, as I said, charge of this province, which consisted of these various types (of people). He subdued those who were enemies; he compelled those who had been enemies most recently to vacate the lands of which they had been stripped; upon the rest, who had often been defeated in great wars, so that they might always be in obedience to the Roman people, he levied in support of the wars which then were being waged by the Roman people in the entire world a great quantity of cavalry, a very large sum of money for their pay, and a very large amount of grain for sustaining the war in Spain. *14* The man who carried this out is summoned to trial; you who were not involved in the matter are trying the case along with the Roman people; those on whom, much against their will, the orders fell are pleading against (us), those who were forced by decree of Cn. Pompey to depart from their lands, those who from the slaughter and rout of war now for the first time dare make a stand against the unarmed M. Fonteius. Tell me, what are the wishes of the Narbonese colonists? What do they think? They want my client to be saved by you; they think that they are unharmed by him. What is the sentiment of the state of the Massiliotes? It accorded my client the highest honours in its gift; though absent, it begs and beseeches you that its conscientiousness, commendation, and authority be seen to have had some weight in your minds. *15* Tell me, what is the wish of the Roman citizens? There is not one of so vast a number who does not think that my client has acquired a strong claim to the gratitude of the province, the empire, the allies, and the citizens. Since therefore, jurors, you have learned what persons want M. Fonteius attacked and who want him defended, now decide what your fairness and the standing of the Roman people require, whether you prefer to give credit to and take counsel for your colonists, your businessmen, your closest and most ancient allies, or those whom you ought neither to credit because of their anger nor honour because of their disloyalty.

16 Tell me: if I produce an even greater supply of most honourable men that could bear witness to my client's courage and innocence, will the collusion of the Gauls nonetheless have greater force than the supreme authority of all? You know, jurors, that when Fonteius was in charge of Gaul, very large armies and highly distinguished commanders of the Roman people were in the two Spains. How many Roman equites, how many military tribunes and legates of what quality and number and in what frequency went to join them! In addition, the very large and distinguished army of Cn. Pompey wintered in Gaul when M. Fonteius held command. Does Fortune herself seem to you to have wanted there to be sufficiently abundant and suitable witnesses and persons cognizant of the exploits performed in Gaul under M. Fonteius' praetorship? What witness from so vast a number of men can you produce in this case? Who from that number is your preferred authority? We shall now use him as encomiast and witness. *17* Will you be in doubt any longer, jurors, that what I laid before you in the beginning is utterly true, that nothing else is at stake in this trial except that, once M. Fonteius has been crushed by the testimonies of those upon whom, much against their will, levies were imposed in the state interest, the rest may hereafter be slower to impose levies since they see those persons attacked without whom the rule of the Roman people could not be safe?

It has been laid to his charge that M. Fonteius profited from road-construction in that he either did not compel it or failed to find construction defective. If all were compelled to build roads and the works of many were denied certification, certainly each charge is false, that a price was given both for immunity since no one was immune and for certification since many were denied certification. *18* Tell me: if we can delegate this charge to excellent men not so as to transfer the guilt to others but so that we may inform (you) that those persons were in charge of the building who can easily take responsibility for and win approval of their performance, will you nonetheless, in reliance on angry witnesses, ascribe all to M. Fonteius? When M. Fonteius was hindered by greater affairs of state and when it was in the public interest for the Via Domitia to be paved, he assigned the task to his legates, outstanding men, C. Annius Bellienus and C. Fonteius; they therefore were in charge; in line with their standing they made demands at their discretion and issued certifications. It was open to you to know this, if not from any other source, at any rate from our correspondence, both sent and received, which you transcribed. If you did not read it previously, find out now from us what Fonteius wrote to his legates about these matters and what they wrote back to him. LETTER SENT TO THE LEGATE C. ANNIUS, TO THE LEGATE C. FONTEIUS, LETTER RECEIVED FROM THE LEGATE C. ANNIUS, FROM THE LEGATE C. FONTEIUS. *19* I think it sufficiently clear, jurors, that the policy of road-construction does not pertain to M. Fonteius and has been handled by those whom no one could criticize.

Now learn about the charge relating to the wine-trade, which the prosecution claim to be the most invidious and greatest. The charge was put in place by Plaetorius in this fashion, that it did not first occur to M. Fonteius in Gaul to establish a duty on wine, but he set out from Rome with this policy already settled upon and planned; that therefore at Tolosa Titurius demanded by way of duty four denarii for each amphora of wine; at Crodunum Porcius and Munius three and a half each; at Vulchalo Servaeus two and a half each; and in these regions a duty was demanded of them if any persons stayed overnight at Cobiomagum, which is a village between Tolosa and Narbo, and did not want to go to Tolosa; that at Elesiodunum C. Annius demanded six denarii each from those who exported to the enemy. *20* I see, jurors, that the charge is large-scale in kind—for it is claimed that a tax has been imposed upon our fruits, and I acknowledge that a rather large sum of money could be collected by that means—and in terms of invidiousness it is very powerful indeed; for his personal enemies have been particularly keen to broadcast the matter by word of mouth. But my view is that the more serious the charge that is shown to be false, the greater the harm inflicted by its inventor. For by the enormity of the matter he aims to seize the minds of the listeners so powerfully that it becomes difficult to arrive at the truth.

ON THE CHARGE RELATING TO THE WINE-TRADE. ON THE WAR AGAINST THE VOCONTII. ON THE DISTRIBUTION OF WINTER-QUARTERS.

21 'But the Gauls deny this.' But the logic of things and the force of the arguments prove it. 'Can a juror, then, disbelieve the witnesses?' He not only can but ought to disbelieve self-interested, angry, conspiring witnesses who have no regard for conscience. If because the Gauls assert it, therefore M. Fonteius must be accounted guilty, what need is there, I should like to know, of a wise juror, a fair presiding officer, an intelligent pleader? 'The Gauls assert it; we cannot deny it.' In this connection, if you think that it is the role of the clever and experienced and fair juror to have to believe without any hesitation because the witnesses assert it, Salus herself cannot protect brave men's innocence. If, however, you think that in judging matters the juror's wisdom serves in no small measure to evaluate every single matter and assess it by its own weight, perhaps your role in reflecting is larger and weightier than mine in pleading. *22* For I must interrogate a witness about each individual point not only once but also briefly; often I must not interrogate at all so as to avoid giving the floor to an angry man or authority to a self-interested one; you can often turn over the same matter in your mind and reflect at length about each individual witness and, if we have declined to interrogate, you ought to judge what was our reason for remaining silent. Therefore if you think that believing witnesses has been prescribed to the juror by law or duty, there is no reason for one juror to be thought better or wiser than another. For a single, simple judgement of the ears has been granted by nature without distinction and in common to the stupid and the wise. *23* Where, then, is there scope for sagacity to shine, where can the stupid and gullible listener be distinguished from the conscientious and wise juror? Surely at the point where the witnesses' assertions are submitted for the jurors to infer and reflect with how much authority, mental balance, regard for moral standards, good faith, conscientiousness, zeal for good reputation, with how much care, how much fear they are pronounced.

Or in the testimonies of barbarians are you going to hesitate to do what the wisest jurors often thought they must not hesitate to do in our own and our fathers' memory concerning the most distinguished men of our community? They did not believe Cn. and Q. Caepio, L. and Q. Metellus as witnesses against Q. Pompeius, a new man; the suspicion of overeagerness (to testify) and enmity removed the credit and authority from their courage, family, and exploits. *24* Is there any man whom we have seen, is there any man we can truly remember equal in counsel, weight, constancy, and the other virtues, in distinctions for honour, genius, and exploits to M. Aemilius Scaurus? Though the earth was practically ruled by his unsworn nod, his sworn testimony was believed neither against C. Fimbria nor C. Memmius: those who were sitting in judgment did not want this path to lie open for enmity, namely that anyone could by testimony banish a man he hated. Who is unaware how high were the moral standards of L. Crassus, what his genius, what his authority? Though his conversation had the authority of testimony, by testimony itself he was unable to prove what he alleged with hostile intent against M. Marcellus. *25* Those jurors had, they had, a divine and unparalleled plan: they thought they were not only passing judgment about the defendant but also about the prosecutor and the witness as to what seemed to be invented, what brought on by chance or circumstance, what corrupted by bribery, what vitiated by hope or fear, what motivated by self-interest or enmity. If the juror does not embrace the totality with his intelligence, is not circumspect in mind and heart, if as each point is pronounced from that place, he thinks it said by some oracle, then surely it will be sufficient, as I said before, for a juror who is not deaf to discharge this task and duty; there will be no reason for some wise and widely experienced man to be called to judge cases.

26 Or did those Roman equites, whom we have seen, who were recently at the height of their influence in the state and the courts, have such spirit and strength as to disbelieve L. Crassus and M. Scaurus as witnesses, while you fear to disbelieve the testimony of the Volcae and the Allobroges? If one should disbelieve an enemy as witness, was Crassus more hostile to Marcellus or Scaurus to Fimbria on the basis of citizens' partisanship and domestic backbiting than the Gauls are to my client? Of the Gauls those in the best position were compelled, much against their will, to provide cavalry, grain, and money once, twice, and more often, some of the others were stripped of their lands after past wars, others were defeated and crushed in this very war. *27* If any people say anything greedily for the sake of gain, it is improper to believe them. A greater gain, I am sure, was in prospect for the Caepiones and Metelli from the conviction of Q. Pompeius, when they would have rid themselves of a critic of their policies, than there is for all Gaul from the disaster of M. Fonteius, with which that province thinks that its immunity and liberty is practically bound up.

Or if it is fitting to look at the men themselves—which ought to have the greatest weight in the case of a witness—is a Gaul of great distinction to be compared not merely with the leading men of our state but with the lowest Roman citizen? Does Indutiomarus know what it is to give testimony? Is he moved by the fear by which each of us is moved when he has been brought forward to that place? *28* Remember, jurors, how greatly you generally exert yourselves not only about what you give as testimony but also what words you use so that no word may seem to be deployed immoderately, no word seem to have slipped out from some greedy impulse. Finally you struggle with your expression so that no hint of overeagerness may appear, so that when you go forward (to testify) there should be a certain tacit reputation for high moral standards and conscientiousness in regard to you and when you stand down that reputation may be seen to have been carefully preserved and retained. *29* In giving testimony Indutiomarus has, I am sure, feared or given thought to these same matters, Indutiomarus, who has eliminated from his entire testimony the word 'I think'—the word most carefully weighed according to our habit, which we use under oath even when we know full well what we are saying—and has said that he 'knows' everything. He feared, of course, that he would lose some portion of his reputation with you and the Roman people, that some such report as this would result: 'Indutiomarus, a man of such quality, spoke so greedily, so rashly; he failed to understand that in his testimony he was bound to present either to his own citizens or our prosecutors nothing except his voice, his face, and his audacity.'

30 Or do you think that in giving testimony those peoples are moved by scrupulous observance of oath and fear of the immortal gods? They differ from the custom and nature of other nations to such an extent that others undertake wars on behalf of their religious observances, these do so against the religious observances of all;

in waging wars others seek peace and pardon from the immortal gods; these have waged wars with the immortal gods themselves! These are the peoples who set out so far from their abodes all the way to Pythian Apollo at Delphi to harry and plunder the oracle of the world. By the same peoples, upright and scrupulous in their testimony, the Capitol was beleaguered as was renowned Jupiter, by whose name our ancestors wanted the credibility of testimonies to be bound. *31* Finally can anything seem to be sacred and a source of religious awe to these people, who, even if they are induced by some fear to think that the gods must be appeased, pollute their altars and temples with human victims so that they cannot even practise religion unless they first violate it by a criminal act? Who is unaware that to this day they retain that monstrous and barbaric custom of sacrificing human beings? Therefore what sort of trustworthiness, what sort of piety do you judge those people to have who think that even the immortal gods can be most easily appeased by bloody crimes against humans?

Will you treat as on the same footing your religious scruples and these witnesses? Will you suppose that anything has been said with integrity or moderately by them? *32* Will your minds, so pure, so uncorrupted, undertake that, though all our legates who went to Gaul during that three-year period, all Roman equites who were in that province, all businessmen of that province, finally all allies and friends of the Roman people who are in Gaul want M. Fonteius to be preserved, commend him under oath publicly and privately, you nonetheless prefer to join with the Gauls in butchering him? In order to be seen to be following what principle? Public opinion? Will the sentiment of our enemies then have greater weight with you than that of citizens? The standing of the witnesses? Can you then give priority to unknown persons before known, unfair persons before fair ones, foreign before domestic, greedy before moderate, hirelings before disinterested persons, impious before religious, bitter enemies to this empire and nation to good and faithful allies and citizens?

33 Or do you doubt, jurors, that all those peoples both cherish and practise deep-seated enmity with the Roman nation? Do you suppose that these men go about here in rough woollen cloaks and breeches with the same downcast eyes and humble spirit as those people customarily do who have suffered wrongs and flee as abased suppliants appealing for aid to a jury? Nothing of the sort! Quite the contrary, they wander about here and there in good spirits and good cheer over the whole Forum with certain threats striking terror with their monstrous barbarian words. I surely would give this no credence had I not heard this several times along with you, jurors, from the prosecutors themselves when they instructed you to beware lest, if the defendant were acquitted, some new Gallic war be stirred up. *34* If in this case M. Fonteius lacked everything, jurors, if he were being summoned to trial, his youth a disgrace, his life disreputable, with the magistracies he exercised in your full view exercised badly, convicted by the testimony of sound men, with legateships conducted shamefully, hated by all his own family, if in that trial he were pressed by the testimonies and account books of the Narbonese colonists of the Roman people, of the Massiliotes, our most loyal allies, of all Roman citizens, nonetheless you would have to take great precaution lest you seem to be frightened of those people and to have been moved by their terrifying threats, even though you heard that they were so crushed by your fathers and ancestors that they ought to be despised. *35* But as things stand, though no sound man damages his reputation, all your citizens and allies commend him, and the same people attack him who have frequently attacked this city and this empire; and though M. Fonteius' enemies are threatening you and the Roman people, his friends and relatives are supplicating you, will you hesitate to show not only your fellow citizens, who are most influenced by glory and praise, but foreign tribes and peoples that in casting your votes you prefer to spare a fellow citizen rather than give ground to the enemy?

36 This is a mighty ground for acquittal, as heaven is my witness, jurors, along with other motives, lest any conspicuous spot of disgrace be attached to this empire if word is spread to Gaul that the senators and equites of the Roman people were moved to pass judgment to please those people not by their testimonies but by their threats. If they try to launch a war, we shall have to raise up C. Marius from the dead, a man who could be the equal in warfare to that threatening and arrogant Indutiomarus; we shall have to raise up Cn. Domitius and Q. Maximus to overwhelm and crush with their arms a second time the tribe of the Allobroges and the remnants of the war, or, since that is impossible, we must beg my friend M. Plaetorius to deter his new clients from embarking on war, to try to avert by prayer their angry hearts and dreadful attacks or, if he cannot, we shall beg his junior colleague M. Fabius to soften the hearts of the Allobroges, since the name of the Fabii enjoys great distinction among them, so that they may be willing either to hold their peace, as conquered and subdued people customarily do, or to understand, when they utter threats, that they are holding out to the Roman people not the fear of war but the hope of triumph.

37 If in the case of a disreputable defendant it would be insufferable for these people to suppose that they have advanced their cause by threats, what do you think you ought to do in the case of M. Fonteius? About this man—for I believe I ought to say this now that the case in its two sessions is almost concluded—about this man not even from his enemies have you heard any invented slander as to scandalous conduct, let alone a charge. Has any defendant, especially one engaged in this type of life, in canvassing for office, in magistracies, in exercising command, ever been accused in such a way that no misconduct, no crime, no disgraceful act arising from lust or wantonness or audacity has been cast in his teeth by the prosecutor, if not a genuine one, nonetheless one invented with some plausible suspicion? *38* We know that M. Aemilius Scaurus, an outstanding man of our state, was prosecuted by M. Brutus. The speeches survive, from which it can be understood that many accusations were made against Scaurus himself—falsely; who denies it? Nonetheless they were pronounced and cast in his teeth by an enemy. How many charges did M'. Aquilius hear at his trial, how many did L. Cotta hear, how many finally did P. Rutilius? This man, though he was convicted, must, it seems to me, nonetheless be numbered among the best and most innocent men. Now that man himself, most revered and most temperate, heard many things in his case tending towards a suspicion of fornication and lust. *39* A speech survives of the man who, in my opinion, was by far the most gifted and eloquent of our people, C. Gracchus; in this speech a great many disgraceful and scandalous things are said against L. Piso. But what a man was the target! He had such great virtue and integrity that even in those best times, when you could find no worthless person, he alone was named 'the Good'. When Gracchus ordered him to be summoned to a public assembly and a traveller asked which Piso, since there were several, he said 'you are compelling me to call my enemy "the Good"'. That man, whom not even his enemy could satisfactorily indicate in naming him unless he had praised him first, whose cognomen by itself showed not only who he was but also what sort of man he was, nonetheless was summoned to a false and unfair accusation of disgraceful acts. *40* M. Fonteius has been accused in two sessions in such a way that nothing was alleged by which a trace of lust, wantonness, cruelty, or audacity could be shown. Not only did they adduce no misdeed of the defendant, but they did not even find fault with any pronouncement of his. But if they had so much intelligence for lying or talent for inventing as they have will for crushing the defendant and licence for abusing him, Fonteius would have fared no better in regard to disgraceful, unmentionable deeds than those whom I previously mentioned. You see, then, a good man, jurors, good, I say, and moderate and temperate in all aspects of life, of high moral standards, full of a sense of responsibility, full of conscientiousness, placed in your protection and power and in such a way that he is entrusted to your protection and given over to your power.

41 Consider therefore whether it is fairer for a most honourable man, a gallant man, an outstanding citizen, to be delivered to deeply hostile and monstrous tribes or to be restored to his friends, especially since there are so many factors that appeal to your hearts on behalf of my innocent client's safety: first the antiquity of his family, which we see has its roots in the very distinguished municipality of Tusculum and is inscribed and noted on monuments of its achievements, then the uninterrupted series of praetorships, which have been marked both with other distinctions and especially with the reputation for innocence, then the fresh memory of his parent, by whose blood not only the Asculans, by whom he was slain, but that entire Social War was infected with the stain of crime, finally the man himself, not only honourable and uncorrupted in all aspects of life but also, in military affairs, of extraordinary sagacity and courage as well as being, of men now alive, among the most practised in waging wars. *42* Therefore if you had need of being warned by me as well, which you do not, I seem justified, given my level of authority, in gently advising you to resolve to take care to retain men whose courage, hard work, and success in military affairs is known. There was once a larger supply of such men in this state; even though this was the case, thought was nonetheless taken not only for their safety but also for their honour. What should you do now, when military pursuits are obsolete among our young men and our gallant men and top leaders are spent, some by age, some by civil discord and the disaster of the state, when so many wars either have been taken on by us of necessity or have arisen suddenly and unexpectedly? Surely you think, do you not, that the man himself should be saved for the doubtful crises of state and others should be fired with enthusiasm for glory and courage? *43* Remember which legates L. Julius had recently in the Italian war, which ones P. Rutilius had, which ones L. Cato, which ones Cn. Pompeius; you will know that at that time M. Cornutus, L. Cinna, L. Sulla, men of praetorian rank, were most skilled in waging war; besides C. Marius, T. Didius, Q. Catulus, P. Crassus were men trained in military science not by literature but by exploits and victories. Come, now turn your eyes to the senate house, look deeply into all parts of the state; do you see nothing that can happen which would cause such men to be missed, or do you think that, should it happen, the Roman people abounds in a supply of men of this kind? If you pay careful heed to this, jurors, you will surely prefer to retain at home for yourselves and your children a man energetic when it comes to the work of war, gallant when it comes to danger, skilled in practice and discipline, prudent in counsel, lucky in chance and fortune, rather than hand him over and surrender him to tribes that are the bitterest enemies of the Roman people and most cruel.

44 But the Gauls are attacking Fonteius virtually in arms and pressing him and hemming him in with utmost spirit and audacity. I see this, jurors; but with your help we shall resist that monstrous and intolerable barbarism with many stout defences. In the first place Macedonia is cast in the way of their onslaught, a province loyal and friendly to the Roman people. Since it asserts that itself and its cities were preserved not only by the counsel but even by the hand of M. Fonteius, as it was defended by him from the arrival and plundering of the Thracians, so from his head it is driving the terrifying attacks of the Gauls. *45* On the other side stands Further Spain, which can not only resist their self-interest by its own religious scruples but even refute the perjuries of wicked men with its own testimonies and testimonials. Moreover, from Gaul itself are drawn the most loyal and most weighty allies. The entire state of the Massiliotes has come to aid the wretched and innocent defendant; it not only strives to render equal thanks to the man by whom it was saved but also because it judges that it was placed in such circumstance and fate in those lands lest those tribes be able to harm us. *46* Fighting with equal zeal for the safety of M. Fonteius is the colony of Narbo, which recently was freed by him from enemy siege and is now moved by the same man's wretched dangers. Finally, as is fitting in the case of a Gallic war, as the laws and customs of our ancestors prescribe, there is no Roman citizen who thinks that he should make any excuse; all tax collectors of that province, farmers, ranchers, the rest of the businessmen are defending M. Fonteius with one accord and one voice.

But if Indutiomarus himself, leader of the Allobroges and the rest of the Gauls, despises such great troops of our allies, surely he will not pluck and drag the defendant from the embrace of his mother, excellent and wretched woman, with you looking on, will he? Especially when on the other side a Vestal Virgin embraces and holds her brother and begs your protection and that of the Roman people, jurors; she who has been occupied for many years with propitiating the immortal gods on your behalf and that of your children, so that she can now propitiate your hearts on behalf of her own safety and that of her brother. *47* What defence, what comfort is left to that wretched woman if the defendant is lost to her? Other women can themselves give birth to their defenders and can have at home an ally and sharer of all their fortunes; what does this Virgin have that can be either pleasant or dear besides her brother? Jurors, do not allow the altars of the immortal gods and of Mother Vesta to be reminded about your tribunal by the Virgin's daily lamentations; take thought that the famous eternal fire preserved by Fonteia's laborious nightly vigil be not said to have been extinguished by the tears of your priestess. *48* The Vestal Virgin is extending her hands to you in supplication, the same ones she stretches out to the immortal gods on your behalf. Beware lest it be risky and arrogant to repudiate the beseeching of that woman since, if the gods reject her prayers, this empire cannot be safe. Do you see all of a sudden, jurors, that most gallant man, M. Fonteius, pour forth tears upon mention of his parent and sister? He who never took fright in the line of battle, who often bearing arms inserted himself into the band and multitude of the enemy since he thought that by such dangers he was leaving to his family the same consolations that his father had left to him, the same man now, his mind troubled, fears lest he not only not be an ornament and aid to his family but even leave behind for the wretches eternal dishonour and disgrace with the bitterest grief. *49* A far different fortune, M. Fonteius, had you been able to choose to suffer death by the arms rather than the perjuries of the Gauls! For then courage would have been the ally of your life, glory the attendant of your death; as things stand, what agony it is for you to pay the penalty for conquest and dominion at the caprice of those who were either defeated by arms or yielded obedience much against their will! Defend from this danger, jurors, a gallant and innocent citizen; take care that you be seen to have given greater credence to our witnesses than foreigners, to have taken greater thought for the safety of citizens than the unbridled greed of the enemy, to have given greater weight to the entreaties of the woman who is in charge of your sacred rites than of those who have waged wars with the sacred rites and shrines of all. Finally, take thought, jurors—the point which has greatest bearing upon the standing of the Roman people—that the prayers of a Vestal Virgin be seen to have prevailed over the threats of the Gauls.

III. Fragments

1. Cus1 What is that point? What logic, what custom, what verisimilitude does it possess? Are we to believe what logic, custom and the nature of the matter rejects?

2. Cus2 Surely this suspicion should not be abandoned to some unfair arbitrator, should it?

3. Cus3 What authority can a witness have who mingles truth with falsehoods in pronouncing testimony?

4. Cus4 By this very argument you ought to repudiate the other testimonies.

5. Cus5 A cover for a lie.

6. Cus6 Cn. Pompey waged war in Spain with exceptional courage and good fortune.

7. Cus7 By hard work and enthusiasm.

8. Cus8 It was done with the support of Cn. Pompey, supreme commander and bravest of men.

9. Aquila Rom. 33.14, Mart. Cap. 482.2 H The greatest amount of grain from Gaul, abundant infantry troops from Gaul, the majority of the cavalry from Gaul.

10. Amm. 15.12.4 . . . that hereafter the Gauls will drink it in a more dilute form, which they thought was poison.

11. Cus9 Why are they fighting, what are they devising, what are they striving for?

12. Julius Victor *RLM* 397.18 If no money has been counted out, of what money is it two percent?

13. Quint. *Inst.* 6.3.51 . . . that while she lived [Plaetorius' mother] ran a school and after her death had teachers.

COMMENTARY

As required by the *lex Cornelia* (see General Introduction sec. 1), C. pleaded Fonteius' case in two sessions (*actiones*). The portion of the speech preserved in the Vatican MS derives from the second session (cf. 37 and 40), to which the Vatican palimpsest material should also be assigned; in spite of Humbert 1925, 216 ff., one need not assume conflation of materials from the two sessions; cf. Lintott 2008, 24 n. 52.

Fonteius was charged with allowing Transalpine Gaul to contract a crushing load of debt during his three-year term as governor (11); subsidiary charges related to corruption in administering road-construction/repair in the province (17–18), the introduction of a duty on wine (19–20), his conduct of war with the Vocontii and distribution of winter quarters for troops (20).

C.'s defence is of the type known in rhetorical theory as the *constitutio coniecturalis*, i.e. he denies that his client committed the crime(s); it was the common approach in extortion cases (cf. *De orat.* 2.105) and inevitably requires undermining the credibility of contrary evidence, in this case the testimony of Gallic witnesses. C. complains that they are Gallic, not Roman (4, 11–12), and that their testimony is unsupported by documents (3, 12). He calls into question the Gauls' scrupulousness in giving testimony and their general piety (27–31) and counters with his own evidence in the form of testimonials furnished by Spain and Macedonia, the provinces where Fonteius served as legate prior to his governorship, and from the Massiliotes, the Roman colonists of Narbo Martius and other Romans living in the province (44–6). The speech concludes in a crescendo of pathos with Fonteius' mother and sister, a Vestal Virgin, supplicating the jurors on his behalf (46–9).

1. Exordium

No verbatim quotation has survived from the exordium, in which C. will have introduced his client and case and will, according to rhetorical theory, have attempted to render the jurors well-disposed, attentive, and receptive (Quint. *Inst.* 4.1.5). Early on he will have taken care to differentiate Fonteius' case from the extortion case of

C. Verres, whom C. had recently prosecuted with success (Jul. Vict. *RLM* p. 400); the cases present some striking similarities, however, as argued by Alexander 2002, ch. 2. The prosecutor M. Plaetorius Cestianus probably sought to link the two cases, perhaps at the same time castigating C. for inconsistency in prosecuting Verres but defending the equally guilty Fonteius; for the prosecutorial tactic cf. Alexander 2002, 35; cf. C.'s reply to a similar charges of inconsistency at *Clu.* 138–42 *Mur.* 3–5, and *Sul.* 2–20. If that is so, C. may have fired back with the riddling criticism of Plaetorius' mother in F 13; cf. Schneider 1876, 43–4; on Cicero's practice of speaking in riddles in his exordia cf. *Cael.* 1 ('a prostitute's resources'), *Rab. Post.* 1 ('royal power and lust'); Klodt 2007, 600 n. 2. Here C. also broached his own very different interpretation of the case, namely that the goal was to dampen other commanders' zeal in exercising authority (cross-reference at 17; cf. Jul. Vict. *RLM* p. 423; Schneider 1876, 42–3; Riggsby 1999*b*; F 11n.). As in the case of *Scaur.*, the state of preservation leaves it unclear whether the speech lacked a formal narrative; cf. Berger 1978, 48 and 210 n. 3.

2. Argumentation/Refutation

I. Remains from the Vatican Palimpsest

Paragraph 34 can serve as a basis for reconstructing the missing parts of the argumentation/refutation. C. will have begun by claiming that Fonteius' youth and life in general were honourable, not disgraceful (*turpis*) or disreputable (*infamis*). When coherent text begins in the Vatican palimpsest, C. has already launched his defence of Fonteius' administration of two offices, moneyer (*triumvir monetalis*) and urban quaestor (the former defence is lost prior to the onset of the palimpsest but alluded to in 5). The text begins in the middle of a complex argument about Fonteius' bookkeeping practices as urban quaestor perhaps in 84 (for the date see below). One of Fonteius' duties was to supervise the account books (*tabulae*: *OLD* s.v. *tabula* 7) kept by scribes (*scribae*) relating to public debt and its discharge; these were analogous to (and probably derived from) private citizens' account books with entries for credits and debits (*codices accepti et expensi*); cf. Thilo 1980, 170–202. In particular he had to administer a law carried by L. Valerius Flaccus (cos. suff. 86) whereby debts were payable at a quarter of the principal; the law may have been, like other measures regulating debt in the late Republic, a response to public pressure to bring debts into line with the value of property and carried in the teeth of opposition from the professional moneylenders and other debt-holders; it was also probably a response to the pressure on the treasury exerted by the Mithridatic and Social Wars; see Bulst 1964, 334–5; Yavetz 1970, 155–6; Barlow 1980; Alexander 2002, 66 and 276 n. 30; another possibility, raised by Badian 1967, 189, is that the law was intended to clear the books of claims of Roman moneylenders against the estate of the deposed king of Egypt, Ptolemy Alexander I, who had made Rome his heir and was killed in a naval battle, presumably in 87. In any case, C. claims that Fonteius followed an accounting procedure established by Hirtuleius, the first urban quaestor to administer funds under the Valerian law. This required an adjustment by which a credit of three-quarters of the principal was deleted and only the quarter that was actually payable remained on the books. This would have allowed the diversion of the 50 per cent difference to the responsible quaestor; this was evidently the charge levelled at Fonteius; cf. Piazza 1987, 290–1; for a different interpretation (based upon the view that *tabulae* = 'receipts') cf. Jouanique 1960.

The bearing of this material on the extortion charge is not *prima facie* clear; it might have been expected in a prosecution for malversation (*peculatus*), though the distinction was not always strictly observed (cf. *Ver.* 2.3.168 and 4.88). This material was, however, part of the accusation (cf. 4: 'What then is that accusation . . . ?'); and C. criticizes the prosecution's inability to produce witnesses (3), something that would not be required if this material had merely been offered as part of a survey of the defendant's prior life (*vita ante acta*) in order to show that his crimes had been foreshadowed; officials' taking of money 'contrary to laws' in general is the target of prosecution in the extortion court and so is properly included here, just as, in prosecuting Verres, C.'s accusation covered not just the governorship of Sicily but also his conduct of previous offices; cf. *Ver.* 2.1.34; Henderson 1951, 76; Alexander 1982, 158; Piazza 1987, 278 ff. The portion of the argumentation/refutation preserved in the Vatican palimpsest can be outlined as follows:

I. In administering funds under the *lex Valeria* Fonteius' practice was the same as that of his predecessors and successors (1)
   A. He made the same use of the 1/4 and 3/4 tables as Hirtuleius (2)
   B. The type of payment was the same [lacuna]

II. The prosecution has adduced no evidence against Fonteius' quaestorship either by witnesses or records (3)
   A. In case of wrongdoing witnesses are always ready to testify
   B. Account books provide sure proof
   C. Large number of potential witnesses (4)
   D. The prosecution is perversely based on foreign rather than domestic evidence

III. No evidence of wrongdoing in administering two offices involving handling of money (5)

IV. Fonteius' legateship in Spain (6) [lacuna]

(1) . . . ought he . . . followed his authority As urban quaestor in 84 Fonteius paid the public debts in accord with the Valerian law, which provided for repayment at 25 per cent of the principal; see above. His policy was criticized by the prosecution but is defended by C. as the same one practised by all officials from the time when the law was carried by L. Valerius Flaccus (cos. suff. 86) down to T. (Quinctius) Crispinus (perhaps qu. 70; cf. *MRR* ii. 128). 'In your . . . quaestorship' would appear to be a reference to the prosecutor M. Plaetorius Cestianus; the date he held the office remains unclear in view of the fragmentary text; *MRR* ii. 601 places it 'by 70' with a query; cf. Münzer, *RE* s.v. Plaetorius 16 1950.49–53; Wiseman 1971, no. 320.

(2) What do you accuse . . . lead you into error For liveliness C. addresses the prosecutor directly; he shifts to make him the subject of third-person verbs but then returns to direct address with a telling point. The reference is to M. Plaetorius Cestianus (pr. 64?), the chief prosecutor (*nominis delator*), who dealt with these charges; cf. *TLRR* no. 186; see also on 36 and Münzer, *RE* s.v. Plaetorius 16. The first quaestor to implement the Valerian law was one Hirtuleius (the praenomen is not attested, the identification with other bearers of the name unclear; cf. Münzer, *RE* s.v. 1; *MRR* ii. 54). From the previous sentence ('my client followed the authority of all his predecessors') and the fact that only one quaestor at a time administered funds under the Valerian law, Ryan 1996 infers that in this policy Fonteius must have had three predecessors, not one or two, and

therefore places Hirtuleius' quaestorship in 86, Fonteius' in 83; but C.'s language here is 'highly rhetorical', as Brennan 2000, 849 n. 238, notes; and in 83 Fonteius was a legate in Spain; see 6 with n. Our passage shows that the Valerian law provided for debt reduction by three-quarters (*dodrantariae* (*tabulae*)) so that a quarter (*quadrantariae* (*tabulae*)) remained to be paid; cf. *OLD* s.vv. *dodrantarius*, *quadrantarius*; Sal. *Cat.* 33 (the revolutionary Manlius citing a recent law providing for repayment in bronze of debts contracted in silver); Vel. 2.23; Rotondi 1912, 347–8; Frank 1933, 270–1; *MRR* ii. 60.

I ask you . . . discharged the same way Beginning with a rhetorical question C. highlights what he sees as a contradiction in Plaetorius' argument: if Hirtuleius' procedure was commendable, as the prosecutor has claimed, then so was Fonteius' since both followed the same policy. *auctor* is originally the 'author' but shades towards 'authority', as here. C. cites as his evidence the public account books (*publicae tabulae*); see the headnote to this section.

You praise him . . . in a single type C. continues to argue for identical policies followed by Hirtuleius and Fonteius without any distinction of types of debts based upon dates when they were contracted, kinds of goods, or the like. Unless Plaetorius was incompetent, however, there must have been more to the charge that C. is concealing or obfuscating.

For when . . . the transit-dues of Aquileia This looks like an argument supporting the preceding assertion (connection with 'for', *nam*) but breaks off before the point is clarified; the mention of the *publicani* in this context suggests, however, that the debt-reduction of the 80s included what the tax-companies owed to the treasury. In Africa the *publicani* had wide scope, not only collecting transit-dues but also rents on the public land (*ager publicus*) that was created on former Carthaginian territory after the Third Punic War and taxes on land sold so as to be private land subject to tax (*ager privatus vectigalisque*); cf. Ürögdi, *RE* Suppl. 11 1194.34 ff. (s.v. *publicani*); Lintott 1992 and *RS* on ll. 66 and 70 of the agrarian law of 111; on the publicans in general cf. Badian 1972; Nicolet 2000, 297–319. 'Had contracted for' (*redemerant*) is Lintott's supplement of the lacunose text. The transit-dues of Aquileia (*Aquileiense portorium*: Mommsen's restoration of the text) are well attested from the late Republic on and were levied on goods travelling up the Adriatic to Illyricum; cf. Vittinghoff, *RE* s.v. Portorium 361.55 ff.

(3)... quickly... No one... in those accounts When coherent text resumes, C. claims that no witness will be found to bribery or skimming of treasury receipts by Fonteius; and there is no trace of theft in the public records. He lends emphasis by emphatic gemination ('No one, no one') and by clauses led in the Latin by negative adjectives separated from their nouns (hyperbaton): 'no indication... no trace'. C. will go on to claim that the absence of such evidence argues powerfully for Fonteius' innocence.

And yet we see... uncorrupted and sound 'Accused in this type of tribunal', i.e. the extortion court (*quaestio de repetundis*); cf. General Introduction sec. 1. For such witness testimony cf. e.g. *Ver.* 2.1.27–8 (Dio of Halaesa). 'Regard for obligation' (*religio*): this is precisely the quality C. will find wanting in the Gallic witnesses against his client at 30–1. 'Deterred by favour': i.e. friendship or regard for Fonteius' reputation, as the next sentence shows. At *S.Rosc.* 28 C. imagines a conversation in which it is alleged that defence counsel would be absent 'because of Chrysogonus' favour' (sc. with Sulla); one wonders whether the absence of defence witnesses in that case was so motivated (ibid. 110). If, however, Fonteius defrauded not individuals but the treasury (see above), that would explain the absence of complaining citizens; cf. Jouanique 1960, 108. The account books are presented as a fallback ('at any rate': *certe*); the reference must be to the official account books supervised by Fonteius as urban quaestor; cf. Thilo 1980, 173.

Assume that all of them... for his reputation C. represents such a widespread conspiracy of silence as unlikely and in any case subject to check against the public records. 'His life': for extortion as a capital offence and the type of punishment actually used at this period cf. 44n.

nonetheless the fact itself... comes to light C. evidently has in mind a case like that of L. Carpinatius' account books, in which the entries in favour of a C. Verrucius all showed an erasure after the second *r*, creating the strong suspicion that they had been tampered with and a fictitious name substituted for that of C. Verres; cf. *Ver.* 2.2.186–91.

They recorded... have been removed 'They' (*isti*) will refer to the recipients of public money paid by Fonteius. C. may be countering a prosecution claim that Fonteius received kickbacks from money he paid out as quaestor. Even if an expense in the same amount as a receipt occurred 'right away' (*protinus*), it would be entered in the appropriate column; nothing can be withdrawn without leaving a record. The argument is weak, however, since Roman bookkeepers sometimes made later insertions, as is shown by the notation *AFPR* (*ante factum post relatum*) for later insertions; cf. *De orat.* 2.280; de Ste Croix 1956, 47. In addition, special circumstances might cause a transaction to be purposely omitted from the account books; such appears to have been the case with a payment of 50,000 sesterces made by the actor Q. Roscius to C. Fannius Chaerea, who kept it out of his account book at Roscius' request; cf. *Q. Rosc.* 1–13 with Stroh 1975, 135–6. For a different interpretation of our passage cf. Thilo 1980, 174–5.

But if they took something... from their strongbox, from... 'They' will be the aforementioned recipients of public money; the 'strongbox' will be their private safe, not the public treasury. Following the second 'from' *ra* remains; *rationibus* ('accounts') is Niebuhr's plausible supplement; cf. Thilo 1980, 174. The following lacuna leaves the precise development unclear, but C. will surely have continued the general point that any embezzlement of public funds must have left traces.

(4) As heaven is my witness... which you see The oath heightens the emotion, as often. The amount of money and number of persons involved should ensure the availability of witnesses if there was any wrongdoing (but see above). The temple of Saturn, located a little to the west of the Forum and easily visible from it, housed the treasury (*aerarium*) under the supervision of the urban quaestors; cf. Coarelli, *LTUR* and Richardson 1992 s.v. Saturnus, aedes. Gemination of the demonstrative ('In that place, that one, I say' *illo illo, inquam, loco*) conveys excitement. C. no doubt accompanied his words with an expressive gesture. For C.'s exploitation in the speeches of things visible to the audience cf. Vasaly 1993: especially 15–26.

Was the money given... copious documentation 'Irregularly' (*extra ordinem*) implies a deviation from standard procedure (cf. *OLD* s.v. *ordo* 15b), in this case without leaving a written record. C. strongly denies any such transaction ('on the contrary': *immo vero*).

What then is that accusation... documents of our own people? A rhetorical question summarizing C.'s objection to the prosecutor's line. 'That accusation': the pronominal adj. *iste* implies contempt, as often: *OLD* s.v. 3; similarly Scaurus 45d ('What the devil is that reason?'; see ad loc.). C. plays variations on the theme that the prosecution is based upon foreign (in particular Gallic) rather than domestic witnesses/records. 'Ascending the Alps' is a metaphor for seeking Gallic evidence. The Ruteni are a Gallic tribe inhabiting the Aveyron region just north of the province, evidently chosen at random (if their complaints played a large role in the case, that material is lost); our passage may point to incorporation of a part of the Ruteni within the Roman province by the time of Fonteius' governorship; cf. Caes. *Gal.* 7.7.4; Rambaud 1980, 304 n. 9. 'Unbridled greed' (*libido*): this is varied by criticisms of their 'greed' or 'greedy' character/behaviour; cf. 21n.; *libido* recurs, however, for emphasis in the peroration (49). 'Barbarians': a recurrent barb in this speech; cf. 33, 44; *Scaur.* 36n.; at *Q.fr.* 1.1(1).27 C. classes Africans, Spaniards, and Gauls as 'barbarian nations'.

(5) An account . . . is discovered The two magistracies held by Fonteius involving the management of public funds were urban quaestor, the subject of the argument since 1, and moneyer (*triumvir monetalis*), presumably discussed previously; cf. *RRC* no. 347; *MRR* ii. 440. 'In full view' renders the set phrase *ante oculos*; cf. *Div. Caec.* 6; *OLD* s. v. *oculus* 3b; it surely refers to his work as quaestor at the *aerarium*; similar is the analogue of a magistrate's conduct of office to an actor's performance onstage; cf. *Ver.* 2.5.35; *Q.fr.* 1.1(1).42. 'Had bearing on many persons' summarizes from 4 ('more than six hundred'). On suspicion as the catalyst of prosecution see F 2n.

(6) The Spanish legateship . . . what manner of . . . Fonteius' legateship in Spain is synchronized with the civil war initiated by Sulla's return in the spring of 83 and continuing to 81; it has been dated as early as 83 (Brennan 2000, 502 and 852–3 n. 298) and as late as 81 (*MRR* ii. 78 and Thomasson 1991, 110, no. 132). Though he served as quaestor under the Cinnan regime, he will have changed sides, though C. says nothing of this in the extant text. In 45 C. specifies the province as Further Spain and indicates that his client's case has received support from that quarter. 'Disorderly condition': cf. *Sul.* 40 'in that most troubled storm of the state'; ibid. 72 'in that grave and disorderly victory of L. Sulla'; similar expressions are collected by Diehl 1988, 167; Marshall 1979, 517, notes allusions to the phrase in letters of Servatus Lupus, abbot of Ferrières in the ninth century ('in this disorderly condition of the state': *Ep.* 24, 43, and 91). In the lacuna that follows C. will have argued that his client conducted himself honourably in that legateship and a subsequent one in Macedonia; cf. 34 with n.

II. Remains preserved in the Vatican MS and its copies

The Vatican MS preserves the last part of the argumentation/refutation (11–43) and the peroration (44–9) of the concluding session (*actio*) of Fonteius' trial. This portion of the argumentation/refutation brings the case forward to the main issue of the trial, the governorship of Transalpine Gaul. In remarks prefaced to this section C. will have alluded to Massilia and its significance for Roman policy in this region; cf. the cross-reference at 13. The remains of the argumentation/refutation preserved in the Vatican MS can be outlined as follows:

I. Allegation that Gaul was crushed by debt (11)
   A. Alleged victims: Roman citizens
   B. Demand for witnesses
II. Survey of Gaul (12)
   A. People recently subdued
   B. Narbo Martius (13)
   C. Massilia
   D. Roman citizens
III. Fonteius' administration
   A. Subjugation of hostile tribes
   B. Assistance for war in Spain
IV. Attitudes of the various groups (14)
   A. Recent enemies
   B. Narbonese
   C. Massiliotes
   D. Roman citizens (15)
V. Many Romans passed through Gaul bound for Spain during Fonteius' governorship: who will testify for the prosecution? (16)
VI. The prosecution aims to weaken Rome's provincial governors (17)
VII. Alleged corruption in the programme for building/repairing roads
   A. No one was given immunity
   B. In many cases completed work was denied certification
   C. Programme managed by legates C. Annius Bellienus and C. Fonteius (18)

VIII. Tax on wine (19)
   A. The policy developed in Rome
   B. Names of toll stations and those in charge of each
   C. This is a large charge, but invented (20)

IX. Topics edited out:
   A. Tax on wine (remaining argument)
   B. War with Vocontii
   C. Distribution of winter quarters

X. Should one always believe witnesses? (21)
   A. Not if they are self-interested, angry, conspiring, and without religious scruples
   B. To do so would level distinctions among jurors
   C. Testimony of distinguished citizens has been disbelieved on grounds of personal enmity (23)
      1. Cn. and Q. Caepio, L. and Q. Metellus against Q. Pompeius
      2. M. Aemilius Scaurus against C. Fimbria and C. Memmius (24)
      3. L. Crassus against M. Marcellus
   D. If the equites could disbelieve Crassus and Scaurus, a fortiori the current jury can disbelieve the Gauls (26): they have greater enmity and more to gain

XI. Indutiomarus compared with a Roman witness (27)
   A. The Roman witness strives to speak moderately and preserve a reputation for modesty and conscientiousness (28)
   B. Indutiomarus shows no sign of fear and says he 'knows' rather than 'thinks' (29)

XII. Gauls have no fear of the gods or regard for oaths (30)
   A. Attacked Delphi
   B. Attacked the Capitol
   C. Practise human sacrifice (31)

XIII. Why should one prefer Gallic to domestic witnesses?

XIV. The Gauls' enmity towards Rome (33)
   A. They strut arrogantly through the Forum
   B. They threaten war in the event of Fonteius' acquittal
      1. Even if Fonteius were guilty, one should not appear to yield to threats (34)
      2. In the event of war C. Marius, Cn. Domitius, Q. Maximus must be summoned from the dead (36)
      3. M. Plaetorius or M. Fabius could intercede with their clients

XV. If even a guilty defendant should be acquitted, how much more so Fonteius? (37)
   A. No character charge has even been invented against him
   B. This is, however, standard procedure in such cases
      1. M. Aemilius Scaurus slandered by M. Brutus (38)
      2. M'. Aquilius, L. Cotta, P. Rutilius similarly
      3. C. Gracchus slandered L. Piso, whose cognomen was 'the Good' (*Frugi*) (39)
   C. No utterance of Fonteius, let alone deed, has been criticized (40)

XVI. Points arguing for Fonteius' acquittal (41)
   A. From an old family of Tusculum
   B. The family has held an unbroken series of praetorships
   C. The memory of his father, killed at Asculum
   D. His skill in warfare; such persons are needed at this time (42)
      1. Such pursuits are out of fashion among the young
      2. Many distinguished commanders have been killed in warfare or civil strife
      3. Catalogue of legates of military distinction in the Social War (43)
      4. Compare that with the current position

(11) . . . that under his praetorship . . . conducted business in Gaul Fonteius was governor of Transalpine Gaul for three years (32), probably 74–72; so with a query *MRR* ii. 117, 111, 104; cf. Badian 1966, 911–12; Clemente 1974, 111; Brennan 2000, 509–11, acknowledges these dates as possible but argues for 77–75, though he admits that the trial occurred 'after 70'; it seems unlikely, however, that the Gauls, if they really were as angry as C. depicts (cf. 15n.), waited so long to bring the case to trial; and the claim that Fonteius' exactions supported Rome's wars 'in the entire world' (13) seems to point to the Mithridatic War, active again from 74 on. Both here and in 16 Fonteius is referred to as 'praetor'; the post-Sullan praetors were, however, initially deployed in Rome; but when their *imperium* was prorogued in the provinces, they were still regularly referred to as praetor, proconsul, or praetor *pro consule*; cf. Coskun 2006, 356–7 n. 8. The pattern by which the Pompeian L. Afranius probably succeeded Fonteius and another Pompeian, M. Pupius Piso, took command in Spain in 71 suggests that Fonteius, too, may have been

Pompey's man; cf. Ebel 1975, 366–7 (with literature), who also emphasizes the timing by which 'Fonteius was sent to Transalpina at about the same time that the Senate was responding to Pompey's demand for more support'. The statement about the crushing debt-load appears in indirect discourse as the prosecutor's allegation. The Latin for debt is characteristically concrete: *aes alienum*, literally 'another's bronze'; it is then varied by *versura* (literally 'the process of turning', in this case, of exchanging one creditor for another: *OLD* s.v. 1 and 3; Rollinger 2009, 152 n. 749). As Ebel 1976, 97, observes, 'As a rule, the tribute imposed by the Romans in the provinces was not oppressive, but in time of crisis it might be raised sharply. When this happened, Roman money-lenders were quick to move in to help the provincials raise the money—at exorbitant rates of interest.' That debt was pervasive in Gaul is confirmed by later indications, including C.'s remarks on Romans' attempts to collect debts in Gaul during Murena's governorship in 64–63 (*Mur.* 42) and the debts of the Allobroges that drove them to take up arms in 66 and 62–61, revolts put down respectively by C. Calpurnius Piso (cos. 67; cf. *MRR ii.* 154) and C. Pomptinus (*MRR* ii. 176), as well as to contemplate allying with Catiline during C.'s consulate (Sal. *Cat.* 40.1). In general, the degree of indebtedness or freedom from debt of subject communities could serve as a yardstick of successful provincial administration; cf. *Q.fr.* 1.1(1).25. Roman businessmen were active in Gaul from the end of the fourth century, as finds of (mostly South Italian) ceramics and to a lesser extent Roman coin-hoards document; see further Clemente 1974, 112–14. C.'s claim that the victims of indebtedness were exclusively Roman citizens is suspect: if so, why were the Gauls complaining, and why does he speak of the prosecution as defending the treasury of the Ruteni (4)?

Why do we not hear . . . the account books of Roman citizens C. again criticizes the prosecution for being unable to produce oral or written evidence from Romans, but as Alexander 2002, 74, points out, since they were supporting Fonteius, they will have suppressed any evidence of his wrongdoing; cf. the suppression of evidence of Verres' guilt by the company that held the contract for collecting the duties at the port of Syracuse and for farming taxes in Sicily (*Ver.* 2.2.176–91) and by the Mamertines, who enjoyed his favour (ibid. 5.48). Support of resident Romans appears to be the typical situation. C.'s only client on extortion charges who faced hostile Roman testimony was Flaccus; C. dealt with it by deromanizing the prosecution's Roman witnesses, just as in his prosecution case he sought to deromanize Verres and romanize his Sicilian clients; cf. Riggsby 1999*a*, 135–6; Vasaly 1993, 212–17. The prosecution could have pointed out, as C. himself did at *Ver.* 2.2.15 and elsewhere, that the extortion law and court had been set up in the interests of the allies (*sociorum causa*) and the jurors were therefore obliged to give their complaints a hearing even if unsupported by Roman evidence. The same terms (*insector* 'harry'; here with *ultro* 'I am going on the offensive') and 'demand' (*flagito*) are likewise used of C.'s attempt to elicit specific information about corruption at *Planc.* 48. The demand for witnesses was also made at 3–4 regarding the urban quaestorship; hence C.'s emphasis on the effort thus consumed. C.'s assertions about the centrality of Roman citizens to the economic life of Gaul are no doubt rhetorically exaggerated but must at least have been plausible to the jury; see previous n. For the phrasing cf. *Flac.* 44: '...no sesterce can stir without five praetors, three quaestors, four treasury officials...'

(12) See to what lengths I am going... what kind of defence? For C.'s frequent tactic of assuming a staggering burden of proof cf. Riggsby 1999*a*, 30 and 56; cf. e.g. *S.Rosc.* 8; *Q.Rosc.* 2 (with similar phrasing 'see how far I am going...'). He has no doubt assured himself that no such indication will be forthcoming; see previous n. He breaks down the Roman citizens into constituent groups (*distributio, diaeresis*; cf. Lausberg 1998, §675) so as to create an emphatic contrast between the many possible sources and the single set of account books demanded. The oath and the exclamation round off the topic.

M. Fonteius had charge...sway of the Roman people Here C. begins a survey of the constituent groups of Transalpine Gaul that continues to the middle of 13: the Gauls, the colonists of Narbo Martius, the Massiliotes, and the Roman citizens. 'To leave aside ancient history' glances at the saga of Manlius' repelling of the Gallic attack on the Capitol in 390; cf. 30n. The 'living memory' (*nostra memoria*) appealed to in oratory was one generation or a bit more in some cases; cf. Morstein-Marx 2004, ch. 3. The discussion of the Gauls focuses exclusively on military encounters and their results, on the Roman side 'triumphs and monuments', on the Gallic side loss of territory and cities in punishment. The attack of the Salluvii on land belonging to Massilia in 125 (Livy per. 60) led to Roman intervention which entailed triumphs of Fulvius Flaccus and Sextius Calvinus and the establishment by the latter of the fort at Aquae Sextiae (modern

Aix-en-Provence): *Act. triumph.* 122, 123; Livy per. 61; further hostilities followed with the Arverni and Allobroges until the major victories won by Cn. Domitius Ahenobarbus at Vindalium (perhaps a bit south-east of Arausio (modern Orange) and north-east of Avennio; see Talbert 2000, 15D1 with query) and by Q. Fabius Maximus at the confluence of the Isar (modern Isère) and the Rhodanus (modern Rhône): *Act. triumph.* 120; cf. Rivet 1988, 39–41. A stone tower marked the site of each victory, but no surviving traces have been found; cf. Flor. 1.36 (III.2); Rivet 1988, 41; very different the 'monuments of the exploits' of Fonteius' family mentioned at 41; see ad loc. Here C. leaves vague which tribes Fonteius fought against; the one name that later emerges is that of the Vocontii (cf. 20 with n.). He is careful to specify that the stripping of land was done 'by the senate' so there can be no question of overreaching on Fonteius' part; in 14, however, it is attributed to Pompey; see ad loc. The confiscated land was distributed to Roman citizens; hence their favourable view of Fonteius' administration. The description concludes with Fonteius' 'copious sweat and labour' by which Gallic territory was added to the Roman Empire. C. thus prepares the ground for the picture he will paint in the sequel of the Gauls as warrior-enemies and of Fonteius as the hard-working (cf. 42n. apropos of *industria*) and loyal servant of Rome's interests. All in all, as Ebel 1975, 366, observes, 'the description of Transalpina which Cicero presents is not one of an organized province, but rather one in the process of being organized'.

(13) There is in the same province . . . those very tribes On the urging of L. Licinius Crassus in 118 Rome moved to establish its first colony beyond the Alps at Narbo Martius; cf. *orat.* 66, no. 15–17; E. Ziebarth, *RE* Suppl. 7 515.29 ff. (s.v. Narbo); Salmon 1969, 121–3; Dahlheim 1977, 141; Gayraud 1981, 120–7; Rivet, 1988, 44. C. describes it as both a look-out post (*specula*) and bulwark (*propugnaculum*) of the Roman people (it would indeed play that role during Vercingetorix's revolt: Caes. *Gal.* 7.7; cf. Grenier 1937, 429). The description thus continues the assumption of hostile relations between Rome and the Gauls and implies the need to defend Italy against them. C. claims Narbonese support for his client in 14 and 46.

There is likewise the city . . . troops and rewards Massilia (modern Marseilles) was not actually part of the Roman province but an independent (Greek) state within it, founded from Phocis *c.*600, with friendly relations to Rome since at least the Hannibalic War. The allusion in this context is, however, justified since maintaining relations with Massilia formed part of the mandate of the governor of Transalpine Gaul. 'About which I previously spoke': the passage is lost in the lacuna prior to the onset of text in the Vatican MS. 'With . . . troops': C. seems to have in mind the garrison established at Aquae Sextiae (see 12n.). The 'rewards' were territorial in nature: when several of Massilia's colonies were attacked in 154 by the Deciates and Oxybii, the Romans intervened and awarded the conquered land to Massilia (Polyb. 33.8–10; Livy per. 47; Rivet 1988, 32–5); later Marius gave Massilia control of the canal his troops dug between the Rhône and the Mediterranean: Str. 4.1.8 (C 183); cf. also 14n. C. cites the Massiliotes' honorary decrees for Fonteius in 14.

There is besides . . . most honourable men The Roman citizens of the province balance the Gauls mentioned at the head of the list and are given weight by final position in the series; their views will be cited in 15. 'Equites' is Clark's insertion; the reference will, however, be to Roman equites, for whom 'honourable' (*honestus*) is a common epithet (cf. Hellegouarc'h 1972, 387–8 and 462–3; Nicolet 1966–74, i. 235–6; Achard 1981, 385), not Gallic cavalry, as Clark suggested ad loc. This group is clearly supporting Fonteius, as one expects from the class heavily engaged in banking and business in general; cf. Nicolet 1966–74, i. 357 ff.; Wiseman 1987, 57–73; Brunt 1988, ch. 3. The bankers lent capital to the Gauls at exorbitant rates and looked to the Roman governor to protect their interests; in Gaul as in Asia they were lightning rods for local resentment and among the first targets in times of revolt; cf. Grenier 1937, 431.

M. Fonteius had . . . various types C. resumes from the point at which he digressed in 12. 'Various types': literally 'variety (*varietas*) of types' cf. on *Scaur.* F 6; the word anticipates the varied reactions to Fonteius' governorship.

He subdued . . . the war in Spain Fonteius' military action is given pride of place, followed by his various administrative measures. For the stripping of lands cf. 12 with n. For Pompey's war in Spain cf. F 5n. 'In obedience to the Roman people': people who surrendered to Roman arms (*dediticii*) were deprived of their statehood but could have it restored, in which case they advanced to the status of 'allies' (*socii*); they were *stipendiarii*, i.e. subject to taxation in money and/or kind, and obliged to provide military assistance, as our passage illustrates. 'The entire world' glances at the third war with Mithridates in Asia, which began in 74; cf. Morstein-Marx 1995, 294 ff., especially 301. 'A very large sum of money and a very large amount of grain':

this corresponds to the emphasis on the need for money and supplies in Pompey's letter to the senate (Sal. *Hist.* 2.98); cf. Ebel 1975, 366.

(14) The man who carried this out . . . the unarmed M. Fonteius Two pictures of Fonteius artfully bookend this sentence: he first appears as the man of (military) action ('the man who carried this out'), then as the unarmed (*inermis*) defendant on trial, whereby his recent opponents have turned the tables and are now trying to reverse their recent military defeat ('from the slaughter and rout of war') by judicial means; cf. the contrast of 'armed' and 'unarmed' at *Caec.* 93. Between the two parties stand the jurors ('you': *vos*) and with them the Roman people, whose interests the jurors protect, as was expected in Rome's 'public courts' (*iudicia publica*); cf. Riggsby 1999*a*, 157–71. 'On whom . . . the orders fell': sc. for support in cavalry, money, and grain as detailed in the previous sentence. The stripping of territory is here attributed to Pompey, previously to the senate (12); no doubt both references are to Pompey's decree ratified by the senate; cf. Ebel 1975, 370, and 1976, 99. These arrangements dated from the fall of 77 when on his way to Spain to face Sertorius Pompey put down a revolt and reorganized territory to benefit Massilia; cf. *Man.* 28 and 30; Caes. *Civ.* 1.34.3 and 35.4; Gelzer 1984, 48; Ebel 1976, 99–100, and in detail 1975.

Tell me . . . unharmed by him The opinions of the other constituent groups of the province are now canvassed in the same order as the inventory at 13; for a similar survey of attitudes towards the defendant cf. *Ver.* 2.2.13–16 and 165–8. In each case the report follows a question introduced with *quid?* ('tell me'). Both here and in 46 C. leaves vague exactly how the colonists of Narbo expressed their support; they could have passed a decree and/or sent representatives to the trial. He presents their view as an appropriate balancing of benefits received and bestowed; cf. 46 apropos Fonteia's service as Vestal; *Scaur.* 39 of Q. Cicero. At 46 C. specifies that his client relieved the colony when it was under siege; see ad loc.

What is the sentiment . . . weight in your minds For the Massiliotes' presence here cf. 13n. C. uses pronouns to contrast how the Massiliotes act *vis-à-vis* Fonteius and the jurors. The honours awarded in such circumstances included public hospitality, honorary citizenship, etc. Such honours could, however, be extorted by a governor, as Verres did in Sicily; cf. *Ver.* 2.2.141–64 (extorted statues) and 2.4.145 (repeal of a decree in his honour by the Syracusan senate). 'Begs and beseeches' (*orat atque obsecrat*): an alliterative pair of which C. was fond in his early speeches; cf. *Quinct.* 10; *S.Rosc.* 10 and 77; *Q.Rosc.* 20; von Albrecht, *RE* Suppl. 13 1303.61–5 and 2003, 100. 'Conscientiousness' (*religio*) in this context is one's adherence to one's sworn oath in providing evidence to the court; cf. Freyburger 1986, 218–22; 45 n. This is precisely the quality that will be denied to the Gallic witnesses against Fonteius at 21 ff.

(15) Tell me, what is the wish . . . the allies and the citizens 'Not one' (*nemo*) occupies the emphatic initial position in the Latin sentence (cf. the first sentence of 3) and contrasts with 'so vast a number'. Two pairs of entities are presented as Fonteius' beneficiaries: the province and the empire of which it is a part and within the province the basic constituents, allies (*socii*: see 13n.) and Roman citizens.

Since therefore, jurors, . . . because of their disloyalty 'Attack' (*oppugno*) can be used in both a literal and, as here, a metaphorical sense; cf. *OLD* s.v.; both senses are juxtaposed in 35. The jurors should be guided, C. suggests, by their own sense of fairness (*aequitas*) and by the standing (*dignitas*) of the Roman people; the latter would be impaired, C. will go on to argue, if the jurors are seen to capitulate to the Gauls' threats (33–6). C. poses a dilemma to the jury: they must side with either of two groups, whereby the work of assimilating the one and alienating the other group is done by the attached epithets: the colonists and businessmen are both qualified as 'your' (*vestris*) and the allies (the Massiliotes) are the 'closest and most ancient' allies. The other side (the Gauls) are denied credibility (*fides*) because of their anger (*iracundia*); this is the first mention of this passion in the extant speech; C. will call the Gauls 'angry' (*irati*) at 18, 21, and 36; cf. Vasaly 1993, 194. Their anger could be regarded as a sign that they genuinely felt themselves to have been victimized. But C. instead couples their anger with covetousness at 21 and wants these passions to be seen as signs of an unstable character; later he will present, contrariwise, the impassiveness of Milo as part of his characterization as a quasi-Stoic; cf. Dyck 1998. The enthymeme continues with the previous conclusion (the Gauls' lack of credibility) as the premiss for the next argument. C. constructs the Massiliotes as 'most faithful' (*fidelissimi*) allies (13) and Macedonia as a 'faithful (*fidelis*) province' (44) for contrast with Gallic 'disloyalty' (*infidelitas*). C.'s claim is in striking contrast to the Emperor Claudius' attribution to the Gauls of 'one hundred years' unwavering loyalty (*fides*) and obedience' (Smallwood 1967: §369.34–5). 'Honour' for the Gauls is not actually at issue before this court, but victory in such litigation could be viewed as such, just as 'eternal dishonour and disgrace' would adhere to Fonteius if convicted (48 *fin.*).

(16) Tell me . . . the supreme authority of all? For 'honourable men' cf. 13n. The Gauls receive no such approving epithet, and with *consensio* ('collusion') C. has chosen a noun that can suggest improper purposes; cf. *Scaur.* 38; *OLD* s.v. 1b: 'plot, subversive agreement, conspiracy'; by a similar strategy he speaks of a 'collusion' (*conspiratio*) and 'conspiracy' (*coniuratio*) among the Sardinian witnesses against Scaurus (cf. *Scaur.* 20n.). In both cases he wants to discredit the foreign witnesses en bloc; cf. Alexander 2002, 63. He goes on to marginalize the Gallic witnesses by opposing them to 'the supreme authority of all'.

You know, jurors, . . . went to join them! For Fonteius' years of service in Gaul cf. 11n. The commanders included Q. Metellus Pius, Sulla's colleague in the consulship of 80, who had since 79 been proconsul of Further Spain. Pompey was appointed to an extraordinary command in Spain in 77 and hastily gathered an army of 30,000 infantry and 1,000 cavalry (Oros. 5.23.9; Sal. *Hist.* 2.98.4); in 74 he successfully appealed to the senate for more troops (cf. the version of his letter at Sal. *Hist.* 2.98). The military tribunes (*tribuni militum*) were mostly of equestrian, occasionally senatorial, family; they were distributed six to a legion and were its highest-ranking officers; the tribunes of the first four legions recruited in a given year were elected, the rest appointed by the commander; cf. in general Suolahti 1955. The legates (*legati*) were officers appointed by the senate on recommendation of the commander; cf. Thomasson 1991. Caesar later enlarged the role of legates at the expense of the military tribunes.

In addition . . . held command This will refer to the second and final time Pompey wintered in Gaul during the campaign against Sertorius, i.e. 74–73 (Sal. *Hist.* 3.46 and Livy per. 93), not 77–76 (Sal. *Hist.* 2.22; App. *BC* 1.109–10.510); cf., however, Brennan 2000, 510, arguing for the earlier date.

Does Fortune herself . . . encomiast and witness Once again C. harps on the prosecution's failure to find supporting Roman witnesses, in spite of the great number of those potentially available; cf. 12 'let them produce a single witness from the number of so many businessmen, settlers, publicans, farmers, cattle-breeders'. In calling them 'suitable' (*idoneos*), he implies, of course, the unsuitability of the Gallic witnesses. For 'authority' (*auctor*) cf. 2n.

(17) Will you be in doubt any longer . . . could not be safe? C. cross-refers to a point made in the exordium, where see n. 'Nothing else is at stake': similar wording at *S.Rosc.* 8. The idea of commands imposed 'against their will' is repeated from 14 but here defended powerfully by invoking the state interest. The reason why future commanders would be slower (*segniores*) in exercising command would be that they see even such a pillar of Roman rule as Fonteius attacked; this sense requires adoption of two readings of the more recent MSS, *videant* ('they see') for *videatis* ('you see') and *oppugnari* ('to be attacked') for *oppugnare* ('to attack') as well as insertion of *sine* ('without') after the latter.

It has been laid to his charge . . . many were denied certification His argument about the Gallic witnesses concluded for now (it will recur from a different angle at 26–40), C. turns to consider a series of specific charges. The first has to do with road-construction, a key component of the Romans' success in creating and binding together their empire; cf. Salmon 1969, 83–4 and 123; Wiseman 1970; Chevallier 1976; Laurence 2001. The noun C. uses here is *munitio*: *OLD* s. v. 3: 'the building up (of a road) so as to give it a firm surface'; this and the related verb (*munire*) may refer either to initial construction or to maintenance; cf. Wiseman 1970, 147 = 1987, 151. Improvements to the road-system were urgently needed to facilitate the movement of troops and supplies to Spain (cf. 18 'in the public interest'; F 9). The costs and labour were, however, the responsibility of the provincials as part of their tribute, as continued in general to be the case under the Empire; cf. Grenier 1937, 430; Kunkel and Wittmann 1995, 365 n. 221. Fonteius is alleged to have profited both by granting exemptions from roadwork ('that he . . . did not compel it') and by taking bribes to certify work done ('that he . . . failed to find . . . defective'); similarly Verres is alleged to have demanded that the farmers of Agyrium pay one sesterce per bushel as a fee for approval of the grain they submitted as a tithe; cf. *Ver.* 2.3.73; such was, in fact, his general practice (ibid. 171). C. meets the first point with a blanket denial that any exemptions were granted; since, however, he makes no attempt to document the claim, it seems 'suspiciously brief' (Alexander 2002, 68). C.'s answer to the second point is also feeble: he merely notes that in many cases roadwork was not certified; but that might merely mean that a few paid bribes but many others refused to do so (so Alexander loc. cit.).

(18) Tell me . . . ascribe all to M. Fonteius? The first sentence of 16 is a question similar in form: in both there is a contrary factor that should be decisive against the negatively characterized Gallic testimony. The Via Domitia (named only here in extant sources) was built by Cn. Domitius Ahenobarbus (cos. 122) following his victories over the Arverni and other tribes of southern Gaul; it went from Narbo south through the Rousillon to the Pyrenees; cf. G. Radke, *RE* Suppl. 13 1668.58–1669.23 and 1672 (s.v. *Viae publicae Romanae*); Radke 1964, 313–14 and 317; finds in the area include a milestone of Domitius discovered at Pont de Treilles (as well as later milestones); cf. Campardou 1949; Duval 1949. Fonteius ordered the road expanded and delegated supervision of the work to the legates C. Annius Bellienus and C. Fonteius. This was, however, not a defence for misconduct, since the governor had to take responsibility for the work of his subalterns; cf. *Div. Caec.* 35; *Ver.* 2.2.26–9; *Q.fr.* 1.1 (1).10; Brennan 2000, 483 and 837 n. 43; Alexander 2002, 69. Hence C. is quick to say that he is not trying to fob off guilt on to them (but see below). For the anger of the Gallic witnesses as discrediting cf. 15n.; contrast Cluentius' prosecution of Oppianicus on the basis of 'the most reliable charges and witnesses' (*Clu.* 10).

When M. Fonteius . . . issued certifications C. is vague about the 'greater affairs of state' that allegedly preoccupied Fonteius; perhaps he alludes to the war with the Vocontii (20). For the Via Domitia see the previous n.; construction on it at this date must indeed have been a state necessity, given the scale of military operations in Spain and the need to send troops and supplies (16 with n.; F 9). C. names two legates, both known only from our speech, C. Annius Bellienus and C. Fonteius, who were in charge of the project; cf. Klebs, *RE* 1.2 2264.38 and Münzer, *RE* 6.2 2842.64 respectively; the latter thinks that C. must have mentioned the relationship if C. Fonteius was his defendant's brother (or did he suppress the fact to enhance the pathos of the peroration? cf. 47 with n.); Schneider 1876, 2, speculates that he was a cousin of the defendant and that the P. Fonteius who adopted C.'s enemy P. Clodius in 59 was his son; cf. Rawson 1991, 235 n. 60; on the legates see also Thomasson 1991, 19 and 110–11 (nos. 140 and 141); *MRR* ii. 105, 530, and 566. 'In line with their standing' (*pro dignitate sua*) they had licence to issue orders and certifications. 'Issue certifications' renders *probo*, the verb regularly used for this process in Roman public works inscriptions (cf. *TLL* s.v. *probo* 1461.66), as is the corresponding Oscan verb in such inscriptions in Oscan-speaking Italy (Untermann 2000: 583 s.v. O.*prúfatted*).

(18–19) It was open to you . . . no one could criticize The Urbino extortion law provides for the prosecutor's collection and delivery to the praetor of relevant documentary evidence (line 34); cf. Mommsen 1899, 432–3. In this case Fonteius' correspondence with his legates has been transcribed and made available for the jurors to review; it is now read out in court for good measure. C. uses these documents to distance his client from road-construction policy ('the policy of road-construction does not pertain to M. Fonteius'). He claims but does not show that the legates should be immune from criticism.

(19) Now learn about . . . most invidious and greatest Transition to the next charge, the toll levied on wine. It is a common tactic to pump up the charge initially and then deflate it in the sequel; cf. *Flac.* 90: 'But Falcidius' charge is huge: he says he gave Flaccus fifty talents'; for the formulation cf. also *Div. Caec.* 30: 'a large charge, a huge amount of money'. The Romans forbade the Transalpine Gauls to plant vines and olives (*Rep.* 3.16); if that prohibition is still in force, the wine in question will be imported from Italy; cf. also the reference to 'our fruits' in 20; de Laet 1949, 82–3; Rivet 1988, 35, however, thinks that the ban applied only to the Oxybii and Deciates, the tribes of Transalpina conquered by 129, the fictive date of C.'s dialogue. For commercial ties between Italy and Gaul at this period cf. Clemente 1974, 21–71; for Italian wine and its trade to Gaul cf. Tchernia 1983 and 1986. Finds of Gallic ceramics at Pompeii show that by AD 79 the roles of importer and exporter were reversed; cf. Leveau in Scheidel *et al.* 2007: 662.

The charge was put in place . . . settled upon and planned For the prosecutor M. Plaetorius cf. 36n. For 'duty' (*portorium*), a tax on goods passing a certain point, cf. Mommsen 1887–8, ii. 440; detailed study by de Laet 1949, especially 76–84 (on Gaul); Cottier *et al.* 2008, 35 (ll. 22 ff.). In general tolls were regulated by law of the censors, which may not, however, have specified locations for toll stations; a provincial governor probably had considerable latitude in this area. So the illegality was probably not the new toll stations *per se* but rather that Fonteius allegedly entered into a secret agreement at Rome whereby he would receive a percentage of the new revenues (see on F 11); cf. de Laet 1949, 80–1; Alexander 2002, 71. The plotting at Rome was probably inferred from the speed with which the new system was implemented; thus C. inferred such plotting by Verres to maximize profits before setting out for Sicily from the speed with which he summoned Dio of Halaesa to his presence; cf. *Ver.* 2.2.17–19. Possibly Fonteius yielded to pressure or bribes from Tolosa to make arrangements favouring that town; cf. Hermon 1993, 288–9, and 1995, 570.

that therefore at Tolosa . . . exported to the enemy This passage, which shows more local knowledge of Gaul than any other in the extant speech (cf. Rambaud 1980, 308), is quoted in indirect discourse from the prosecutor. It comprises a list of four towns in which toll stations were established and those in charge of each. Of these C. Annius is evidently Fonteius' legate (see 18); the others may also have been of that rank (rather than publicans, as is sometimes assumed). Thus Brennan 2000, 510, suggests that Titurius may be identified with the moneyer L. Titurius L.f. Sabinus (*RRC* no. 344 dated to 89) and the legate Titurius charged by Pompey with commanding a winter camp in Celtiberia perhaps in 75/74 (Sal. *Hist.* 2.94; Thomasson 1991, 110, no. 137); the others named are otherwise unknown; at Crodunum Porcius and Munius may have commanded in succession over the course of Fonteius' three-year tenure. The current identifications of the towns are as follows: Tolosa = Toulouse, Vulchalo = Carcassonne, Crodunum = Castelnaudary, and Elesiodunum = Montferrand; there is also a destination without a toll station, Cobiomagum (= Bram); cf. Hermon 1993, 285–6; Rancoule 1985, 265–7. The Roman denarius was created as a silver coin with its half piece the quinarius in 211; the latter was revived and struck in large quantities engraved with a victoriatus type in 101 and 99–97 and widely circulated in both Transalpine and Cisalpine Gaul ('victoriatus' is here rendered as 'half'); Cf. *RRC* 621–30. The fees quoted are evidently based upon distance travelled. 'The enemy' probably refers to the Ruteni, the tribe outside the province closest to Elesiodunum, not to Sertorius' army. cf. Clemente 1974, 133–7.

(20) I see, jurors, . . . by word of mouth C. concedes that this is a large-scale matter and that much ill-will (*invidia*) can accrue to it. For a 'tax' (*vectigal*) of this kind cf. Mommsen 1887–8, ii. 434–43 and iii. 731–2 and 1115. 'Our fruits': Roman wine is evidently in question; see above. The potential ill-will is shown by the keenness of Fonteius' private enemies (*inimici*) to spread the story. Who were these enemies? Ward 1968, 803–5, and 1970 suspects the Metelli; Gruen 1971, 12–13 (cf. 1974, 268 n. 28), however, points out that there is no evidence that the prosecution received Metellan support.

But my view . . . to arrive at the truth In spite of the concession just made, C. is not prepared to admit the truth of the charge itself; rather, he insists that the invention of a large falsehood is a greater injustice since it 'seizes (*occupare*) the minds of the listeners' and thus makes it difficult to find the truth; cf. *Ver.* 2.4.113: 'so great a superstition seized (*occupavit*) the minds of all the Sicilians'.

On the charge . . . winter-quarters These are rubrics referring to topics omitted either by C. himself or an ancient editor of the speech; cf. Dyck 2011. The topic of the tax on wine, broached in the preceding sections, evidently continued, since C. has asserted but not yet proven that the charge is false. C. has referred vaguely to Fonteius' military campaign (12–13); here we find out the name of one tribe of his enemies, the Vocontii, who were subdued in 118 but rebelled in 109 and again during Fonteius' governorship; cf. H. Rolland, *RE* 9A1 705.48–55 (s.v. Vocontii). Brennan 2000, 510, thinks this war against one of the first tribes encountered in the province may have occurred early in Fonteius' governorship to secure the transit-routes for troops bound for Spain. Since most troops were committed to Spain, Ebel 1976, 97, suspects a minor engagement: 'perhaps he was making forcible "requisitions" of supplies'. After Caesar's conquest, the Vocontii were, like Massilia, an allied state; they were later incorporated in Narbonensis; cf. H. Rolland, *RE* 9A1 705.60 ff. (s.v. Vocontii). 'The distribution of winter quarters' may have involved his own troops, but as the responsible governor, Fonteius may also have determined the location of Pompey's winter camps in Gaul in 74/73; see 16n.; on the damage that could be entailed cf. *Man.* 38.

(21) 'But the Gauls deny this.' . . . prove it Here C. introduces arguments of an imaginary objector, a feature of popular rhetoric; cf. *Scaur.* 18n. What do the Gauls deny? Lintott 2008, 24, takes it to be C.'s responses 'to the prosecution's charges regarding the tax on wine, the war with the Vocontii, and the allocation of winter-quarters'. But it seems unlikely that C. had a single reply to these diverse charges that could be summarized as 'this' (*hoc*). The reduction to rubrics implies omission of fairly considerable matter and complex argument under each head. Also relevant here is whether the rubrics were added by C. himself or a later editor; see previous n. What does seem clear is that the Gauls' 'denial' will have been given during the questioning of witnesses at the end of the first session (*actio*) of the trial: Lintott, loc. cit. For the conflict between logic and

witness testimony cf. F 1, possibly from the immediately preceding argument.

'Can a juror ... regard for conscience The dialogue with an imaginary objector continues. C. lists four disqualifying traits, all claimed for the Gauls: they are first called 'self-interested' (*cupidi*) here and again at 32; cf. 45 (*cupiditas*); 'unbridled greed' (*libido*) in 4 and 49 intensifies the idea; for their anger cf. 15n.; 'conspiring' (*coniuratis*) was adumbrated by the reference to their 'collusion' (*consensio*) at 16; cf. *Scaur.* 38n.; 'have no regard for conscience' (*religio*): i.e. the conscientious fulfilment of the witness's oath. C. will argue this point in detail at 27–32, where *religio* broadens its meaning to regard for the cult of the gods generally.

If because the Gauls ... we cannot deny it' 'Guilty' renders *nocens*; *innocens* is attested much earlier (Naev. *trag.* 9), whereas *nocens* apparently developed as its antonym only in C.'s time; cf. *OLD* s.vv.; *TLL* s.v. *innocens*. C. argues that a blanket acceptance of witness testimony would rob court proceedings of their point. Here and elsewhere 'juror' renders *iudex* so as to avoid confusion with the presiding officer; for the 'wise' *iudex* cf. 23 and e.g. *Caec.* 8; in general Hartung 1974. 'Presiding officer' renders *quaesitor*, the president of one of the *quaestiones* (standing courts) of Rome; the word is also used loosely of any of the jurors in such a court; cf. *OLD* s.v. *quaesitor* 1; Mommsen 1899, 187 n. 3 and 206–7. Though the extortion court was always headed by a serving praetor, a *quaesitor* (in the narrower sense) presided e.g. over the murder court.

In this connection ... brave men's innocence 'Clever and experienced and fair' are meant to stand as attributes of a good juror; 'clever' (*ingeniosus*) does not so function elsewhere in C.'s speeches; cf. 39, where it is an epithet of C. Gracchus. 'Experienced' (*peritus*) is often found in the set phrase for 'legal expert' *iuris peritus*; but here C. evidently uses the term in a broad sense; cf. 25; *Clu.* 115. Verres is ironically a 'fair (*aequus*) judge' at *Ver.* 2.1.73; the phrase is used without irony ibid. 3.164 and at *Rab. perd.* 7. As a common noun *salus* is a person's 'safety, well-being' or the like (*OLD* s.v. 1); the defendant's *salus* is regularly spoken of as being at risk in legal proceedings; cf. e.g. *Planc.* 3 and 69, *Mil.* 102, *Deiot.* 1. Salus is also from an early date an Italian goddess prayed to in order to guarantee one's safety; cf. Wissowa 1912, 131–3 and 308–9; Winkler 1995. Under this hypothesis even innocence and prayers to Salus would be without effect.

If, however . . . than mine in pleading An alternative view of the judge's role (introduced by *sin* 'If, however'). The text adopted here is Fleckeisen's restoration, whereby *valere existimatis* ('you think . . . serves') is inserted following *iudicis* ('juror's'), it being assumed that the scribe's eye skipped from *-is* to *-is*; for the sense of *valeo* see *OLD* s.v. 7b: 'to tend effectively to a result, serve towards'. 'Perhaps' renders *videte ne* + subj., literally 'take care (that not)'; cf. *OLD* s.v. *video* 17a. Here, as sometimes elsewhere, C. reflects on the division of labour between the jurors and the defence counsel; cf. e.g. *S.Rosc.* 10 and 36, where it is differently conceived.

(22) For I must interrogate . . . reason for remaining silent Here C. offers an explanation for his previous assertion ('for', *enim*). There is a quantitative difference in the two roles: C. interrogating 'once' (*semel*) or not at all, whereas the jurors must 'often' (*saepe*) reflect on the same matter and infer the reason for C.'s decision to forego interrogation. The comparison is of unlike entities, however, holding up C.'s actions in court for contrast with the jurors' thought processes; he ignores the fact that the advocate must think long and hard about his case. By denying cross-examination to an angry or self-interested witness, C. implicitly acts upon the principle established in 21 that such a person is not credible (though the real reason may rather have been his inability to discredit the testimony; cf. *Scaur.* 19). He thus hints that the jurors should not expect detailed cross-examination of the prosecution's Gallic witnesses, just as Hortensius declined to question the Sicilian witnesses against Verres at the latter's trial; cf. *Ver.* 2.3.41 and 5.155; Alexander 2002, 73 and 278 n. 48; similarly *Scaur.* 20. Both advocates were probably following an already established playbook for dealing with hostile foreign witnesses.

Therefore if you think . . . the stupid and the wise This restates from 21 with emphasis on the juror the point about the levelling of generally accepted distinctions ('If because the Gauls . . . we cannot deny it').

(23) Where, then, is there . . . they are pronounced 'Conscientious' (*religiosus*) applies to the juror no less than the witness (cf. 21 'regard for conscience'), since the juror is sworn to render a true verdict; cf. *Scaur.* 17n.; for the 'wise juror' cf. 21n. For C.'s call for jurors to engage in *coniectura*, i.e. the drawing of inferences, cf. *Ver.* 2.4.34; *Scaur.* 15n. The indirect questions 'with how much authority . . . they are pronounced' are loosely appended as the content of the jurors'

reflections. 'With how much authority' is the ultimate question and is broken down into components by *divisio* (cf. 12n.). 'Mental balance' (*aequitas animi*) is a criterion that would, of course, exclude witnesses infected with the self-interest and anger attributed to the Gauls; cf. 21n. At 27 ff. C. will examine in detail the demeanour of the chief Gallic witness, Indutiomarus, and find it wanting in modesty, etc.

Or in the testimonies of barbarians . . . men of our community? An implicit a fortiori argument from the treatment of the testimony of eminent Romans. For the Gauls as 'barbarians' cf. 4n. For the 'usable memory' invoked in public oratory at Rome cf. 12n.

They did not believe . . . courage, family and exploits Rhetorical theory defines example as a technical proof introduced from outside the case; the historical example is the commonest type since it enjoys the greatest credibility; cf. Quint. *Inst.* 5.11.1 and 17. From here through 27 C. offers examples of famous Romans being disbelieved by juries; at 38–40 he gives instances of outrageous charges made against famous Romans; the former is an a fortiori argument that scepticism of Gallic testimony is warranted; the latter is a foil for Fonteius, who has been subjected to no such charges. On C.'s use of historical examples see further Schönberger 1911; Sinkovich 1974; Brinton 1988; Bücher 2006, part 3; van der Blom 2010, ch. 6. Q. Pompeius (cos. 141) was, as C. notes, 'a new man' (*novus homo*), i.e. without family background in politics; on his rise cf. Wiseman 1971, 3. He served in Spain as consul and proconsul and after an unsuccessful campaign concluded a peace with the Numantines that he later denied; cf. *MRR* i. 477 and 480; Richardson 1986, 144–6. When prosecuted *c.*138 for misconduct in Spain, he was acquitted in spite of hostile testimony by representatives of formidable noble families (*TLRR* 8), namely two pairs of brothers, Cn. Servilius Caepio (cos. 141) and Q. Servilius Caepio (cos. 140) and L. Caecilius Metellus Calvus (cos. 142) and Q. Caecilius Metellus Macedonicus (cos. 143); on the forensic activity of the 'two Caepiones' at this time see also *Brut.* 97. 'Suspicion' is the personified subject; cf. F 2 with n. Personal enmity (*inimicitia*) was a potent force in Roman politics; cf. Epstein 1987, especially (on this case) 99 and 105–6. The enmity already felt between them was exacerbated when Pompeius succeeded Macedonicus as governor of Nearer Spain; his complaints that his predecessor deliberately left the army in poor condition ruined Macedonicus' chances for a triumph (cf. V. Max. 9.3.7); on the political background cf. Gruen 1968, 34–7. It is doubtful, however, that self-interest (*cupiditas*) in a material sense was an important factor in the prosecution; at 27 C. defines the potential gain for the Caepiones and Metelli in terms of political interests ('when they would have rid themselves of a critic of their policies').

(24) Is there any man . . . M. Aemilius Scaurus? For the elder Scaurus and C.'s admiration for him in his youth cf. on *Scaur.* F 2–5.

Though the earth . . . banish a man he hated As leader of the senate (*princeps senatus*; cf. *Scaur.* 46n.), Scaurus exercised great influence; hence C. hyperbolically assimilates him to the traditional picture of Jupiter, whose nod indicated assent; cf. e.g. Virg. *A.* 9.106: 'he nodded and with his nod shook the whole of Olympus'. C. alludes to two trials of uncertain date, both for extortion (this is evidently what V. Max. 8.5.2 means in saying they were tried 'under the same law'). Memmius had provoked Scaurus in 109 when the latter served as advocate for L. Calpurnius Bestia, under indictment by Memmius for treason in his dealings with Jugurtha as consul in 111 (*MRR* i. 540; *TLRR* 54; *De orat.* 2.283; Gruen 1968, 149). Memmius in turn was called to account for his conduct of the praetorship (104? cf. *MRR* i. 549 with 562 n. 4); he was assassinated as a candidate during the consular elections of 100; cf. Münzer, *RE* s.v. Memmius 5. C. Flavius Fimbria (cos. 104) was prosecuted by M. Gratidius, the brother of Cicero's paternal grandmother (Münzer, *RE* s.v. Gratidius 2), presumably for extortion as governor of a province; C. will have known of the case from family tradition; cf. Münzer, *RE* s.v. Flavius 87. Both men were acquitted despite Scaurus' testimony; cf. *TLRR* 60 and 61; Gruen 1968, 174–5. D'Arms 1972 argues that the recollection of our passage with its juxtaposed examples of Pompeius and Scaurus led C. to compare the two men at *Mur.* 16.

Who is unaware . . . against M. Marcellus Another of the young Cicero's heroes was L. Licinius Crassus (cos. 95), immortalized as the main speaker of *On the Orator*, where C. expatiates (1.121–2) on Crassus' modesty (*pudor*). The defendant was evidently the M. Claudius Marcellus who, as legate of C. Marius, was a participant in the great victory at Aquae Sextiae (102; Thomasson 1991, 108, no. 95); on his further career cf. Münzer, *RE* s.v. Claudius 226. The date of the trial and the charge are not attested; Crassus' death yields a lower terminus of 91; cf. *TLRR* 87; Gruen 1968, 194 and n. 26.

(25) Those jurors . . . self-interest or enmity For gemination of the verb to create excitement cf. Wills 1996, 103; similarly *Scaur.* 25 and 49. 'Divine' (*divinus*) is fairly frequent as a high commendation;

cf. e.g. *De orat.* 1.40: 'I recall Servilius Galba, a man of prodigious eloquence' (*divinum hominem in dicendo*); *OLD* s.v. 3b. The judges in the cited cases, according to C., took a comprehensive view and considered the various possible corrupting factors on both sides. Similarly, Q. Mucius Scaevola Pontifex held that it took a great judge to decide cases involving 'good faith' (*bona fides*) since the possibility of a countersuit demanded a comprehensive view of the rights and wrongs at issue (cf. *Off.* 3.70). 'Invented' (*fictum*) could apply either to the prosecutor's charge (cf. e.g. *S.Rosc.* 128 'invented charge', *ficto crimine*) or the testimony of witnesses. For 'circumstance' (*tempus*), often political, as a factor in prosecution cf. *S.Rosc.* 28 with Dyck 2010 ad loc. Hope, fear, and financial gain are among the paths of influence at *Off.* 2.21–2; hope, fear, and reward are among the standard topics brought to bear against witnesses according to *Part.* 49. Bribery could, of course, be used to motivate either a prosecutor or witnesses (cf. C.'s complaint at *S.Rosc.* 30). Rewards (*praemia*) were available for those who aided successful prosecution in some types of criminal trial of the late Republic. Thus under the *lex Acilia* foreigners not of Latin status could hope for citizenship and immunity from military service or, if they preferred, the right of appeal against a magistrate's decision (*provocatio*) and immunity from military service (lines 76–9); admission to citizenship seems, however, to have been confined to Latins under one of the Servilian laws (*Balb.* 54); cf. Alexander 1985. Self-interest and enmity occupy final position for emphasis, since C. claims that they are at play in the present case.

If the juror does not . . . to judge cases 'Embrace . . . with his intelligence': similarly *Ver.* 2.2.1: 'I embraced [it, i.e. the Sicilians' case] with my mind somewhat more fully'. 'Is not circumspect' renders *circumspiciet* ('does not look about'), often used metaphorically for 'consider carefully' and modified to show that a mental process is meant; cf. e.g. *Agr.* 2.45; *Sul.* 70. 'From that place' was presumably said with a gesture to the tribunal, from which, after being summoned by the herald, the witness gave testimony; cf. Mommsen 1899, 431; David 1995 (history of the tribunal); Bablitz 2007, 59 (reconstruction of a large courtroom); Citroni Marchetti 1995, 21, 24, and 30 (on the way the tribunal is figured in the speech). 'As I said before': C. reprises from 22 the argument about the levelling of distinctions among jurors.

(26) Or did those Roman equites . . . the Volcae and the Allobroges? That earlier witnesses possessed greater authority but were nonetheless disbelieved was also a standard argument against witnesses (*Part.* 49). 'Recently' (*nuper*) is a term of some elasticity which Cicero sometimes uses deceptively. The equites had not enjoyed exclusive control of the juries since 91. C. Gracchus removed the extortion court from senatorial control and gave it to the equites in 122 (the Sempronian Law: Rotondi 1912, 313–14), and the matter remained contentious for some fifty years. In 106 the Servilian Law created mixed juries of senators and equites (ibid. 325), but the equites regained control in 104 or 101 (the *lex Servilia Glauciae*: cf. Lintott, *CAH* ix. 94). Under the Plautian Law (89: Rotondi 1912: 342) there were mixed juries with senators, equites, and ordinary citizens serving side by side. Sulla gave the senate control once again (the Cornelian Law of 82: ibid. 351). Most of C.'s forensic cases, like ours, were tried under the Aurelian Law providing for juries divided equally among senators, equites, and the *tribuni aerarii* (another citizen group meeting a property qualification) (70: ibid. 369). cf. Nicolet 1966–74, i. 467 ff.; Brunt 1988, 151–60. The height of equestrian influence in the state should perhaps be dated from *c.*107, the first consulship of C. Marius, who was himself an eques by birth and marked out a policy in opposition to that of the established nobility; cf. Lintott, *CAH* ix. 90–2; *Rab. perd.* 20, referring to the power of the equites, including control of the courts, in 100; *S.Rosc.* 140, describing the supporters of the Sullan revolution as 'those who could not abide the distinction of the equites'; some equites, like Cicero's friend T. Pomponius Atticus, preferred on the whole to stay out of politics; cf. Brunt 1988, 155. C. alludes again to the cases of Crassus and Scaurus cited in 24: the equestrian jurors did not allow themselves to be bowled over by the authority of such formidable nobles; the a fortiori argument is that the present jury should be at least as sceptical of the testimony of Gallic tribesmen. Indutiomarus, one of the principal witnesses, was leader of the Allobroges; hence their appearance here. C. takes a very different view of their credibility at *Sul.* 17 ('the most truthful witnesses') and 36 ('behold the care of the Gauls'), since he relied on their testimony against the Catilinarian conspirators but is at pains to show that their evidence need not damage his client; cf. Schmitz 1985, 150–1. If the Volcae or their representatives played a major role in the case, our passage is the only surviving trace; cf. 46n.; the group in question here, the Volcae Tectosages, settled in the region of Tolosa

in Languedoc; cf. Bannert, *RE* Suppl. 15, 937.16 ff., especially 945.29 ff. (s.v. Volcae).

If one should disbelieve . . . to my client? C. adverts to the principle laid down at 23–4 that personal enmity compromises the credibility of testimony and repeats two of the examples from 24. The tacit premiss is that enmity within the body politic ('citizens' partisanship and domestic backbiting') is less bitter than that against foreign enemies (and the damage to credibility if testimony is set aside is therefore also less).

Of the Gauls . . . crushed in this very war Fonteius' policies are repeated from 13, this time ranked by their impact on the subjects ('those in the best position . . . others . . . others . . . ').

(27) If any people . . . to believe them 'Gain' renders *emolumentum*, originally the 'output from a mill' and used in a broad sense in Latin, whereas the English derivative is specialized as 'pay'; cf. *OLD* s.v. For the principle that personal interest vitiates testimony cf. *Q.Rosc.* 45; Quint. *Inst.* 5.7.5; Greenidge 1901, 482 and n. 5.

A greater gain . . . is practically bound up 'I am sure' (*credo*) signals irony, as often; cf. *OLD* s.v. 8c. For the judicial assault of the Caepiones and Metelli on Q. Pompeius see 23n. 'Policies' renders *studia*; cf. *OLD* s.v. *studium* 5b. 'Immunity' (*immunitas*) is 'exemption from tax or tribute': *OLD* s.v. 'Immunity and liberty' are combined here, as they generally were in practice (though theoretically separable); cf. Dahlheim 1977, 255–61. Though some peoples of the province may have enjoyed status as 'free and exempt' (*liberi et immunes*), it was, of course, naïve for the Gauls to suppose that their tributary status was Fonteius' personal imposition, rather than the policy of the Roman state. They are evidently projecting their own tribal and quasi-feudal notions of conquest onto Rome, which is, rather, imposing a developed imperial bureaucracy; cf. Doyle 1986: 135–6 for a typology of relations between periphery and metropole. For a similar overestimation of the power of individual officials attributed to the Sardinians cf. *Scaur.* 36n. For a different interpretation cf. Ward 1968, 804, not registering the irony.

Or if it is fitting . . . the lowest Roman citizen? This follows from the classification of Gauls as barbarians (cf. 4n.); C. will dilate on the topic in the sequel. The distinction between Gauls and Romans was, however, not so absolute as he pretends. Thus one of the Vocontii, Cn. Pompeius Trogus, grandfather of the historian, was granted citizenship by Pompey for services in the war with Sertorius (Just.

Phil. 43.5.11 = Pomp. Trog. fr. 165); cf. Rambaud 1980, 309 and n. 23; in addition, Sulla is known to have granted citizenship to some Gauls (*Arch.* 25). Badian 1958, appendix B, has compiled a list of those known to have been granted citizenship individually in the late Republic; cf. Brunt 1971, 204–5. Some Western provincials were also granted citizenship as a group, e.g. the *turma Salluitana*, i.e. a cavalry troop composed of Salluienses (who lived in the region of modern Zaragoza; cf. Richardson 1983, 35–6; Birks *et al.* 1984, 47), that fought with distinction at Asculum in 89: *ILS* 8888; cf. Badian 1958, 257 and 262 n. 1. On the Gauls' assimilation of Roman culture see Woolf 1998. C. has been defended against charges of racism (Rambaud 1980, 314–15), but his forensic speeches should not be taken for his real views (*Clu.* 139); he is, however, exploiting prejudices in the jurors' minds for the benefit of his case; cf. Citroni Marchetti 1995, 14; in general Vassaly 1993, ch. 6. The 'lowest . . . citizen' (*infimus civis*) can serve as a foil for others at the upper end of the sociopolitical spectrum, such as the praetor governing a province (*Ver.* 2.3.74) or Caesar (*Phil.* 2.109).

Does Indutiomarus know . . . to that place? Indutiomarus, leader of the Allobroges, is known only from our speech; he is not to be confused with the homonymous leader of the Treveri who instigated a revolt against Caesar in 54; cf. Münzer, *RE* s.v. 1–2. As the sequel shows, he travelled to Rome for the trial and testified in person. He will presumably have turned first to the Fabii, who, since the conquest of the Allobroges by Q. Fabius Maximus as cos. in 121 (cf. 12n.), were their traditional Roman patrons; hence M. Fabius' participation in this case as *subscriptor*; cf. 36; Münzer, *RE* s.v. Fabius 26 and 110. 'What it is to give testimony': the idea is expanded at *Flac.* 9 (apropos of Asiatic Greeks): 'that nation has never cultivated scrupulous good faith in testimony, and they do not know what is the force, the authority, the weight of this entire matter'; similarly ibid. 23 'a nation by no means scrupulous in pronouncing testimony'. 'With . . . how much fear' testimony was pronounced was one of the points to be considered by the judge at 23; see also 29n. 'That place' is again the tribunal; cf. 25n.

(28) Remember, jurors, how greatly . . . some greedy impulse This chapter aims to influence the jurors' judgment on the witnesses' diction and demeanour; no account is taken of linguistic or cultural differences; rather, Gallic witnesses are expected to conform to Roman norms. Avoiding the appearance of greed is important since

an obviously self-interested (*cupidus*) witness loses credibility; C. will claim that the Gallic witnesses fall foul of this rule; cf. 21 with n.

Finally you struggle . . . preserved and retained The visage (*vultus*) is highly expressive, as the ancients were well aware; cf. Swain 2007, especially 180–1. 'Modesty' (*pudor*) and 'conscientiousness' (*religio*) are the qualities sought, overeagerness (*cupiditas*) to be avoided; cf. the previous n.; on the psychology of *pudor* in giving testimony cf. Kaster 2005, 59–60. At *Ver.* 2.4.16 C. is at pains to assimilate his Sicilian witness, C. Heius, to Roman behaviour: 'A man of impeccable nobility in his own community who would wish you to hold a true opinion about his conscientiousness (*religio*) and public standing (*dignitas*) . . .'

(29) In giving testimony . . . he 'knows' everything 'I am sure' (*credo*) again adds an ironic colour; cf. 27n. The witness's 'fear', as appears from this passage, is not so much the fear of divine punishment in the event of perjury as it is the fear of loss of standing if one's testimony is suspected of being tainted; not dissimilar is the fear of the conscientious prosecutor as described at *Div. Caec.* 41–2. The Gauls had their own courts and forensic culture, as various passages in Caes. *Gal.* show. Perhaps an appearance of unshakeable conviction was as helpful to a witness in a Gallic court as an appearance of modesty was (according to C.) in a Roman one. It is difficult to avoid the conclusion that C. is trying to penalize Indutiomarus for cultural differences. The argument from a Roman witness's 'I think' (*arbitror*; cf. *Luc.* 146) vs. Indutiomarus' 'I know' (*scio*) is a bit ironic since C.'s own attitude of supreme certitude, symbolized by his proud assertion 'I know' (*comperi*) with regard to the plans of the Catilinarian conspirators, would be an object of scorn for his detractors; cf. *Cat.* 1.10.2–4 with Dyck 2008 ad loc.; it also touches merely the form, not the content, of Indutiomarus' testimony; cf. Schmitz 1985, 51 n. 29.

He feared, of course, . . . his face and his audacity' The verb for 'fear' is *vereor*, 'a mild and strategic sort of fear, which manifests itself above all in circumspection and the wish to avoid drawing attention to oneself in an improper way' (Kaster 2005, 16); the related noun is *verecundia* 'an attitude of restraint (arising from respect for others or a proper humility on one's own part)' (*OLD* s.v. 1). 'Of course' (*videlicet*) signals irony, as often; cf. *OLD* s.v. 3. The (Roman) witness's concern for preserving reputation (*existimatio*) appears at *Ver.* 2.2.177; cf. also 28. 'A man of such quality' (*talis vir*): C. regularly uses the phrase of the jurors in court (e.g. *S.Rosc.* 72) and other exalted persons; a Roman would be unlikely to use it non-ironically of a foreigner. 'So greedily (*cupide*), so rashly': for the Roman witness's effort to avoid appearing immoderate or greedy cf. 28, where 'over-eagerness' renders *cupiditas*. 'He failed to understand . . . his audacity': the irony continues, C. having already argued that there is a far higher standard for credible testimony in a Roman court. 'Face' (*os*) is often used in Latin, as in English, as a metaphor for audacity or shamelessness; cf. *OLD* s.v. 8b.

(30) Or do you think . . . fear of the immortal gods? 'Those peoples': the pronominal adj. *iste* is used with contempt here, as often; cf. 4n.; for the Gauls as barbarians cf. 4n. The Romans took a people's religious observances as a measure of their degree of barbarism or civilization. Thus at *ND* 1.62 'Cotta' argues that many peoples are so savage as to be without a concept of god. The early conception is that perjury is an offence against the gods and punished by them; by the late Republic this remained the Roman view, and there were legal consequences for perjury in only a few cases; cf. *Leg.* 2.22.6 ('let the divine punishment for perjury be ruin, the human one disgrace') with Dyck 2004 ad loc.; Robinson 1973, 360–1. Lucilius thus attributed the perjury of wicked Romans to their atheism: fr. 1138–41 W. Other peoples were less scrupulous; Polybius 6.56.13–14 remarks that Roman magistrates under oath tend to be much more trustworthy in financial dealings than their Greek counterparts; on the whole topic cf. Latte, *RE* s.v. Meineid.

They differ from the custom . . . with the immortal gods themselves! C. seeks to create a vast chasm between the Gauls and other peoples ('to such an extent', *tantum*) both by nature and by custom: not only do they have no fear of the gods but they engage in impious war against them; cf. the characterization of Verres as the 'enemy of sacred rites and religious practices' (*Ver.* 2.1.9; similarly 4.72, 75, and 112). The point will recur in the peroration as a contrasting foil for the piety of Fonteius' sister, a Vestal Virgin (49). The Roman ritual procedures for initiating wars performed by special religious functionaries called *fetiales* can be seen as a means of seeking peace and pardon from the gods when waging war; cf. *Off.* 1.36 with Dyck 1996 ad loc.; Harris 1979, 166–75. The 'peace of the gods' (*pax deum*) was a state free of divine anger; that state was breached by any offence against divine law, and atonements (*piacula*) were then required in order to restore the *pax deum*; cf. *OLD* s.v. *pax* 2; Ehlers, *RE* s.v. *piaculum*, especially 1181.12 ff.; *TLL* s.v. *pax* 865.3 ff. and

866.23 ff.; for 'peace and pardon' ibid. 865.13–14; *Rab. perd.* 5; Wissowa 1912, 389–90.

These are the peoples . . . the oracle of the world The Volcae Tectosages left their homeland in the Hercynian Forest in Germany and divided into two groups, one settling in Gaul (cf. 26n.), the other, led by Brennus and Acichorius, entering the Balkans; there in 278 they were drawn by rumours of great treasures to Delphi. Probably after sacking the shrine they were driven away by defenders hastily assembled from nearby Greek communities; then they proceeded to Thrace and crossed to Asia Minor, where they finally settled in the eastern part of Great Phrygia, which came to be called Galatia; cf. Will and Heinen, *CAH* vii. 114–15 and 422–5 respectively; Brandis, *RE* s.v. Galatia; Pomtow, *RE* s.v. Delphoi; Bannert, *RE* Suppl. 15 945.29 ff. (s.v. Volcae); and on the various traditions and Rome's use of them Williams 2001: 157–70. 'Set out': Latin *proficiscor* is to set out with a definite goal; cf. Fordyce on Catul. 46.10; *OLD* s.v. 1b; C. thus makes it appear that the Celts were bent on attacking the oracle from the start of their journey. Apollo received the epithet 'Pythian' (*Pythius*) after slaying the dragon Python that guarded the oracle; cf. [Apollod.] *Bib.* 1.4.1; Ov. *Met.* 1.438 ff. By calling it 'the oracle of the world' C. emphasizes its international character; similarly Livy 38.48.2 refers to it as 'the shared oracle of the human race'; similarly at *Ver.* 2.4.115 C. presents the Sicilian cults violated by Verres' actions as 'the common religious observance of all peoples'. Though well past the pinnacle of its influence, the Delphic oracle was still consulted by Greeks and foreign visitors; cf. in general Parke and Wormell 1956; Plut. *Cic.* 5.1 claims that C. consulted the oracle; Flacelière 1977 is sceptical in view of *Div.* 2.57, but there the context is polemical; *Ver.* 2.4.4 and 135 strongly imply a visit to Thespiae, presumably en route between Athens and Delphi.

By the same peoples . . . testimonies to be bound 'Upright' renders *sanctus*; cf. *OLD* s.v. 4a. C. alludes to the saga of Manlius, awakened to defend the Capitol by the honking of the geese of Juno (the temple of Juno Moneta was on the Arx, that of Jupiter, Juno, and Minerva on the other summit; cf. Richardson 1992 s.v. *Capitolinus Mons*); cf. Livy 5.47.1–8 with Ogilvie's n.; Fluss, *RE* 14.1 1170.25–1171.14 (s.v. Manlius 50); and on the remodelling of the sack after the Gallic raid on Delphi cf. Williams 2001: ch. 4. Our passage (among others) shows that witnesses' depositions were given under oath; cf. Freyburger 1986, 221. As the all-seeing god of heaven, Jupiter was naturally invoked in oaths (cf. Enn. *trag.* 350 J.) and soon received the epithet *Fidius* 'sworn by in oaths'; cf. Wissowa 1912, 118.

(31) Finally can anything . . . violate it by a criminal act? Since 30 C. has implicitly asserted that the Gauls do not fear the gods (and hence would have no scruples about violating oaths). Here, however, he acknowledges that they sometimes act out of fear of the gods but claims that they nonetheless pervert religious practices. 'Pollute': *funesto* is 'pollute by murder, stain with blood', first attested here in extant Latin; similar usage at *Rab. perd.* 11; *Mil.* 90; cf. *OLD* and *TLL* s.v. 'Human victims' (*humanis hostiis*): in the Latin phrase the epithet precedes for emphasis.

Who is unaware . . . sacrificing human beings? The attribution of a 'barbaric custom' to the Gauls comes as no surprise after they have been classified as barbarians (4). The Gauls' practice of human sacrifice was a commonplace of ancient ethnography; cf. *Rep.* 3.15, Caes. *Gal.* 6.16, and later testimonies collected by Clemente 1974, 149; it is confirmed by archaeological finds at Entremont and elsewhere; cf. Rambaud 1980, 307 and n. 16. The practice may also have occurred at Rome if the reports of the sacrifice of two pairs of male and female victims, one Greek, the other Gallic, in the Forum Boarium deserve any credit; cf. Plut. *Marc.* 3; Oros. 4.13.3; Futrell 1997, 197–203; Williams 2001, 173–5.

Therefore what sort of . . . by bloody crimes against humans? 'Trustworthiness' (*fides*) is emphasized since the quality of the Gauls' testimony is the issue before the court, but the larger question of the quality of their piety (*pietas*) in general is also implicated; cf. 30n. 'Bloody crimes' renders *scelere et sanguine*, literally 'crime and blood', by hendiadys.

Will you treat as on the same footing . . . moderately by them? By accepting the Gauls' testimony the jurors would, C. argues, be accepting them as on the same footing with Romans in religious observance, whereas their practices, just described, from a Roman point of view, stand religion on its head. 'With integrity' renders *sancte*, i.e. in accord with their oath by the gods; cf. 30n. on *sanctus*. For speaking moderately (*moderate*) as a concern of a Roman witness cf. 28.

(32) Will your minds . . . in butchering him? C. poses a dilemma to the jurors as to which group they wish to join and makes siding with the Gauls as unattractive as possible; similarly he seeks to end solidarity with Chrysogonus at *S.Rosc.* 140 ('Let them cease to share their cause with Chrysogonus') and 142 ('that reprobate partisan of

Chrysogonus who thinks that the cause is shared with him, is harmed when he is separated from the lustre of the cause'). 'Pure' (*castus*) refers to ritual purity; 'uncorrupted' (*integer*) provides an ethical complement. As in 12, dividing the Roman citizens into sub-groups (legates, equites, businessmen) gives them added weight; cf. ad loc. 'Three-year period' (*triennio*): this is our one piece of evidence for the duration of Fonteius' governorship; for the probable dates cf. 11n. 'Allies and friends' (*socii . . . atque amici*) glances above all at the Massiliotes (on their special relation to Rome cf. Mommsen 1887–8, iii. 669–70, and 13n.), though other communities in Transalpina, especially Greek cities along the coast, may also have enjoyed such status, as did the Aedui and apparently others outside the province. 'Butcher' renders *iugulo*, a particularly brutal word for murder, originally referring to the cutting of the throat (*iugulum*) of a gladiator or sacrificial victim; cf. *OLD* s.v. *iugulo*.

In order to be seen . . . faithful allies and citizens? C. considers and rejects two possible rationales for preferring the testimony of the Gauls. If one wants to follow 'public opinion' (*voluntas hominum*), their opinion as enemies is worth less than that of citizens (cf., however, *Sul.* 25, where C. states that his policy is to follow the interest (*utilitas*) rather than the opinion (*voluntas*) of the people). Their 'standing' (*dignitas*) is also lower than that of Fonteius' witnesses in seven respects, indicated by seven pairs of opposed attributes; here the contrast enemies/citizens-allies is repeated in final position. Only here in the extant speech does C. allege that the Gallic witnesses are 'hirelings' (perhaps of Fonteius' enemies; cf. 20; for hired witnesses cf. also *Clu.* 192); for rewards granted in criminal prosecutions cf. 25n. For 'allies' see previous n.

(33) Or do you doubt . . . with the Roman nation? For enmity (*inimicitia*) vitiating testimony cf. the examples cited at 23 and 24. 'Practice' (*gero*): the verb is used of enmity also at *Div. Caec.* 66; the addition of this verb to 'cherish' (*habeo*) serves emphasis; C. may also wish to suggest the idea of 'waging war' (*bellum gero*); cf. *OLD* s.v. 4 and 8b. 'Nation' renders *nomen*, often so used; cf. *Scaur.* 45n.

Do you suppose . . . to a jury? C. uses their native dress ('in rough woollen cloaks and breeches': *sagatos bracatosque*) to set the Gauls apart as unRoman in aspect as in attitude; similar strategy appears regarding the Sardinians at *Scaur.* 45d and o; cf. in general Dyck 2001. The 'expected' attitude is, of course, formulated for stark contrast with their actual behaviour. Riggsby 1999*a*, 148, observes that in portraying the Sicilians in the *Verrines* C. 'strikes precisely the plaintive and humble tone' that he desiderates here; cf. e.g. *Ver.* 1.28: 'the Sicilians, timid and afflicted people'.

Nothing of the sort! . . . Gallic war be stirred up Far from being 'with eyes downcast and humble spirit' (*animo demisso atque humili*), the Gauls are 'in good spirits and good cheer' (*laeti atque erecti*). 'Over the whole Forum' is added as an aggravating circumstance, the Forum being the convergence of many roads and considered the heart of the city (cf. Richardson 1992 s.v. Forum Romanum); as Citroni Marchetti 1995, 25, observes, C. pictures them as an enemy presence within the city; cf. the disapproving picture of Chrysogonus and his retinue 'gadding about here and there through the Forum' (*S.Rosc.* 135); on rights of foreigners resident at Rome cf. Mommsen 1864–79, i. 319–54. C. does not explain the Gauls' attitude, merely leaving the impression that they are arrogant and over-confident; cf. 36 'that threatening and arrogant Indutiomarus'. These are, as Rambaud 1980 argues, pro-Roman Gauls; they are apparently confident that their wrongs will be redressed by the Roman court. The epithets 'barbarian' and 'monstrous' are repeated from 31, where they described the custom of human sacrifice. The remarks about a future war may not have been threats so much as a prognosis that their anti-Roman opponents would exploit a defeat in court as an excuse to launch another war; cf. ibid. 313. The imputation of 'barbarian' behaviour is by now expected; cf. 4, 23, 27, 31. The prospect of a 'new Gallic war' might well set Romans' teeth on edge, given that within living memory they had incurred horrendous casualties in the war with the Cimbri and Teutones, who were thought to be Gauls, rather than Germans, until Caesar; cf. Walser 1956, 37 and n. 8; on the Romans' (irrational) fear of the Gauls cf. also Bellen 1985; Williams 2001: 170–82.

(34) If in this case M. Fonteius . . . they ought to be despised An unreal supposition in which the protasis stands C.'s entire case on its head: even if all that C. has shown were untrue . . . On the help provided by this passage for reconstructing the missing parts of the speech see headnote to the Vatican palimpsest. The point about the magistracies having been conducted 'in your full view' (*ante oculos vestros*) is repeated from 5, and the absence of witnesses to any financial malfeasance was argued in 3–4. 'Sound men': cf. *Scaur.* 43-4n. The discussion of Fonteius' legateship in Spain begins in 6 but is truncated; see ad loc. This was followed by a legateship in

Macedonia; see further 44n. C. deploys the support of his client's family, in particular his sister, a Vestal Virgin, and his mother, to good effect in the peroration (46–9); elsewhere he similarly commends his client as 'a son approved by his own people' (*S.Rosc.* 152) and answers the prosecution's charge that his client is 'not approved by his own people' (*Cael.* 5); cf. also *Planc.* 29. 'Pressed' (*premo*) conceives the defendant as spatially confined by adverse testimony; similarly 44 and *Scaur.* 17: 'to hem me in (*urgere*) with charges'. For Fonteius' support by the Narbonese, the Massiliotes, and the Roman citizens cf. 14–15. 'Most loyal' (*fidelissimus*) was already the Massiliotes' epithet at 13; similarly 45. In the much briefer apodosis C. invokes, as he often does, the ancestors as a standard of comparison: he warns the jurors against appearing to fear peoples on whom the ancestors had inflicted a devastating defeat; cf. 13n. On the importance the Romans generally attached to maintaining the standards of their ancestors cf. Earl 1967, 28; Flower 1996, ch. 7; on the achievement of the ancestors in creating the empire, often praised by C., cf. Roloff 1938, 114–20; Bücher 2006, 169–71.

(35) But as things stand . . . . rather than give ground to the enemy? 'But as things stand': *nunc vero* marks a return to reality after a counterfactual; cf. Risselada 1996, 113–14. 'Sound man': see previous n. The division of opinion between citizens and allies on the one side and the Gauls on the other continues from 13–15. There is a pun on 'damage' (*laedere*) and 'commend' (*laudare*); similarly *Ver.* 2.2.114 and 4.19; *Q.Rosc.* 19; *Flac.* 6; *Phil.* 3.18; cf. Holst 1925: 79, no. 264, and 80, nos. 273 and 281. 'Attack' (*oppugno*) is used here both metaphorically of prosecution in court and literally of military action. It is, in fact, C.'s tactic to represent the prosecution as a continuation of the Gauls' war against Fonteius/Rome by other means; cf. 14, 44, and F 11; Rambaud 1980, 306. Fonteius' friends and enemies are represented as adopting the opposite tactics of supplication and threat; the judges are given choices correspondingly (sparing a citizen vs. yielding to an enemy) without reference to laws or evidence; and the whole scene plays out before an audience of Roman citizens and foreign peoples whose behaviour will be influenced by the jurors' choice. For the magnetism of glory and praise cf. *Arch.* 26; the point is that his fellow citizens should be shown that Fonteius' virtue is rewarded and external peoples that the Romans cannot be intimidated.

(36) This is a mighty ground . . . by their threats If in the previous argument C. was concerned with the reaction of 'foreign peoples' in

general, here he focuses specifically on the Gauls. 'As heaven is my witness' renders *mehercules*; cf. *Scaur.* F 9n.; the form with the -*s* is archaic and prevailed in C.'s youth. 'Spot of disgrace': literally 'spot and disgrace' (*macula atque ignominia*), by hendiadys. The public courts (*iudicia publica*) of Rome had to think of the state interest in general; hence this argument; cf. Riggsby1999*a*, ch. 6. 'Senators and equites' is a shorthand for the jury, the *tribuni aerarii* being elided; cf. 26n. Our sources often lump the equites and *tribuni aerarii* together: the two groups met the same property qualification, and the distinction between them is contested; cf. Bleicken 1995, 12–14.

If they try to launch a war... the remnants of the war C. Marius is mentioned for his victory over the Teutones at Aquae Sextiae in 102 (on the ethnic confusion cf. 33n.), Cn. Domitius and Q. Maximus as victors over the Allobroges in 121; cf. 27n. 'Remnants (*reliquias*) of the war': 'of the war' (*belli*) is Clark's insertion, any further campaign in this region being represented as a mere mopping-up operation in the aftermath of the victories of the named commanders; Lambinus, however, substituted *reliquas* for *reliquias*, in which case the reference would be to the 'other (sc. nations)' besides the Allobroges. Why the exercise in necromancy (cf. *Scaur.* 47–8n.)? C. again holds up the exploits of the ancestors as a model (cf. 34 with n.), but he apparently also assumes Fonteius' conviction and a consequent dearth of living commanders; cf. 42–3; Riggsby 1999*a*, 147. For Indutiomarus' arrogance cf. 29, for the Gauls' threats 33 with n.

or, since that is impossible... the hope of triumph The two members of the prosecution team, M. Plaetorius Cestianus and M. Fabius, are represented as bearing different relations to their clients, Plaetorius having just taken them on ('his new clients'), whereas Fabius has inherited the role of patron; cf. Meyer 1957, 219, and in general on the heritability of such relations 213; Badian 1958, 263–4. Whether the assistant prosecutor was a direct descendant of the victor of 121 or a more remote relation may be left open; it seems in any case excluded by this context that he was of Gallic origin; cf. Alexander 2002, 62–3 with 275 n. 13. In spite of the harsh criticism of his adversary's mother (F 13), C. claims (ironically?) that he is Plaetorius' friend; such claims of friendship with the opposing counsel were a fairly common forensic tactic of C.'s; cf. Craig 1981. Though rather junior at the time of the trial (for his possible quaestorship cf. 1 with n.), Plaetorius pursued a political career; by the end of 51 he suffered some misfortune (*Att.* 5.20(113).8, sometimes interpreted as a conviction on extortion charges) and is not heard of again; cf. Münzer, *RE* s.v. Plaetorius 16. 'As conquered and subdued people customarily do': once again C. faults the Gauls for behaving inappropriately; cf. 33. 'Hope of a triumph': C. concludes the topic with a defiant flourish. The greatest Roman public occasion, the triumph involved a victorious general leading his legions, captives, and plunder in procession down the Via Sacra, through the Forum and up the Capitoline Hill to the temple of Jupiter Optimus Maximus; cf. Versnel 1970; Itgenshorst 2005; Beard 2007.

(37) If in the case . . . let alone a charge C. has just completed the argument that, even if Fonteius were guilty as charged, it would be disgraceful for the jurors to convict him and thus appear to be yielding to the Gauls' threats (34–6). Now taking back the counterfactual hypothesis, he advances the argument that the case for Fonteius' acquittal is much stronger in view of the facts. The 'two sessions' (*actiones*) are mentioned also in 40: the *lex Servilia Glauciae* and subsequent enactments required extortion cases to be argued in such form; cf. *Ver.* 2.1.26; Greenidge 1901, 422 and 499–502; Riggsby 1999*a*, 121; for the relation of the extant remains to the court proceedings see the headnote to the speech. C. distinguishes between a charge (*crimen*), i.e. an actionable offence that can form a basis for prosecution, and slander (*maledictum*); cf. *Cael.* 6: 'But it is one thing to engage in slander, another to prosecute: prosecution requires a charge (*crimen*), to define the subject, mark the individual, prove with argument, confirm by testimony; slander (*maledictio*) has no purpose except insult . . . ' So strong is the presumption that the prosecution will seek to blacken the defendant's character that C. uses the absence of even an invented (*fictum*; cf. 25n.) slander as a sign of his client's innocence; cf. Craig 2004, 193.

Has any defendant . . . with some plausible suspicion? 'In this type of life' i.e. the active life (*vita activa*) of politics and public service as defined by the following items. 'Magistracies' renders *potestates*, literally 'powers', an instance of abstract for concrete; cf. *OLD* s.v. *potestas* 3. C. lends weight to the rhetorical question through the use of quasi-synonyms, three each for criminality and its source. As in the previous sentence, the absence even of invented charges is stressed.

(38) We know that M. Aemilius Scaurus . . . by an enemy The son of one of the men who laid the foundations of Roman law, M. Junius Brutus became a professional prosecutor; C. gives vent to his disapproval of the man at *Brut.* 130 and *Off.* 2.50; see Dyck 1996 ad loc.

He prosecuted Scaurus for extortion, probably in the year following the campaigns of his consulate (115) in the Apennines and Alps; cf. Bloch 1909, 26–7; *TLRR* 37 with literature; cf. also *Scaur.* F 2n.

How many charges did . . . L. Cotta hear . . . ? The extortion trial of M'. Aquilius was famous for the *coup de théâtre* by which his advocate, M. Antonius, parted his tunic to display the wounds his client had suffered face to face with the enemy; cf. *TLRR* 84, dating the trial with a query to 97; Leigh 1995, 205 and n. 29; on Aquilius see further *Scaur.* 2n. L. Aurelius Cotta (cos. 144) was acquitted in 138 on extortion charges brought by Scipio Aemilianus; cf. *TLRR* 9.

how many finally did . . . fornication and lust C. justifies Rutilius' inclusion with the previous defendants who had been acquitted on grounds that his conviction was unjust; he was accused of extortion in the aftermath of his service as legate of Q. Mucius Scaevola Pontifex in Asia; cf. Thomasson 1991, 108, no. 87, who dates the legateship to 94 with a query, whereas Broughton, *MRR ii.* 8, prefers 97; Morstein-Marx 1989 argues convincingly for the earlier date. The conviction represented the revenge of the equites in view of his opposition to exploitation of the provincials by the tax-farmers; his life was regarded as a model of Stoic austerity; cf. *Scaur.* F 3n.; Dyck 1996 on *Off.* 3.9.

(39) A speech survives . . . against L. Piso The speech was an invective against a leading opponent of the grain dole that Gracchus carried as tribune (123); cf. Rotondi 1912, 307–8; for surviving fragments cf. *orat.* pp. 186–7; the following (fr. 43) perhaps gives the tone: 'your boyhood was a dishonour to your youth, your youth a disgrace to your old age, your old age a scandal to the commonwealth' (the attribution is, however, rejected by Stockton 1979, 220). 'Most gifted' (*ingeniosissimum*): C. often uses *ingenium* ('inborn nature, natural talent') with reference to orators, e.g. *Cael.* 45 'his talent shone forth' (of M. Caelius Rufus). C. gives a detailed and positive assessment of Gracchus' oratorical powers at *Brut.* 125–6; at *Har.* 41 he tempers praise for the oratory with disapproval of his policies; that same tension is implicit in our passage. On C. Gracchus' oratory cf. in general Suerbaum 2002, 500–4.

But what a man . . . accusation of disgraceful acts As often, C. uses the exclamation as a vivid characterization; cf. *Leg.* 3.20 with Dyck 2004 ad loc. He tends to idealize the Rome of two generations past, though that age, too, had its scoundrels; cf. e.g. *Scaur.* F 9n. L. Calpurnius Piso Frugi (cos. 133) carried as tribune (149) the first law against extortion, which provided the model for the subsequent standing courts; cf. Rotondi 1912, 292. His second cognomen *frugi* was a commendation, especially for slaves: 'good, honest, thrifty' or the like; cf. *OLD* s.v.; for an example of his care in dealing with state property cf. V. Max. 4.3.10. This anecdote is not attested elsewhere; perhaps C. heard it from his grandson L. Calpurnius Piso Frugi (pr. 74), whom he mentions favourably (*Div. Caec.* 64) and to whose son he would engage his daughter Tullia in 67; cf. Münzer, *RE* s.v. Calpurnius 93, 96, and 98; Treggiari 2007, 41–2. Another possible source would be M. Pupius Piso (cos. 61), who was by birth a Calpurnius Piso Frugi and to whose care C. was entrusted as a young man; cf. Asc. 15C; A. Stein, *RE* 23.2 s.v. Pupius 10.

(40) M. Fonteius has been accused . . . whom I previously mentioned For the two sessions required for such a trial cf. 37n. Lust (*libido*), wantonness (*petulantia*), and audacity (*audacia*) are taken up from 37, with cruelty (*crudelitas*) now added; they are the qualities that lead to crime and so are targeted in prosecutions for extortion (for cruelty cf. *Scaur.* F 6–13n.); their opposites, abstinence (*abstinentia*), self-control (*continentia* or *temperantia*), and clemency (*clementia*), are praised in good governors; cf. *Q.fr.* 1.1(1).9, 13, 18, 32, 45; *Att.* 5.16 (109).3; 5.18(111).2. The absence of a misdeed (*facinus*) is likewise repeated from 37, now augmented by an offending pronouncement (*dictum*). Nonetheless the prosecutors are not praised for their honesty but criticized for lacking the courage to lie and a talent for invention, in contrast to the accusers cited in 38–9.

You see, then, a good man . . . given over to your power 'A good man' renders *frugi*, on which cf. 39n.; the word leads the Latin sentence and is repeated for emphasis. 'Modesty' (*pudor*) and 'conscientiousness' (*religio*) were said to be characteristic of Roman witnesses; cf. 28 with n. On the jurors' good faith engaged by their oath cf. *Scaur.* 17n. For the defendant or his affairs given over to the jurors' power cf. *Flac.* 4; C. often refers to their power (*potestas*); cf. e.g. *S.Rosc.* 22, 129, 154; *Mur.* 83; *Cael.* 79.

(41) Consider therefore . . . restored to his friends The epithets attached both to Fonteius and the nations accusing him tilt the balance strongly towards acquittal. C. makes this sound as though *deditio*, the surrender to the enemy of a military commander who made an unauthorized treaty with that enemy, was in question and not simple exile (cf. 44n.); the famous recent example was that of C. Hostilius Mancinus (cos. 137), who was surrendered to the Numantines but sent back by them; cf. Rosenstein 1986. 'Hostile' (*inimicissimis*) may

refer to enmity against the Roman people generally (as in 32) or the defendant in particular (that the friends are the opposite pole suggests the latter). 'Monstrous' renders *immanis*, used in 31 with reference to the practice of human sacrifice.

especially since there are so many . . . monuments of its achievements C. mentions the antiquity of his client's family at *Clu.* 43 and *Flac.* 106. Tusculum was one of the first, if not the first, municipality (*municipium*) of Italy to receive Roman citizenship; cf. Livy 8.14.2–4; Sherwin-White 1973, 59–60; McCracken, *RE* 7A2, 1467.55 ff. By C.'s day it had produced more consuls than all other municipalities combined (*Planc.* 19). 'Inscribed and noted on monuments of its achievements': on the epigraphic and numismatic evidence for the Fonteii cf. Taylor 1960, 214–15; contrast the monuments commemorating the Gauls, described at 12.

then the uninterrupted series . . . the reputation for innocence The family can be traced as far back as M. Fonteius pr. 166 (*MRR* i. 437); the defendant himself was evidently praetor in 75 (ibid. ii. 97 with a query); C. implies that his father and grandfather were also praetors, though there is no further evidence; cf. Münzer, *RE* s.v. Fonteius 2, 11 and 12; Alexander 2002, 61 and 274 n. 4.

then the fresh memory . . . the stain of crime Fonteius *père* (the praenomen is not attested) was in Asculum as legate of the praetor Q. Servilius in late 91 or early 90 when both were killed by an angry mob, the *causa efficiens* of the Social War; cf. Münzer, *RE* s.v. Fonteius 2; Thomasson 1991, 108, no. 90; *MRR* ii. 20 and 23.

finally the man himself . . . in waging wars Unfortunately, C.'s account of the war with the Vocontii has been edited out (cf. 20n.) and the discussion of his campaign in Macedonia (cf. 44) lost so we do not have details corroborating this claim; it was, however, a standard argument in defence of provincial governors; in *Ver.* 2.5 C. prepared material to rebut the point if raised on Verres' behalf; cf. Berger 1978, 136 with 216 n. 43; Frazel 2009, ch. 3; C. adapts the argument to Milo's case at *Mil.* 69–70.

(42) Therefore if you had need . . . is known As a relatively junior figure C. is careful to avoid giving offence by denying that the warning is needed and offering it 'gently' in view of his (sc. limited) authority; for invocation of the state interest as a consideration before a public court (*iudicium publicum*) cf. 36n. 'Courage' (*virtus*) and 'success' (*felicitas*) often appear as qualities sought in a military commander, whereby (good) fortune (*fortuna*) varies *felicitas* (cf. *Man.* 27, 47,

49, 51), 'hard work' (*industria*, also in F 7; cf. 12 on Fonteius' 'copious sweat and labour') less often (*Man.* 29).

There was once a larger supply . . . glory and courage? The contrast between 'safety' (*salus*) and 'honour' (*honor*) glances at Fonteius' plight with his very safety at risk in this trial; cf. 21 with n and 46. Similarly at *Cael.* 39–40 C. comments on the obsolescence of the old-time morals and discipline that made Rome great, albeit without specific reference to military culture; for the perceived decline in military men cf. *Ver.* 2.5.2 and 25; *Man.* 27; *De orat.* 3.136; Roloff 1938, 66. The 70s had seen the protracted war in Spain (cf. F 6n.), the renewal of war against Mithridates in 74 (cf. 13n.) and Spartacus' sudden and unexpected slave revolt (73–71). C. claims that acquittal would procure the double benefit of preserving Fonteius for future military assignments and showing Rome's young men that military prowess is still valued.

(43) Remember which legates . . . exploits and victories C. cites the depth of experienced commanders available during the Social War as a contrasting foil to the present. L. Julius and P. Rutilius were the consuls of 90 (*MRR* ii. 25), L. Cato and Cn. Pompeius those of 89 (ibid. 32). Under them served three legates of praetorian rank (M. (Caecilius) Cornutus (pr. by 90), L. Cinna (pr. 90), and L. Sulla (pr. 93)) and four consulars (C. Marius (cos. I 107), T. Didius (cos. 98), Q. Catulus (cos. 102), and P. Crassus (cos. 97)); cf. Thomasson 1991, 14 n. 37 and 108–9, nos. 91–4, 97, 104–5; *MRR* ii. 25–6, 28–9, 32, 36; on the rarity of legates of consular rank (except in times of crisis) cf. Badian 1993, 205–6.

Come, now turn your eyes . . . most cruel 'Look deeply into all parts of the state': cf. *Leg.* 3.41, where C. declares that a senator must know the state and its resources. 'Do you see . . . men of this kind?': C. hints that in an emergency there might well be a shortage of experienced and competent commanders. 'Happen' renders *accido*, usually implying misfortune; cf. Engl. 'if something should happen to me'. 'Energetic (*impiger*) when it comes to the work of war': cf. 42n. 'Gallant . . . skilled': he applies this characterization to C. Cassius at *Phil.* 11.35. For being 'lucky' (*felix*) as a quality of a commander cf. 42n. apropos of good fortune (*felicitas*). 'Rather than hand him over . . . ': for the formulation reminiscent of *deditio* see 41n. ('Consider therefore . . . restored to his friends'). While, as Riggsby 1999*a*, 147, notes, C. 'never explicitly privileges' state interest over the question of guilt or innocence, he does strongly suggest that the state interest should trump other considerations, as he does also in Murena's case, on which see Craig 1986.

3. The Peroration (44–49)

The peroration typically combines a summary of the case with an attempt to move pity; cf. Quint. *Inst.* 6.1; Winterbottom 2004. Here C. figures the forensic struggle as a battle for Fonteius between attackers (the Gauls) and defenders (Macedonia, Further Spain, Massilia, Narbo, Fonteius' mother and sister); he thus neatly summarizes the case and adds a dollop of drama and pathos. The contents may be outlined as follows:

I. Fonteius has stalwart defenders against the Gauls' attack (44)
   A. Macedonia, saved by Fonteius from the ravages of the Thracians
   B. Further Spain (45)
   C. Massilia, saved by Fonteius and in general a buffer against Gallic threats to Rome
   D. Narbo, freed from siege by Fonteius (46)
   E. All Roman citizens of the province
   F. Fonteius' mother
   G. His sister, a Vestal Virgin
      1. She has interceded with the gods on behalf of you and your families
      2. Her brother is her sole support (47)
      3. Do not cause her to lament and dowse the eternal fire with tears
      4. It would be arrogant to spurn her intercession (48)

II. Fonteius' tears over the fate of his mother and sister if he is convicted

III. Better for him to have died from the Gauls' missiles than their perjuries (49)

IV. Final appeal for acquittal

(44) But the Gauls . . . many stout defences Again the Gauls' forensic attack on Fonteius is figured as a military expedition; cf. 14, 35, and F 11n.; Winterbottom 2004, 228; for the imagery of spatial confinement cf. 34n. 'With your help': C. is careful to involve the jury; cf. the

appeal at *S.Rosc.* 10. For the Gauls as 'monstrous' (*immanis*) cf. 41 with n.; for their barbarism cf. 4n.

In the first place Macedonia . . . attacks of the Gauls For vividness Macedonia and the other communities supporting Fonteius are personified. As legate in Macedonia Fonteius helped fend off marauding Thracians; this was probably under the Ap. Claudius Pulcher (cos. 79), governor in 77 and 76, who is known to have battled the Thracians; cf. *MRR* ii. 89 and 94; Münzer, *RE* 6.2 2844.11 ff. (Fonteius 12); Brennan 2000, 529, has, however, suggested that it was under Cn. Dolabella (cos 81), governor 80–78 (*MRR* ii. 80, 84, and 86), so as to free Fonteius for an earlier tenure of Transalpine Gaul; cf. 10n. Like Massilia (13), Macedonia is qualified as 'loyal' (sc. to Rome), in implicit contrast to the Gauls. 'From his head': *caput* is used of 'the life of a person, especially when endangered' but also 'one's life as forfeit for various offences', albeit in the late Republic exile ordinarily substituted for the death penalty for Roman citizens: *OLD* s.v. 4 and 5. Here the prior meaning accords with the martial imagery of the passage, the latter with the legal position: extortion was perhaps treated as a capital offence in the *lex Servilia Glauciae* and the provision retained in the *lex Cornelia* under which Fonteius is being tried; cf. Lintott 1981, 198–202; cf. also the reference to the defendant's 'safety' (*salus*) being at risk (42 with n.).

(45) On the other side stands Further Spain . . . testimonies and testimonials As a juristic person a province could provide public testimonies (*testimonia publica*) to the court; in this case they took the form of testimonials to Fonteius' good character (*laudationes*); these were commonly presented by sworn legates and so engaged the 'religious scruples' (*religio*) of the community; on the procedure cf. Mommsen 1899, 411, n. 4 and 441 and Greenidge 1901, 489–91. On Fonteius' Spanish legateship cf. 6n.; the Spanish contribution to the defence case is non-specific, simply countering negative qualities assigned to the Gauls. For the Gauls' self-interest (*cupiditas*) cf. 21n. C. cast grave doubt on the Gauls' scrupulousness in giving testimony and general piety at 27–31; hence it is no surprise that here and in 49 he denounces them as wicked and their testimony as perjured.

Moreover, from Gaul itself . . . to harm us The loyalty of the Massiliotes is implicitly contrasted with Fonteius' accusers; cf. the n. before last apropos of Macedonia. 'Wretched' (*miser*) is one of the 'words that recur obsessively in perorations': Winterbottom 2004, 223; this is the first of a cluster of occurrences of *miser/miseriae* ('misfortunes') referring to Fonteius and members of his family; cf. 46, 47, 48. Fonteius' services to Massilia, for which he received the honours mentioned in 14 as well as the testimonials recorded in our passage, are not otherwise attested; the language ('by whom it was saved') suggests military intervention, as in the case of Narbo (46). The Massiliotes' defence of Fonteius is depicted as part of their general policy of buffering Rome against Gallic tribes; cf. *Off.* 2.28 and *Phil.* 8.18; in general H. G. Wackernagel, *RE* 14.2 2132.34 ff.

(46) Fighting with equal zeal . . . wretched dangers The sentence is led by the verb, and the vigorous action is underlined by alliteration (*propugnat pariter pro*). When some of the Gauls rebelled, Fonteius thwarted a siege of Narbo, perhaps by the Volcae; cf. 26 and Rivet 1988, 57. 'Wretched dangers': literally 'misfortunes and dangers' (*miseriis ac periculis*), by hendiadys; see the previous n.

Finally, as is fitting . . . one accord and one voice 'Gallic war' (*bellum Gallicum*) is non-technical; the technical expression would be 'Gallic disturbance' (*Gallicus tumultus*), the proclamation of which expedited the levying of soldiers to meet the emergency; cf. Mommsen 1887–8, i. 695. C. alludes to the fact, spelt out at *Phil.* 8.3, that in a 'Gallic disturbance' no exemptions from service (*vacationes*) are valid (sc. because of the potential danger to Rome itself); cf. Mommsen 1887–8, iii. 241–2; Osthoff 1952, 10–16; Williams 2001, 175–6. So all relevant Roman citizens (again broken down into groups to give them added weight; cf. 12n.) are active in support of his client.

But if Indutiomarus himself . . . will he? Indutiomarus was chief only of the Allobroges; C. means that he is the chief witness on the Gallic side; his contempt is evidently inferred from his demeanour on the witness stand and the Gauls' threats of military action; cf. 29 and 33 with n. Though the father has died (cf. 41 with n.), the defendant's mother has appeared in court to support her son; for her epithet 'wretched' cf. 45n. C. imagines the conflict as a struggle for possession of Fonteius between Indutiomarus and his client's mother; the jurors are spectators ('with you (pl.) looking on') and implicitly invited to intervene; similarly at *S.Rosc.* 12 he imagines the courtroom as the scene of a bloodbath unless the jurors take a firm line.

Especially when on the other side . . . that of her brother Having a sister who is a Vestal Virgin is virtually ideal for a defendant; here C. begins to exploit the situation rhetorically; cf. Winterbottom 2004, 221. 'Embraces and holds': the scene will have been staged before the court to match C.'s description. 'Protection' renders *fides*, often so used as object of a verb of begging or the like; cf. Freyburger 1986, 69–74. 'For so many years': at least twenty since, in view of the requirement of having both parents alive, Fonteia must have been dedicated to the service of Vesta from 91/90 at the latest, the date of her father's death; cf. 41n.; Gel. 1.12.2; Rüpke 2008, no. 1733. The major duty of the Vestals was to maintain the eternal flame in the temple of Vesta, regarded as a talisman of the safety of Rome; cf. Koch, *RE* 8A2 1732.25 ff.; Wildfang 2006, ch. 1. The jurors are reminded of a benefit (*beneficium*) conferred on the state by Fonteia and given opportunity to repay it, a topos with a long history in Greek and Roman rhetoric; cf. North 2000, 360 n. 5.

(47) What defence, what comfort . . . besides her brother? 'Wretched woman': cf. 45n. Vestals were taken into service between the ages of 6 and 10 and discharged after thirty years; at that point it was open to them to marry, but few did so; cf. Koch, *RE* 8A2 1733.7 ff. Unlike most Roman women, they thus remained dependent on their birth families; in Fonteia's case, in view of her father's death (cf. 41n.), that meant the defendant, who, C. implies, is her sole sibling; but M'. Fonteius, moneyer of 85, has been suspected of being an additional sibling (*RRC* no. 353), and the relation of the legate C. Fonteius (18) remains unclear.

Jurors, do not allow . . . the tears of your priestess As often in the peroration, C. pictures the consequences of a conviction for a relative of the defendant; cf. e.g. *Cael.* 79 'place before your eyes the old age of this wretched man who relies upon this his only son' etc. The image of the sacred fire dowsed by the Vestal's tears has been called 'perhaps the most frigid conceit in [C.'s] entire corpus': North 2000, 360 (a competitor for that title would be *Ver.* 2.5.92: 'It was one and the same night in which the praetor burned with the flame of shameful love and the fleet of the Roman people burned in a conflagration set by pirates'); the conceit was, however, adapted to Tarpeia at Prop. 4.4.45–6; Hutchinson 2010, 105 n. 16, compares the apostrophe of the Alban mountains and groves at *Mil.* 85 as a similar 'religious fantasy'.

(48) The Vestal Virgin is extending . . . this empire cannot be safe This is doubtless staged so that Fonteia performs the act of supplication as C. describes it. For a straightforward plea not to despise a supplication cf. *Ver.* 2.4.113; our passage is more powerful in that the plea is turned into a warning against haughtiness in view of the

previous benefit and combined with a suggestion of appropriate reciprocation; cf. 46n. 'This empire': literally 'these things' (*haec*), no doubt accompanied by a sweeping gesture; cf. North 2000, 363.

Do you see all of a sudden . . . with the bitterest grief C.'s 'staging' of Fonteius' predicament is conventional and quite different from that of Milo, though both are depicted as brave men. He claims that Milo remains unmoved by C.'s tears and indeed refuses a tearful defence (101 and 105), part of his depiction as a quasi-Stoic hero; see further Dyck 1998. Fonteius' tears, C. makes clear, are not for his own plight: he has faced great danger in battle without flinching; rather, they are for his mother and sister, who will be bereft of him. 'Not be an ornament': in the Roman conception a member who produced estimable achievements was an ornament to the family; cf. *S.Rosc.* 147 (of Caecilia Metella): 'by her virtue she brought it about that with as much honour as she was supplied by [her male relatives'] standing she returned to them equally great ornaments from her good reputation'. 'The wretches': cf. 45n.

(49) A far different fortune . . . much against their will! As in 14, C. underlines the irony of Fonteius' answering charges brought by his former battlefield enemies. 'To suffer death': for extortion as a capital crime under the *lex Cornelia* cf. 44n. 'Perjuries': cf. 45n. 'As things stand': for *nunc vero* returning to reality after a counterfactual cf. 35n. For the Gauls as a defeated enemy yielding unwilling obedience cf. 12–14.

Defend from this danger . . . the threats of the Gauls 'Gallant and innocent' summarizes the way C. wants his client to be seen: at 16 he offered a greater number of witnesses to Fonteius' courage and innocence; cf. also the allusion to 'brave men's innocence' at 21 and the family's 'reputation for innocence' (41). 'Greater credence to our witnesses than foreigners': C. was at pains to delineate a marked difference in the way Romans and foreigners give testimony (28–9). For Fonteius' safety (*salus*) being at risk cf. 42n.; recurring from 4, 'unbridled greed' (*libido*) heightens previous complaints about the Gauls' self-interest (*cupiditas*) or their being *cupidi*; cf. 21n. The stark contrast between 'the woman who is in charge of your sacred rites' and 'those who have waged wars with the sacred rites and shrines of all' has been prepared at 30–1 and 46–8. On the Gauls' threats and the importance of not yielding to them cf. 33–6.

FRAGMENTS

(F 1) An attack on the credibility of an argument advanced by the prosecution. At *Scaur.* 14–16 C. argues that an 'argument proper to the matter' (*argumentum . . . proprium rei*) is the true argument (as opposed to witness testimony). The dichotomy between logic and witness testimony becomes explicit at 21; this fragment might perhaps have been part of the immediately preceding argument. C. concedes that prosecution should be brought when it is 'likely' (*verisimile*) that a crime has been committed; hence the denial of verisimilitude (*similitudo veritatis*) here calls into question the validity of the prosecution (based on this particular argument). Similar points are scattered in other defences; thus e.g. at *S.Rosc.* 45 he claims that the prosecutor Erucius is arguing 'against the nature of things, against human custom and against the opinions of all'.

(F 2) 'Suspicion' (*suspicio*) is what leads a prosecutor to file charges; cf. *S.Rosc.* 8 with Dyck 2010 ad loc.; 'this suspicion' will refer to suspicion that a specific crime has been committed. In default of context it is unclear whether C. is referring to the prosecutor as an 'unfair arbitrator' (*iniquissimo disceptatori*) or is merely raising a hypothetical possibility.

(F 3) C. attempts to discredit a witness's entire testimony on the grounds that part of it is false.

(F 4) Possibly continuous with F 3; 'you' is pl., referring to the jurors. C. presumably seeks to discredit en bloc the testimony of all the Gallic witnesses; similarly his argument at *Scaur.* 17–20 that it is unnecessary for him to refute the Sardinian witnesses individually; cf. also 22n.

(F 5) Possibly C. so refers to the intermingling of truthful elements (see F 3). Similarly *Tull.* 10–11 'He thought it necessary . . . to remove that subterfuge' (*latebram*); *Cael.* 53 'all the coverts (*latebras*) of suspicion' (tr. Austin); with different relation of ideas *Div.* 2.111 'covert of obscurity'; different syntax at *Off.* 3.106 'a cover for perjury' (*latebra periurio*); cf. *OLD* s.v. *latebra* 3; *TLL* s.v. 993.48 ff.; a similar idea is expressed in different terms at *Q.Rosc.* 51: 'another retreat (*deverticulum*) for fraud and treachery' (tr. Freese).

(F 6) Initial placement in the Latin sentence lends emphasis to Pompey's name. Campaigning in Spain from 76 to 71, Pompey defeated the rebels Sertorius and Perperna; cf. Gelzer 1984, 46–54;

Seager 2002, 32–5. Though 'there is no sign that Pompey gave specific support to Fonteius at his trial' (Lintott 2008, 102), C. will try to connect Fonteius with Pompey as much as possible so as to present the former's harsh measures as militarily justified; cf. 8 and 16, for his courage cf. detailed argument at *Man.* 29–35, for his good fortune ibid. 47–8.

(F 7) Presumably further qualities contributing to military success, probably, given the order of fragments, Pompey's rather than Fonteius' (for the latter's 'hard work' (*industria*) cf. 42n.).

(F 8) Again Pompey's name is at the head of the sentence (cf. F 6 with n.).

(F 9) 'From Gaul' emphatically punctuates each member of the tricolon. The point is that Gaul was the chief source of supplies and troops used in the war in Spain and the demands made upon the populace correspondingly severe (but necessary for Roman victory, C. will have insisted); cf. the claim at 18 that work on the Via Domitia was 'in the public interest'.

(F 10) Another fragment quoted out of context but clearly part of C.'s argument about the duty Fonteius levied on wine; cf. the abbreviated discussion of the topic at 19–20. He falls back on a stereotype of the Gauls as tipplers (Polyb. 2.19.4; Posid. F 67 E-K and later sources cited by Paterson 1978, 454 n. 12) and ironically claims that the duty will benefit them since they will now overcome their phobia ('which they thought was poison') and dilute their wine, as other peoples do, rather than drinking it neat; cf. Alexander 2002, 70–1.

(F 11) The Gauls are evidently the subject; the first verb, 'fight' (*pugno*), is deliberately ambiguous; it is used metaphorically of the court proceedings but also suggests the warfare the Gauls have so recently waged against Rome, a point C. stresses; cf. 12–14, 36, 44. The motif becomes ominous when C. discusses the Gauls' threat of war in the event of Fonteius' acquittal (33–6). C. uncovers what he sees as their hidden motive: the weakening of the authority of Roman governors generally (17, cross-referring to an earlier discussion, of which this is perhaps a remnant).

(F 12) The context is unclear. The prosecution appears to have charged Fonteius with assessing a 2 per cent rake-off for a payment; C.'s defence is that no such payment was exacted. Alexander 2002, 70, connects the fragment with the administration of the road-building programme (17–19), but there is no sign of a lacuna in that sector. This point may, rather, have been curtailed from the discussion of financial offices in the Vatican palimpsest (so Schneider 1876, 47),

since that is where C. denies that any relevant financial transactions can be shown (3).

(F 13) A jest at the expense of Plaetorius' late mother, in spite of C.'s ostensible friendship with the prosecutor (36 with n.); for possible context see on the exordium. C. puns on two senses of *ludus* 'school' and 'brothel' (*OLD* s.v. 6a) and of *magister* 'teacher' and 'liquiditor of debtors' property' (*OLD* s.v. 8 and 5c respectively); cf. Holst 1925, 34. Such caustic banter (*dicacitas*) could be a powerful weapon; cf. *De orat.* 2.216–34, especially 218–19.

On Behalf of Marcus Aemilius Scaurus

INTRODUCTION

1. Sardinia: From Carthaginian Colony to Roman Province

A large Mediterranean island west of Italy, Sardinia is endowed with iron, copper, lead, and silver deposits, and metallurgy was important from the earliest stages of its civilization.[1] Remains of large stone towers called *nuraghi* bear witness to a local culture beginning in the early second millennium; it was a civilization that 'flourished in those areas where the combination of soil, water, and rainful provided maximum opportunities for substance and surplus' (sc. of cereals, especially barley).[2] From around the ninth century BC Phoenician settlements appear on the coast. The Carthaginians annexed Sardinia to their empire *c.*500; though they seem to have dominated it incompletely, their cemeteries concentrated in the west and especially the south of the island, they probably introduced, as in Sicily, a tax paid in kind, i.e. primarily grain.[3] When Rome and Carthage came into conflict, Sardinia's strategic significance became apparent to the Romans: the distance from the northern city of Olbia to Latium was only 188 km,[4] so that Sardinia could be, and was, used as a base of naval operations against the Italian coast during the early phases of the First Punic War.[5]

In the aftermath of that war the Carthaginian mercenaries revolted, among them those based in Sardinia, who called in Roman help. After some initial reluctance, the Romans intervened, dispatching forces to the island in 238 or 237 and continuing the campaign to 231, when

[1] Rowland 2001: 42. [2] Ibid. 36.
[3] Ibid. 295 (fig. 46) and 91. [4] Ibid. 1. [5] Ibid. 87.

the island was subjugated. In 227 it was organized as one of Rome's first overseas provinces, to be governed by a magistrate (praetor or propraetor) sent from Rome. In 215, during the Second Punic War, with Carthaginian support, a certain Hampsicoras led a revolt against Roman rule, but it was put down by the propraetor T. Manlius Torquatus. Further revolts followed in 181 and 178, the latter finally quelled by the proconsul Ti. Sempronius Gracchus in 175 with enormous reported casualties (80,000). In the aftermath Gracchus reorganized the province, doubling the tax (*vectigal*) paid by previously stipendiary communities and collecting a tax in grain, presumably in addition to the previous tithe. This set the pattern for Sardinia under Roman rule, which, together with Sicily and Africa, was to be one of Rome's three major suppliers of corn (Cic. *Man.* 34).[6]

Our speech presents a divided portrait of the Sardinians: on the one hand, some members of the local elite such as C.'s guest-friend Cn. Domitius Sincaius were clearly assimilating Roman identity (43–4); but on the other hand, C. is able to depict the Sardinians generally as crude and uncouth in their dress and attitudes (especially 15, 17, 42, 44, 45d and o), cultural stereotypes that suggest that a Punic identity may have continued to flourish in the countryside.[7]

2. The Aemilii Scauri in Roman Society and Politics

The Aemilii were one of Rome's oldest patrician families; they gave their name to the Aemilian tribe and occupied the consulate within the first three decades of the Republic.[8] The Scauri were a younger branch, attested from the second century BC onwards, named, apparently, for their prominent ankles.[9] The earliest known representative was L. Aemilius Scaurus, a lieutenant of L. Aemilius Regillus in the war against Antiochus (190), possibly grandfather of the *princeps senatus*.[10] The latter was born into poverty but by his energy, determination, and careful cultivation of his public image became the

6 Ibid. 89–92.

7 Cf. van Dommelen 1998, esp. 44–5.

8 Cf. Klebs, *RE* s.v. Aemilius.

9 Porph. on Hor. *Sat.* 1.3.47; Kajanto 1965, 242.

10 So Klebs, *RE* s.v. Aemilius 138; Henderson 1958, 195, however, thinks that this man cannot have been a direct ancestor of C.'s client because Asc. 23C denies any public offices as far back as the great-grandfather.

first member of the family in three generations to hold office (cf. Asc. 23C).

This is not the place for a full biography of M. Aemilius Scaurus *père*,[11] but since at his trial his son was still, to a considerable degree, basking in the glow of his father's reputation (cf. *Scaur.* 2–5, 46, 49–50; Asc. 20C), it is worth surveying the main components of his career and character. After seeing military service in Spain and Sardinia, the elder Scaurus began his public career with election as augur in 123 (Rüpke 2008, no. 527); he served as curule aedile in 122, the year of C. Gracchus' second tribunate. The optimate trend of his policies comes into focus early on, for he is said to have sharpened the consul L. Opimius against Gracchus in 121.[12] In the aftermath of Gracchus' fall Scaurus reaped benefit by election as praetor for 120 or 119.[13] Though he suffered defeat in the consular elections for 116 (with ensuing suit and countersuit for electoral malfeasance (*ambitus*) with his successful opponent P. Rutilius Rufus: *TLRR* 34–5), he won election the following year. His consulate (115) was marked by his humiliation of the praetor P. Decius Subulo, the erstwhile prosecutor of Opimius (*TLRR* 27), campaigns against the Gauls and Ligurians, and legislation concerning the voting rights of freedmen and limiting senatorial luxury (*MRR* i. 531); at the end of his year of office he was named leader of the senate (*princeps senatus*), a position he retained for the rest of his life and did not hesitate to exploit to advantage (cf. F 4n.). His prosecution by M. Brutus for extortion presumably followed soon thereafter but resulted in acquittal (*TLRR* 37).

In the years following his consulship Scaurus continued to participate fully in affairs of state. Thus he served on a senatorial commission dispatched in 112 to mediate between Jugurtha and Adherbal. The following year saw him return to Africa as a legate of the consul L. Calpurnius Bestia (*MRR* i. 539 and 541; cf. Thomasson 1991, 107, no. 74); influenced by bribery, however, Scaurus and the other legates concluded a shameful peace with the king. In 109 a bill carried by C. Mamilius Limetanus empanelled a special court to investigate treason in dealings with Jugurtha (*MRR* i. 546), but Scaurus managed

[11] Cf. detailed studies by Bloch 1909 and Bates 1986 as well as Klebs, *RE* s.v. Aemilius 140.

[12] *Vir. illustr.* 72.9 with Bates 1986, 253.

[13] *MRR* i. 526, gives the latter date with a query.

to get himself appointed as one of the three investigators (*quaesitores*).[14] He served as censor the following year with M. Livius Drusus; they promoted such public works as the construction of the Via Aemilia and repair of the Mulvian Bridge; but Scaurus refused to vacate the office on his colleague's death until the tribunes threatened him with imprisonment (*MRR* i. 545). In 104 he was given a special mandate to facilitate the supply of grain to the capital through the port of Ostia, the quaestor L. Saturninus having been relieved of that charge at a time of high prices;[15] and during Saturninus' revolt of 100, he urged the consul C. Marius to take action and appeared with other senators under arms in the Comitium.[16]

Much of the political debate of the last decade of the second century and first decade of the first played out in the courts, with Scaurus, as expected, taking a large role. At a popular tribunal convened in 103 Q. Servilius Caepio was convicted for the devastating defeat the Romans suffered two years previously at Arausio (modern Orange); the trial, presided over by C. Norbanus, was marred by violence, however, and Scaurus himself was injured by a thrown rock; Norbanus was later called to account with Scaurus as a witness against him but was acquitted; cf. *TLRR* 66 and 86. In two other cases of the last years of the second century Scaurus is found testifying against *popularis* politicians, namely C. Memmius and C. Flavius Fimbria (cos. 104); cf. *Font.* 24 and 26; *TLRR* 60–1. He was prosecuted on charges of extortion in late 92 or early 91 by Q. Servilius Caepio (son of the general defeated at Arausio) and Cn. Cornelius Dolabella (pr. 81), possibly in connection with a bribe allegedly tendered by Mithridates, and again in 90 under the *lex Varia*; cf. F 3 and 4; *TLRR* 96 and 100.

Scaurus must have married well before his consulship since by 102 he had a son of military age (born *c.*120?). Serving in that year under Q. Lutatius Catulus, who was campaigning against the Cimbri, young

[14] Sumner 1976 raises the attractive possibility that the M. Scaurus chosen as *quaesitor* of the Mamilian court of inquiry was actually M. Aurelius Scaurus (cos. suff. 108) and Sal. *Jug.* 40.4 confused him with M. Aemilius Scaurus; Gruen 1968, 147–9, offers an account of Scaurus' role without resorting to that conjecture.

[15] Cf. *MRR* i. 560; Chandler 1978, 330–1; in the late Republic the *quaestor Ostiensis* had charge of the reception, storage, and shipment of imported grain to Rome and appears also to have exercised judicial powers; cf. Meiggs 1960, 298–9. Was Saturninus seeking to exploit the situation for (anti-senatorial) political advantage?

[16] Cf. Cic. *Rab. perd.* 21; V. Max. 3.2.18.

Scaurus fled from battle and was subsequently disowned by his father and committed suicide.[17] This son was evidently by a wife previous to Caecilia Metella, daughter of L. Caecilius Metellus Delmaticus[18] and mother of C.'s client and of his sister Aemilia.[19] Scaurus *père* had evidently died by the latter half of 89 since Sulla appears to have married Metella shortly after his election as consul for 88.[20] She bore him the twins Faustus and Fausta (as well as a son who predeceased her).[21]

Scaurus' political coming-of-age at the time of C. Gracchus' tribunate set him on a course that he was to follow consistently through the rest of his career. The 'singular severity' of his public demeanour (Cic. *Off.* 1.108) was related to those political struggles as well as his personal struggle as an impoverished patrician who had to work for his honours 'just like a new man' (Asc. 23C). Metella will, however, have brought him a substantial dowry, and he was evidently not above the general level of officials of the time when it came to accepting bribes (see above). For the much younger C. he was not so much a personality in his own right as a personification of the senate whose interests he consistently defended; cf. 46 'the renowned senate house bears you witness about the authoritative and gallant headship of his father'.

The younger Scaurus will have been born *c.*96 if he held the quaestorship of 66 at the minimum age (30). Upon his father's death, when he was about 11 years of age, he became the stepson of Sulla, recently elected consul for the first time. He is said to have behaved moderately at the time of Sulla's victory in the civil war, neither accepting gifts nor profiting from the proscriptions (Asc. 18C), though his mother was less scrupulous (Plin. *Nat.* 36.116). Shortly after his appointment as dictator in 82 Sulla arranged for the marriage of Scaurus' sister Aemilia to Pompey; though she died soon afterward giving birth to the child of her first husband,

[17] Cf. Klebs, *RE* s.v. Aemilius 137.

[18] Cf. Münzer, *RE* s.v. Caecilius 91 and 134.

[19] She may have been born *c.*100, given that she was already married and pregnant by her husband in 82 when compelled by Sulla to divorce and marry Pompey; see below.

[20] This is inferred from Plutarch's ordering of events (*Sull.* 6.10).

[21] Ibid. 34.3 (birth of the twins), 37.2 (the son who died), and 35.2 (her death during the feasting following Sulla's triumph in 81).

M'. Acilius Glabrio,[22] the family connection with Pompey was to be important. Scaurus came to public notice for the first time in 78 when at the age of about 18 he successfully prosecuted his father's enemy Cn. Cornelius Dolabella (pr. 81; *TLRR* 135). He is next heard of as Pompey's quaestor in Asia (dated to 66 with a query at *MRR* ii. 153), where he remained as a promagistrate until 61; in 63 Pompey left him in command in Syria and Palestine when he himself went to Pontus (ibid. 159, 163, 168, 175, 180; cf. 45d n.). Though Scaurus must have received a substantial inheritance from his mother and stepfather,[23] he could now powerfully augment his fortune, receiving 400 talents from Aristobulus, a pretender to the Maccabean throne, and another 300 from Aretas, who bribed Scaurus to desist from waging war against him (*MRR* ii. 163 and 175). After returning to Rome, he married Mucia, daughter of Q. Mucius Scaevola, whom Pompey had divorced in 62. Elected aedile for 58, he offered the most lavish spectacles the city had ever seen (ibid. 195), so lavish that, in spite of his wealth, he fell into massive debt (Asc. 18C). As praetor in 56 he presided over Sestius' trial for violence (*Sest.* 101 and 116; *MRR* ii. 208). The following year as governor of Sardinia (ibid. 217–18) he appears to have tried to recoup losses and lay up a war chest for the consular campaign of 54. Within days of his return from Sardinia Scaurus defended C. Porcius Cato on charges connected with his tribunate of the plebs in 56 (*TLRR* 286). He had little time, however, to savour his victory in that case; two days after the verdict he was himself indicted for misconduct as governor of Sardinia (ibid. 295).

After his acquittal in our case (see below), Scaurus was prosecuted for misconduct in the consular elections for 53, was convicted, and went into what must have been a comfortable exile (*TLRR* 300 and 319; for the sale price of his house on the Palatine cf. 45i n.). His son by Mucia, also named M. Aemilius Scaurus, betrayed his stepbrother Sextus Pompey in 35 to Antony's generals[24] and fought with Antony at Actium; his life was spared, however, on his mother's intercession (Dio 51.2.4–5). Mamercus Aemilius Scaurus (cos. suff. AD 21) was the son of Antony's partisan; he married Aemilia Lepida, by whom he

[22] Ibid. 33.3; Plut. *Pomp.* 9.1–2.

[23] For the legacies cf. Plin. *Nat.* 36.116; Shatzman 1975, 290, estimates them to have amounted to 'tens of millions of denarii'.

[24] App. *BC* 5.142; Hadas 1930, 158–9; possibly this was in revenge for his father's abandonment by Pompey; cf. nn. 64 and 65 below.

sired a daughter (Tac. *An.* 3.23). Accused in AD 34 of adultery with Livilla and consultation of astrologers, he forestalled the verdict by suicide, thus entailing the extinction of the Aemilii Scauri.[25]

3. The Roman Plebs and the Grain Supply

Grain, principally wheat, was a staple of the Roman diet.[26] The bulk of the supply came from Rome's overseas provinces, Sardinia, Sicily, and, after 146, Africa.[27] Getting a sufficient supply to market in the city to feed the growing numbers of citizens resident there was, even in good times, a challenge.[28] Such factors as poor weather, warfare, piracy, hoarding, speculation, and a convergence of people on the city for a special occasion, such as C.'s return from exile in August 57, could easily create a shortage, which could, if the plight of the plebs grew desperate, lead to rioting. The crisis could be met by a special distribution, as e.g. in 75 when Q. Hortensius Hortalus as aedile distributed grain to the people (*MRR* ii. 97). It was only in 123 that C. Gracchus as tribune of the plebs carried a law providing for monthly distribution of grain to adult male Roman citizens in the capital in quantities of 5 *modii* each at the fixed price of 6⅓ *asses* per *modius*[29] and establishing public granaries to store supplies.[30] The price must have been subsidized; hence criticism of the policy by conservatives like C. as a raid on the treasury (*Off.* 2.72). Nonetheless it was a popular measure; the grain distribution remained in place, with interruption between 81 and 73 and in times of war, until the end of the Republic.[31]

In addition, in times of shortage special measures might be adopted, such as the directive to Verres as governor of Sicily to

[25] Sen. *Suas.* 2.22; cf. in general von Rohden and Klebs, *RE* s.v. Aemilius 139 and 142.

[26] Cf. Rickman 1980, 3–8; thus grain was the basic provision of the Roman legionary soldier, distributed in quantities of 2/3 *medimnos* = *c*.4 *modii* (see n. 29 below) each per month: Polyb. 6.39.13; see further Liebenam, *RE* 6.2 1663.50 ff. (s.v. *exercitus*).

[27] Rickman 1980, ch. 5.

[28] On the rising urban population cf. *ESAR* i. 108–214; Brunt 1971, 134 ff., 383 ff., and 705.

[29] Roman dry measure = 8.733 litres = 1.1 peck.

[30] Rotondi 1912, 307–8; Rostovtzeff, *RE* 7.1173 (s.v. *frumentum*); Stockton 1979, 126–9.

[31] Cf. in general Garnsey 1988, 198–217.

purchase a second tithe of 3 million *modii* at 3 sesterces per *modius* and another 800,000 *modii* for 3½ sesterces (*Ver.* 2.3.163) or Pompey's appointment in 57 on C.'s motion to a special five-year commission to supervise the grain supply (*cura annonae*: *MRR* ii. 200). Problems persisted, however, with fresh rioting instigated by Clodius on 7 February 56 (*Q.fr.* 2.3(7).2); possibly the rioting at the Megalensian Games in early April was also related to the shortage;[32] then on 5 April the senate awarded Pompey 40 million sesterces to carry out his work (*Q.fr.* 2.6(10).1).[33] Against this background Triarius' emphasis on Scaurus' handling of the grain supplies, about which he questioned all his witnesses (21), appears to be well advised. He aimed to rouse indignation against a defendant depicted as a *bon vivant* (cf. 45i, l, n.) who at the same time manipulated the grain supply to the disadvantage of Roman citizens.

4. Cicero's Political Position between the Council of Luca and the Defence of Scaurus

The constellation of forces that determined the main lines of policy at Rome from the summer of 60 to the 50s, with perhaps the exception of 58 to the Council of Luca, was the coalition of Caesar, Pompey, and Crassus. C. was slow to recognize this fact, however,[34] and thought that he had space for independent action because of his services as consul and his influence with Pompey. C.'s first warning of the true power relations occurred when P. Clodius, whom he had alienated by testimony at the Bona Dea trial of 61 (*TLRR* 236), was given a free hand to change from patrician to plebeian status, then was elected tribune of the plebs, agitated against C. for putting Roman citizens to death without a trial during the suppression of the Catilinarian conspiracy, and forced him into exile.[35] Upon his return in August 57 after seventeen months of exile C. tried to resume his previous independence and opposition to Caesar's policies but was brought sharply to heel after the members of the coalition met and reaffirmed

[32] So Tatum 1999, 212.

[33] The loss of grain in the flooding of the Tiber that sent Pompey in search of new supplies prior to Gabinius' trial, which had its *divinatio* on 12 Oct. (*TLRR* 303), was evidently subsequent to our trial, which ended 2 Sept. (ibid. 295); cf. Dio 39.63.3.

[34] Cf. Sanders 1932.

[35] Cf. Tatum 1999, chs. 3–6.

their alliance at Luca in April 56. After the meeting Pompey travelled to Sardinia, where he met with Quintus Cicero, who was still active there as his legate (cf. 39n.), and reminded him that prior to the recall from exile Quintus had gone surety for his brother's good behaviour; he now expected C. to suspend his opposition to Caesar's consular policies;[36] he presumably also required support for Caesar's recent demands.

For the next several years C. felt himself obliged, in order to secure his own position against the continuing threat of Clodius, to support the basic lines of policy laid down by the coalition. The first sign of this volte-face was at a senate meeting in May when C. moved that the four legions Caesar recruited on his own initiative be supported by the treasury (*Balb.* 61); he followed this up in June with praise of Caesar's conquests in the speech *On the Consular Provinces*, which he published but withheld from Atticus as an embarrassing palinode (*Att.* 4.5(80).1 with Shackleton Bailey's n.). In July senatorial debate on a recent opinion of the haruspices, the Etruscan soothsayers functioning as an advisory body to the Roman state,[37] gave C. opportunity to put his own gloss on the current political position.[38] In particular he used the haruspices' warning about 'discord of the optimates' to justify his attempts to reconcile Caesar, Pompey, and Crassus with the optimates in opposition to Clodius' efforts to drive a wedge between the two camps (*Har.* 40, 47–55). An example of how the coalition was able to harness C. to their ends is the defence around this time of L. Cornelius Balbus, one of Caesar's key aides, in which C. collaborated with Crassus and Pompey (*TLRR* 276).

Amid the optimates' sniping at Caesar, the joint consulship of Crassus and Pompey in 55 was meant to clear the air. C. began the year resolved to follow Pompey's line (*Fam.* 1.8(19).2). He even reconciled with his enemy P. Vatinius, elected praetor for the year (*Fam.* 1.9(20).19). Work on the dialogue *On the Orator*, to be published in November (*Att.* 4.13(87).2), kept C. occupied on his estates on the Bay of Naples during the spring. In spite of his previous public

[36] Cf. *Fam.* 1.9(20).9; Ruebel 1975; Gelzer 1984, 131–3; Seager 2002, 117–21.

[37] Cf. North in Beard and North, 1990, 49 ff.; Wissowa 1912, 543 ff.

[38] I follow the dating established by Meyer 2003; for interpretation cf. Corbeill 2010.

restraint, the return in September from Macedonia of L. Calpurnius Piso Caesoninus, Caesar's father-in-law and one of the consuls who presided over his exile, caused C.'s pent-up anger to burst through all dams; it found expression in the scurrilous *Against Piso*, a masterpiece of character assassination. Unwelcome attendance at the opening of Pompey's theatre (*Fam.* 7(24).1.2–3), a burdensome defence, at Pompey's request, of L. Caninius Gallus (*TLRR* 280), and a flare-up of bad feeling between C. and M. Crassus over allegations raised during the investigation of the Catilinarian conspiracy, followed by a reconciliation (*Fam.* 1.9(20).20), round out the year's notable events.

The following year sees new links binding C. to Caesar, including Caesar's loan of 800,000 or 820,000 sesterces (*Att.* 5.1(94).2, 4(97).3, 5(98).2, 6(99).2),[39] the sending of Q. Cicero to serve as legate in Caesar's army in Gaul (*Fam.* 1.9(20).21; Thomasson 1991, 114, no. 209), and Caesar's dedication to C. of his grammatical treatise *On Analogy* (*gram.* F 1 and 3). At the same time the reconciliation with Crassus holds firm: C. reports defending the latter's interests in the senate against the stubborn opposition of both consuls and many consulars (*Fam.* 5.8(25).1 and 1.9(20).20). C. was busy in the courts this year (this is the year he speaks of writing speeches during the games and holidays: *Planc.* 66). Some of these tasks, such as the defence of the Reatines' interests before a special commission (cf. 27n.), were owed to old clients and readily accepted; similarly the cases of C. Messius and M. Cispius, two of the tribunes of 57 who had earned C.'s thanks through their efforts on behalf of his recall (*TLRR* 279 and 289). Others, undertaken at Caesar's request, were less welcome, such as the defence of M. Livius Drusus Claudianus and especially, in spite of their recent reconciliation, that of P. Vatinius (*TLRR* 290 and 292).[40] The same letter announces both the defence of Vatinius and the pending case of Scaurus, with whom C. had no particularly strong ties (*Q.fr.* 2.16(20).3).[41]

[39] Cf. Shatzman 1975, 416–17; Rollinger 2009, 149–53.

[40] C. complains around this time of enforced work as an advocate in general terms at *Fam.* 7.1(24).4.

[41] Hence C. could write to Quintus 'I have laid Scaurus under heavy obligation by the favour of a defence' (*Q.fr.* 3.1(21).16).

5. The Trial of Scaurus

a. The Prosecution: Its Motive and Strategy

Scaurus returned to Rome from his province on 28 June 54 and was indicted eight days later (Asc. 18–19C). The chief prosecutor (*nominis delator*) was P. Valerius Triarius, son of the governor of Sardinia who had resisted Lepidus' attempt to establish a toehold there after the defeat of his revolt.[42] He was assisted by the *subscriptores* L. Marius, possibly to be identified with the quaestor of 50,[43] and the brothers M. and Q. Pacuvius Claudius, about whom nothing is known beyond their involvement in this case and the immediately following trial for *calumnia*.[44]

The indictment occurred just prior to the consular elections,[45] in which Scaurus intended to stand, apparently with the support of Pompey.[46] The timing was not an accident: the aim was to hinder Scaurus' election. This is confirmed by the fact that the prosecutors declined to use the thirty days each allocated for investigation of the charges in Sardinia and Corsica (Asc. 19C; cf. *Scaur.* 23). It has been thought that the mere indictment would not have prevented Scaurus from standing but the empanelment of the jury would.[47] On 27 July, as he is preparing for the litigation, C. foresees difficulties for the case unless his client is already consul-designate (*Att.* 4.15(90).9), without

[42] Volkmann, *RE* s.v. Valerius 363 and 367; *MRR* ii. 89 and 91.

[43] Münzer, *RE* s.v. Marius 4 and 20; *MRR* ii. 250; cf. Courtney 1961, 155, who remarks of this man that 'the very name ... seems significant when one recalls the relationship of Scaurus to Sulla and the exertions of Faustus Sulla on his behalf'.

[44] Münzer, *RE* s.v. Pacuvius 4 and 5; the brothers' name, combining two gentile names, is dubious and much debated; Cladus 'lame' or Caldus (derived from *calidus* 'warm' and attested as a cognomen of the Caelii) is often substituted for Claudius; cf. Courtney 1961, 154; Gruen 1974, 333 n. 107; Shackleton Bailey 1975, 442; Rawson 1977, 348–9 = 1991, 235–6; Marshall 1985, 123–4; Lewis 2006, 218; Claudi<an>us might be worth considering. For the procedure and punishment for *calumnia* cf. Mommsen 1899, 491–8; Greenidge 1901, 468–70; Levy 1933, 153–77.

[45] They were normally held at this period on or soon after 10 July; cf. Mommsen 1887–8, i. 584.

[46] *Att.* 4.15(90).7 albeit with the qualification that it is dubious whether he supports him 'with his face or his heart' (*fronte an mente*); Courtney 1961, 156, notes Scaurus' service under Pompey in the East and the fact that both men had children by Mucia, albeit the fact that Scaurus married her immediately after Pompey divorced her rankled (Asc. 20C). Plut. *Pomp.* 42.7 states that Pompey never gave grounds for the divorce but that C. indicates that it was adultery in a (non-extant) letter.

[47] The hypothesis of John 1876, 426–7.

any hint that the empanelment of the jury would disqualify his candidature.[48] Perhaps the prosecution's goal was, rather, to procure a conviction before the election or at the very least to distract Scaurus in his canvassing and thus make him a less formidable contender.[49] Hence it is no surprise that C. identifies the consular elections as the motive for the prosecution (*Scaur.* 31–5). Nor did the prosecutors deny that the consular elections were a factor: they claimed that their goal was to prevent Scaurus from buying the election with his ill-gotten gains, enjoying immunity as consul, and after his year in office going off to plunder another province before he could be brought to book (Asc. 19C). C.'s explanation of the political background is rather different. He claims that the consul Ap. Claudius was pulling the strings behind the scenes in order to procure the election of his brother Gaius, who could not otherwise prevail against Scaurus in canvassing for the one consular seat open to a patrician;[50] he adds that Appius persists, even after Gaius has suspended his campaign, out of personal pique (*Scaur.* 31–5). The true reason, later disclosed, was that Appius was in league with the consular candidates C. Memmius and Cn. Domitius Calvinus (*Att.* 4.17(91).2).[51]

Beyond organizing the timetable so as to hinder or complicate Scaurus' election as consul, the prosecution aimed to shock the jury with sensational charges of cruelty, greed, and unbridled lust, in particular that Scaurus had murdered Bostar for his money and forced Aris of Nora to flee and his wife to commit suicide because he had designs on her (F 7–8, 1–12). In this Triarius painted a picture not unlike C.'s own portrait of Verres in the famous prosecution of 70. Likewise similar to the case against Verres was Triarius' emphasis on Scaurus' exactions regarding the grain supply (21), charges that might have been expected to resonate in light of the recent shortage (see sec. 3 above). Triarius evidently concluded his case in a crescendo

[48] C.'s calculation is evidently based on the prestige that the election would carry rather than a law immunizing magistrates-designate from prosecution except on charges of electoral malfeasance (*ambitus*); against the existence of such a law cf. Weinrib 1971 against Shackleton Bailey 1970.

[49] Cf. Cicero's confession at *Ver.* 1.24: 'I could not devote my undivided attention to canvassing because of the trial' (sc. of Verres).

[50] But, in view of the timing, this was probably a mere pretext, as Courtney 1961, 154, remarks: 'The prosecution was launched on July 6, the election was originally set for the end of the month (*ad Att.* IV.15.8–9); how could C. Claudius get back from Asia and conduct a campaign?'

[51] Courtney 1961, 154; cf. also Tatum 1999, 232.

of indignation, claiming that Scaurus illegally enriched himself to support a lavish lifestyle, featuring an outsize house fitted with columns so colossal that they had to be brought in on wagons (45i, l, n.).[52]

b. The Defence Team

Besides speaking on his own behalf Scaurus was defended by no fewer than six advocates (Asc. 20C). C. disapproved of such large panels on principle (*Brut.* 207) but participated nonetheless. It has been supposed that the number of defence counsel 'shows the general unwillingness of the aristocracy to encompass or see the ruin of one of their own class';[53] perhaps, but it also suggests that the case was perceived to be weak[54] and may reflect a strategy of appealing to various segments of the jury. The advocates, besides C., were the following:

(1) M. Calidius, who, as praetor in 57, supported C.'s recall from exile (*MRR* ii. 200). The family had strong ties to the Metelli going back to the advocate's father Q. Calidius (tr. pleb. 98), who moved the recall from exile of Metellus Numidicus (*MRR* ii. 5) and enjoyed the support of the son, Metellus Pius (cos. 80), for the praetorship of 79 (*MRR* ii. 83).[55]

(2) M. Claudius Marcellus (cos. 51), a reliable optimate. He warned C. of an attempt on his life during the Catilinarian conspiracy (*Cat.* 1.21; Plut. *Cic.* 15.1) and in 56 defended Milo against a prosecution on charges of violence brought by Clodius (*TLRR* 266); later he would participate in the defence of Milo for the murder of Clodius (ibid. 309). In his consulate he was uncompromising in his opposition

[52] For the reconstruction of the case against Scaurus see further Alexander 2002, ch. 4.

[53] Brunt 1965, 15.

[54] Cf. Brennan 2000, 494: 'Scaurus' command needed all the defending it could get'; cf. also the (probably) ten character witnesses, including Pompey, and the eleven persons supplicating the jury: *TLRR* 295; ten appears to have been the licit number of character witnesses (*Ver.* 2.5.57); hence the uncertain status of the testimonials supplied by Cn. Domitius Sincaius and the 'good men from Sardinia' (included with a query in *TLRR*).

[55] Cf. Münzer, *RE* s.v. Calidius 4 and 5.

to Caesar's plans; his later pardon by Caesar was celebrated by C. in the extant speech mistitled *On Behalf of Marcellus.*[56]

(3) P. Clodius Pulcher (aed. cur. 56). He might have been expected to support the case launched by his brother Appius (cf. C.'s needling at 36); Tatum 1999, 233, sees Clodius' participation as an effort to distance himself from Appius as word of the unsavoury electoral bargain leaked out (see above).

(4) Q. Hortensius Hortalus (cos. 69). By contrast, his presence is no surprise here: Rome's second-best orator of the time is often found collaborating with C. during and after the latter's consulate and defending the cause of his fellow nobles.[57]

(5) M. Valerius Messalla Niger (cos. 61, cens. 55). He was the cousin of Sulla's fifth wife Valeria and may have owed his pontificate to Sulla;[58] he persuaded C. to undertake the defence of the dictator's nephew P. Sulla (*Sul.* 20), possibly also that of Sextus Roscius (cf. *S.Rosc.* 149 with Dyck 2010 ad loc.). The policies of his consulate earned C.'s praise (*Att.* 1.13(13).2 and 3, 14(14).6), as does his forensic oratory at *Brut.* 246, by which time (46) he was dead; though C. speaks there of his handling of 'many cases', ours is the only known example.[59]

c. Cicero's Speech

There was massive Sardinian testimony to Scaurus' wrongdoing during his year as governor (55: *MRR* ii. 217–18),[60] particularly his manipulation of the grain supply, a grave charge given the recent shortage at Rome (see sec. 3 above). If C. had a cogent refutation of this charge, it is not

[56] Cf. Münzer, *RE* s.v. Claudius 229.

[57] See further Dyck 2008b; Courtney 1961, 155, however, remarks that 'to argue from relationships alone one would expect to find Hortensius on the side upheld by Servilia', his mother-in-law (*Ver.* 2.2.24), whom Courtney identifies with Cato's sister, whose ties to Triarius are noted by Asc. 19C; but the mother with the elder Catulus of Hortensius' wife Lutatia was probably rather the sister of Caepio the consul of 106 (so Münzer, *RE* s.v. Servilius 97 and 1999, 228, 262–3 and 318) or of the Caepio who opposed Drusus in 91 (Münzer, *RE* s.v. Servilius 50); the latter is argued by Badian 1964, 218 and 232–3.

[58] *Har.* 12; but Rüpke 2008, no. 3411 n. 7 observes that he would have been very young for cooptation in 81.

[59] Cf. Münzer, *RE* s.v. Valerius 266.

[60] The prosecutor claimed that he could call the 120 witnesses allowed by law and that he would agree to an acquittal if Scaurus could name that number of provincials from whom he had *not* taken money (V. Max. 8.1 abs. 10).

extant. The prosecution's portrait of Scaurus as arrogant and addicted to luxury rings true, in spite of C.'s attempts to disarm such criticisms with humour (45l, 45n.).[61] C. offers a luminous portrait of the defendant's father in both the exordium and peroration, a scurrilous attack on the chief prosecution witness as a murderer of his wife and on his new wife as the murderer of her own son (9–12 and F 10), commonplaces on the unreliability of witness testimony (14–17), criticism of the prosecutor for hasty preparation (23–30), a general attack on the character of Sardinians as unreliable and mendacious (38–44), an analysis of the case as politically motivated (30–7), and a fond reminiscence of his client's lavish aedileship (sch. Bob. on *Sest.* 116). The remains suggest that C. has constructed an elaborate machine designed to distract the jurors from the serious underlying charges and make them feel that it was all right to ignore the Sardinians' complaints.[62]

d. The Outcome

In the event Scaurus was overwhelmingly acquitted by all three categories of jurors (Asc. 28C; *Att.* 4.17(91).4; V. Max. 8.1 abs. 10). Indeed, the following day the presiding praetor M. Cato opened deliberations as to whether the prosecutors should be convicted of calumny,[63] but no majority was found (Asc. 29C). To Atticus C. takes some pride in his performance ('in my best style' (*ornatissime*) tr. Shackleton Bailey: *Att.* 4.17(91).4). C. reports to Quintus from Arpinum in September that the speech has already been written up (*Q.fr.* 3.1(21).11). Besides C.'s speech, the trial may have had one other permanent outcome. Triarius had put his finger on a weak point in the Roman constitution, namely the ability of officials holding *imperium* to evade accountability for years (and presumably also escape conviction when the cases against them had grown cold). Whether spurred by his arguments or not, a Pompeian law of the year 52 established a five-year interval between urban and provincial *imperium.*[64]

[61] Similarly Brennan 2000, 495.

[62] For a similar strategy in Murena's case cf. Craig 1986.

[63] If the jurors returned a large majority in favour of the defendent the presiding officer was virtually bound to entertain a charge of calumny against the prosecutors afterwards before the same jury; on the procedure cf. Mommsen 1899, 491–8; Greenidge 1901, 468–70; Levy 1933, 153–77; Berger 1953 s.v. *calumnia*.

[64] Rotondi 1912, 411–12; Brennan 2000, 496; the case of Caesar, cos. 59 and then for years proconsul in Gaul, was, of course, much more striking.

As to Scaurus himself, in spite of the efforts of his kinsman the tribune Scaevola to postpone the elections by watching for ill omens (*Att.* 4.17(91).4), Scaurus' candidature went flat (*Q.fr.* 3.3(23).3).[65] Indeed, he was indicted for electoral malfeasance by the same Triarius and, in spite of C.'s defence, convicted and exiled in 52 (*TLRR* 300 and 319).[66]

6. The Surviving Text

Apart from fragments quoted in literary and grammatical texts,[67] *Scaur.* survives in folios of two manuscripts written in the fifth century and reused at Bobbio in the seventh century. There they remained until the seventeenth century when the MSS were transferred, one to Milan, the other to Turin. In 1814 Angelo Mai detected Ciceronian speeches beneath Sedulius' Easter poem in the Milan MS (Ambros. R 57 sup., now S.P. 11.66) (A); the writing is continuous rustic capital, three columns per leaf, twenty-four lines per column, each line accommodating twelve letters; *Scaur.* occupies six leaves.[68] The Turin MS D IV.22 (T) contains a text of Augustine; in 1820 A. Peyron discovered the lower text consisting of ten Ciceronian speeches, all from a single book written in two columns of rustic capitals, among them four and a half leaves of *Scaur.* The text was photographed before being destroyed by fire in 1904.[69] While A shows more superficial carelessness than T, the two witnesses seem to be of about equal weight.[70]

Some of the fragments of our speech derive from Asconius' commentary (mid-first century AD), the text of which is based upon some thirty fifteenth-century Italian manuscripts, all derived from a lost ninth-century archetype from St Gall. The text in current use is Clark

[65] Pompey had already turned against him; cf. *Q.fr.* 3.6(26).3 (end of Nov.): 'Pompey cast Scaurus away long ago'.

[66] On the apparent revival of the trial by Pompey as sole consul in 52 with retrospective application of the Pompeian law on bribery cf. Henderson 1958, 203–4.

[67] Listed by Olechowska 1984, pp. xi–xii.

[68] Mai 1814.

[69] Peyron 1824; cf. Olechowska 1984, pp. v–vi; Rouse and Reeve in Reynolds 1983, 56; reconstruction by Reeve 1992.

[70] So Olechowska 1984, pp. ix–x.

1907; Lewis 2006 reprints Clark with translation and commentary, but a new critical edition is needed.[71]

TRANSLATION

(F 1) M. Scaurus had above all to hope, jurors, that he might, without incurring anyone's enmity, without giving offence or causing distress, hold on to the standing of his line, his family, and his name, which is what he was always particularly eager to do.

(F 2) He also underwent a trial before the people with the tribune Cn. Domitius conducting the prosecution.

(F 3) He was prosecuted by Q. Servilius Caepio under the Servilian law when the equestrian order controlled the courts and, in light of P. Rutilius' conviction, no one seemed to be too innocent to fear them.

(F 4) That guardian of the free commonwealth was also charged with treason by the same man under the lex Varia; he was harassed by Q.Varius, tribune of the plebs.

(F 5) I did not merely admire that famous man, as all have done, but I was also particularly fond of him. When I was burning with a keen desire for glory, he gave me the first impulse to hope that, without the backing of a fortune, I could arrive at my goal by hard work and consistent application.

(F 6) Since the prosecution was heaped up in a kind of pile of charges, without any distinction or variety of type.

(F 7) Now he said that a certain Bostar of Nora, fleeing from Sardinia . . . Scaurus' arrival . . . he was buried before the defendant's dinner was removed.

(F 8) If finally he could by no means have appropriated those goods except upon Bostar's death . . .

(F 9) By Hercules, gentlemen of the jury, if I were pleading on behalf of L. Tubulus, whom we have heard was the most wicked and brazen man in all history, I would nevertheless not be afraid if it were alleged that he had administered poison to a dinner guest when Tubulus was neither the man's heir nor angry with him.

[71] Reeve in Reynolds 1983, 24–5.

(F 10) . . . than what he had was offered for sale. Come, I have defended Scaurus, Triarius: you defend the mother.

(F 11) . . . that you were afraid that you were insolvent, finally that the defendant wished to retain the goods which had been advertised for sale unless . . .

(F 12) . . . since Aris refused to give . . . he attempted to flee from Sardinia clandestinely.

(F 13) they ransom themselves by that part of the body because of which they are most sought.

(1) We have heard about those matters, but we remember and have practically seen the following: P. Crassus of the same line and name committed suicide so as not to fall into the hands of his enemies.

(2) Though he enjoyed the same honours, Manius Aquilius, a man of great martial bravery, was unable to imitate the deed of the illustrious elder Crassus; <rather,> he fouled <the glory of his courageous> exploits with the disgrace of his old age. Tell me: in that same period were the distinguished Julii or M. Antonius, endowed with supreme command, able to imitate the second Crassus? *(3)* In all the monuments of Greece, which are more embellished in words than facts, who, apart from Ajax and characters in plays, who, as the poet says, 'though an insolent victor, could not for pain of the disgrace suffer himself to be defeated', besides Themistocles of Athens, punished himself with death? *(4)* But the Greeklings invent many tales, among whom they say that Theombrotus of Ambracia flung himself from a very high wall, not because he had suffered some bitter misfortune but, as I see written, since he had read the supreme philosopher Plato's book about death, written with authority and elegance, in which, I believe, Socrates discourses at length on the very day on which he had to die, that what we believe to be life is death since the soul is held confined by the body as if by a prison, but that is life when the same soul is released from the chains of the body and has returned to the place of its origin. *(5)* Now surely that Sardinian woman you mention did not know or read Pythagoras or Plato, did she? They themselves, however, praise death with the reservation that they prohibit one to escape life and assert that this is contrary to the compact and law of nature. You surely will find no other just cause for suicide. Moreover, the prosecutor recognized this, for at a certain point he tossed out that that woman preferred to be stripped of her life than her chastity. *(6)* But he instantly retreated and said nothing more about chastity fearing to provide us an opening for

ridicule and jest. For it is agreed that that lady was not only supremely ugly but also in extreme old age. So, however witty that Sardinian woman may have been, how can there be any suspicion of a love affair?

(7) So you may not suppose, Triarius, that I am inventing the content of my speech and not learning the case from the defendant, I will explain to you what views there were in Sardinia about that woman's death—for there were two—so that even more easily . . .

(8) . . . as I said a little bit earlier, for a considerable time he loved the lustful and reprobate woman in an infamous and notorious adultery. Although he feared his wife, a wealthy and shrewish old woman, he neither wanted to keep her married to him because of her repulsivess nor divorce her because of her dowry. So in agreement with Bostar's mother he formed the plan that each would go to Rome; he gave assurance that there he would find a means to marry her.

(9) In this connection two views, as I said, were held, one of them in accord with the state and nature of things: Aris' wife was already upset by the disgrace of the adultery; when she heard that Aris had gone to Rome with his beloved pretending to flee in fear—so not only had there previously been a relationship between them but they would even be joined in matrimony—she flared up with a woman's rage and preferred to die rather than endure it. *(10)* The other view, no less probable and, I believe, even more believed in Sardinia, is that that witness and guest-friend of yours, Triarius, upon his departure for Rome, gave his freedman the task not of laying violent hand upon the old woman—for that would not have been the right thing to do to one's patron—but of squeezing her neck with two little fingers and surrounding it with a bit of rope so that she would be thought to have died by hanging. *(11)* This suspicion prevailed all the more because she was said to have been hanged by the freedman at the time when the citizens of Nora were celebrating the Parentalia and all had according to their custom departed the city. The solitude of their departure was, however, optimal for one who suffocated his patron, not for a woman bent on suicide. *(12)* The suspicion received confirmation since, upon the old woman's death, the freedman immediately proceeded to Rome as if his task had been accomplished and as soon as the freedman reported his wife's death Aris immediately married Bostar's mother.

(13) There you have it! To what families, how foul, how polluted, how disgraceful, are you handing over this family, jurors! Moved by

what witnesses do you suppose you must forget in the case of what man, what family, what name you are casting your votes! You see the crimes of mothers against their children, of husbands against their wives, you see acts of boundless lust mixed with cruelty. You have the authors of the two principal charges, by which this entire case has been shaped before ignorant or spiteful persons, fouled with every crime and disgrace.

(14) By now, jurors, surely no residue of suspicion lingers in these charges does it? Have they not been cleared away, refuted, broken? How did this happen? Because, Triarius, you have given me something to refute, on which to argue, about which to dispute; since the type of charge was not such that it wholly depends upon witness testimony but that the judge himself might weigh it on his own. *(15)* Nor, jurors, in the case of an unknown witness ought we to do anything else than inquire by argument, inference, and suspicion into the force and nature of the facts themselves. Not only an African or Sardinian witness, if they prefer to be so designated, but even someone more discerning and scrupulous can be impelled, intimidated, moulded, turned; he who has free licence to lie is the master of his own will. *(16)* The argument appropriate to the matter—nothing else can truly be called an argument—is the voice of the facts, the footprint of nature, the mark of the truth; whatever it is, it must remain immutable; it is not invented but taken by the speaker. Therefore if I am bested in a prosecution of that kind, I would yield and give way; for I would be defeated by the facts, by the case, by the truth. *(17)* Would you confront me with a succession of Sardinians in hordes and try not to hem me in with charges but to intimidate me with the roar of Africans? I will not be able to dispute, but I will be able to flee for refuge to these men's good faith and clemency, to the jurors' oath, to the fairness of the Roman people, who wanted this to be a leading family in this city, to implore the divine power of the immortal gods who have always shown favour to this line and name.

(18) 'He demanded, commanded, snatched, extracted'. If you teach us on the basis of account books, since the preparation of account books itself involves a kind of series and order of contracted business, I shall pay close attention and I shall see what I must do in the course of offering my defence. If in the end you are relying on witnesses—I will not say good and approved men—let them only be known, I shall consider how I must contend with each. *(19)* But if all the witnesses have a single colour, a single voice, a single nationality, if

they attempt to confirm their allegations not only with no arguments but not with any kinds of documents public or private—albeit even this can be fabricated—where, jurors, am I to turn, or what am I to do? Am I to argue with them individually? Tell me: did you have nothing to give? He will say that he had. Who will know it? Who will judge? There was no cause. He will invent one. How will we refute it? He could refuse to give it if that were the case. He will claim it was extorted by force. What eloquence can refute by argument the impudence of an unknown person? *(20)* Therefore I shall not deal with that collusion of the Sardinians and with the perjury that has been forced out, compelled, and subtly elicited, nor shall I gather up some fine-drawn arguments, but I shall meet their onslaught with my onslaught and come to blows. Each of them need not individually be dragged out from their line of battle; I need not struggle and do battle with individuals; I must lay low their entire battle line with a single onslaught.

(21) The single most weighty accusation of Sardinia as a whole is that which concerns the grain supply. On this question Triarius has interrogated all the Sardinians, and the charge has been confirmed by a single compact among the witnesses and by agreement of them all. Before I touch upon this charge I ask you, jurors, to allow me to lay, as it were, the foundations of our entire defence. If these shall be well founded and set in place, as I reckon and suppose, no part of the prosecution case holds any terrors for me. *(22)* I shall speak first about the type of prosecution itself, afterward about the Sardinians, then briefly also about Scaurus. When these points have been expounded, then and only then shall I broach this dreadful and terrifying charge about the grain supply.

(23) What manner of accusation is this, Triarius, that, in the first place, you have not gone to investigate? What was the basis of that confidence, so savage, so assured, that you could crush my client? When I was a boy I believe I heard that L. Aelius, an educated and witty freedman, when he was avenging the wrongs done his patron, filed suit against Q. Titius Mutto, a most disreputable person, <with . . . as the investigating magistrate>. When he was asked by him what province or what deadline he was demanding for witnesses, he demanded the eighth hour until he could hold an inquiry in the Cattle Market. *(24)* Did you suppose that you should do the same in the case of M. Aemilius Scaurus? He says 'Because the case was brought to me at Rome'. Well, did the Sicilians not bring Sicily's

case to me at Rome? But what men! Prudent by nature, practised by experience, deeply educated. Nonetheless I thought that I must get to know and learn the province's case in the province itself. *(25)* Should I not have become acquainted with the complaints and wrongs of the arable-farmers among the crops and fields themselves? I traversed, I traversed, I say, Triarius, in the harshest winter the valleys and hills of the Agrigentines. That renowned and fertile Leontine Plain itself practically taught me my case. I visited the farmers' huts; people conversed with me at the ploughshare. *(26)* And so that case was extracted in such a way that the jurors seemed not to be hearing but seeing and practically touching my argument. It seemed to me neither justifiable nor true when I had undertaken the defence of the most faithful and ancient province, to learn the case like that of an individual client in my bedchamber.

(27) Recently when the Reatini, who are my clients, wanted me to argue their public case about the streams and channels of the Velinus before the present consuls, I did not think that I would do justice either to the standing of the respected prefecture or to my own pledge unless not only the people but also the place itself and the lake had taught me that case. *(28)* Nor would you have done otherwise, Triarius, if those Sardinians of yours had wanted it: these people who were by no means minded for you to come to Sardinia so that you would find out that everything was far different from what was reported to you, that there was no complaint of the masses in Sardinia, no popular enmity against Scaurus . . .

(29) . . . by <whose> breath they say Aetna burns, so I crushed Verres with the testimony of the whole of Sicily. You concluded your pleading in the first session with a single witness produced. But what a witness, immortal gods! Was it not enough to have concluded with a single man, an unknown man, an insignificant man? Did you even conclude the first session with the witness Valerius, who, granted citizenship by gift of your father, expressed his thanks to you not with distinguished duties but manifest perjury? *(30)* But if the omen of your name perhaps guided you, nonetheless we, according to the custom of the ancestors, since we think it of good augury, interpret it not for destruction but for salvation. But all that speed and haste, the fact that you did away with the investigation and the entire previous session, revealed and made clear what was nonetheless not hidden: this trial has been organized not for the sake of a trial but for the sake of the consular elections.

(31) In this context I will at no point, jurors, cast aspersions on Appius Claudius, a gallant consul and distinguished man, bound to me, as I hope, by a reliable and firm reconciliation. For that role might have been appropriate for him whom a sense of grievance and his own suspicion compelled to do it or him who demanded this role for himself because he either failed to notice whom he was harming or thought he would effect an easy reconciliation. *(32)* I will say so much as may satisfy the case and be least harsh or bitter towards him. What disgrace is there in Appius Claudius' being an enemy to M. Scaurus? Tell me: was his grandfather not an enemy to P. Africanus? And he (Appius) likewise to me? And I to him? These enmities once perhaps brought pain to each of us, but surely never dishonour. *(33)* The predecessor envied his successor; he wanted him to be as odious as possible so that his own memory might stand out all the more—a circumstance not only not unaccustomed but even ordinary and quite widespread. Indeed this everyday circumstance would not in itself have moved Appius Claudius, a man endowed with such culture and wisdom, except that he thought that the defendant would be the electoral rival of his brother, C. Claudius. *(34)* Whether the latter would be a patrician or a plebeian—he had not yet arrived at a fixed decision—he thought that he would be in competition with the defendant; Appius, on the other hand, thought the competition still more acute since he recalled that he had been a patrician in candidature for the pontificate, for the Salian priesthood, and in other matters. Therefore he did not want his brother to be defeated in his consulate and, if he were a patrician, he saw that he would be unequal to Scaurus unless he struck him with some fear or disgrace.

(35) Would I not think that this ought to be granted to a brother where a brother's highest office is concerned, especially since I feel the strength of a brother's love almost beyond all others? 'But his brother is no longer canvassing'. Tell me, then: if, held back by the whole of Asia as a suppliant, beseeched by businessmen, by tax-farmers, by all allies and citizens, he placed the interests and well-being of the province ahead of his own holding of office, do you on that account suppose that a mind once wounded can be so easily healed? *(36)* And yet in all these matters, especially with barbarians, opinion often carries greater weight than the fact itself. The Sardinians are convinced that they can do nothing more pleasing to Appius than to diminish Scaurus' reputation. They are also led on by the hope of many benefits and rewards. They think that a consul can do anything,

especially when he makes promises spontaneously. I will now say no more on this point. *(37)* And yet I said what I have just said as if I were his brother—not the one who is his brother and has said a lot—but the brother I have always been towards my own brother. Therefore, jurors, you ought to resist the entire type of prosecution in which you see nothing has been undertaken in the customary way, moderately, with deliberation, with integrity, on the contrary everything has been undertaken in a base, disorderly, hasty, rapid way by collusion, command, authority, hope, and threats.

(38) I come now to the witnesses. I shall teach you that they not only lack all credibility and authority but do not even have the appearance or semblance of witnesses. In the first place their credibility is destroyed by their very unanimity; this was made manifest when the Sardinians' conspiratorial pact was read out; in the second place by that well-known greed, which was prompted by the hope and promise of rewards; finally by the people themselves, whose mendacity is such that they think freedom is distinguishable from slavery by nothing other than the licence to tell lies.

(39) Not that I say that we ought never to be moved by the Sardinians' complaints. I am neither so inhumane nor so unfeeling towards the Sardinians, especially since my brother recently took his leave from them after having had charge of the grain supply on Pompey's orders. He consulted their interests with his habitual good faith and humanity and was in turn greatly loved and esteemed by them. *(40)* Let this refuge be kept open for their grievance and for their just complaints, let the way be blocked to conspiracy and barriers set up against intrigue; and let this be no more so among the Sardinians than among Gauls, Africans, Spaniards. T. Albucius and C. Megabocchus were condemned on their return from Sardinia even though some Sardinians commended them. The variety (of testimonies) itself enhanced credibility: they were convicted by fair witnesses and authentic records. *(41)* Now there is a single voice, a single sentiment, not forced out by a grievance but feigned, not stirred up by wrongs committed by my client but by promises and rewards held out by others. 'But the Sardinians once carried conviction'. And they will perhaps do again one day if they present themselves as persons of integrity, uncorrupted, voluntarily, not at someone's instigation, under no obligation to anyone, and free men. If they should acquire such qualities, let them nonetheless rejoice and marvel that they carry conviction; with all these qualities lacking, will they nonetheless have

no regard for themselves, will they not shudder at the reputation of their race?

(42) All records of antiquity and all histories have shown us that the race of the Phoenicians is utterly untrustworthy. The Carthaginians, descended from them, have shown by their many rebellions, the many treaties they have violated and broken, that they have degenerated not at all. The Sardinians were not settled into Sardinia and established there by the Carthaginians of mixed African race but were colonists banished and rejected by them. *(43)* So when there was no soundness in this race in its unadulterated state, how foul do we imagine it became through so many infusions? In this connection my host and friend Cn. Domitius Sincaius, a man of great distinction, will pardon me, so will . . . , likewise granted citizenship by Pompey, the commendation of all of whom we nonetheless enjoy, so too will other sound men from Sardinia; *(44)* I trust there are a few. When I speak of a people's vices, I certainly make exceptions. But I have to discuss the general type; within it, by their character and culture, some may have conquered the vices of their line itself and their people. The facts themselves show clearly that the majority is without credibility, without partnership and bond with our nation. What province is there besides Sardinia that has no community that is a friend to the Roman people or free? *(45a)* Africa herself, that well-known parent of Sardinia, which fought a great many bitter wars with our ancestors, defended itself from participation in the Punic Wars not only by its loyal kingdoms but even in the province, as Utica testifies. By the death of the Scipios Further Spain . . .

(45b) poor in resources, its populace untrustworthy.

(45c) (peoples) have been found of such type as to be called brothers of the Roman people.

(45f) when this name had been heard, which spread throughout all nations

(45h) When, out of many, a single paternal enemy remained for him, Dolabella, who had joined with Q. Caepio, his relation, in prosecuting the elder Scaurus, that feud not taken up by him but inherited . . .

(45d) What the devil is that reason?

Would the sheepskin coat of the Sardinians change the man whom royal purple failed to move?

(45i) especially since the proximity and populousness of the place removes the suspicion of idleness or greed.

(45l) Further I, who have Alban columns, transported them by panniers.

(45n) Did you have no house? But you had one. Did you have surplus capital? But you were in want. You have insanely run into columns, you have raged insanely at other people's property; you have set a higher value on a sunken, dark, prostrate house than yourself and your own fortunes.

(45o) Although you could not escape these points, will you nonetheless struggle and demand that M. Aemilius with all his public standing, with the memory of his father, with the glory of his grandfather, be surrendered to a most disreputable, mendacious, unreliable people and, I might almost say, witnesses covered with skins?

(46) On whatever point my mind and even my eyes alight, from all sides, matter for my defence of Scaurus is supplied. The renowned senate house bears you witness about the authoritative and gallant headship of his father. My client's grandfather, L. Metellus himself, is seen to have established the most hallowed gods in that renowned temple in your field of vision, jurors, so that they may beg you for the safety of his grandson since they themselves have often supported by their aid many who were in difficulties and imploring them. *(47)* The renowned Capitolium, distinguished by three temples, the access way of Jupiter Optimus Maximus, Juno Regina, Minerva, adorned by lavish gifts of his father and also of my client, . . . M. Scaurus before . . . of that illustrious L. Metellus, pontifex maximus, who, when that temple was ablaze, hurled himself into the midst of the fire and snatched from the flames the renowned Palladium which is held in the custody of Vesta as a pledge of the safety of us and our empire. If only he could briefly rise up: *(48)* he who snatched from that conflagration . . . would surely snatch his own scion from these flames.

(49) but I also see you, Marcus Scaurus, I see, I say, I do not merely contemplate you in thought, not without great mental anguish and pain, when I saw the sordid raiment of your son I remember you and if only, as you have passed before my eyes in this entire case, you might now present yourself to the minds and cling to the hearts of these men. A sight, as god is my witness, . . .

. . . even if perchance he had not known him, he would nonetheless assert that he was the first citizen of the community.

(50) How am I now to address you? As a man? But you are not among us. As one dead? But you are alive and in full vigour and are active in the hearts and on the lips of all, and moreover the divine

mind had nothing mortal, nor could any part of you die except for the body. Therefore whatever way . . . you . . .

Fragments of Uncertain Location

(1) This, I say, jurors, is the case: nor is this a new claim raised by me but it has been investigated by others.
(2) in general terms

Unplaced Testimony

. . . Sardis and Sardiniensis. And yet in Cicero in the *Scauriana* we find this distinction concerning the Sardi and Sardienses: he teaches that the one group are the inhabitants, the other the immigrants.

COMMENTARY

C.'s defence of M. Aemilius Scaurus survives in a highly fragmentary state. If the extant remains are representative, however, the case appears to be weak (see Introduction 5c). The contents can be outlined as follows:

I. Exordium (F 1)
II. Digression: Scaurus *père*
   A. Indicted by Cn. Domitius (F 2)
   B. Indicted by Q. Servilius Caepio (F 3)
   C. Indicted and harrassed by Q. Varius (F 4)
   D. C.'s regard for him (F 5)
III. Preliminary refutation of charges: Bostar and Aris' wife
   A. Criticism of disorganized prosecution case (F 6)
   B. Bostar allegedly killed for his property by Scaurus at dinner (F 7–9)
   C. Accusation of Bostar's mother (F 10–11)
   D. Aris attempts to flee Sardinia, leaving his wife behind (F 12–13)

- E. Aris' wife unlikely to have committed suicide to escape Scaurus' advances
  - 1. Suicide rare except among Romans
    - a. P. Licinius Crassus Mucianus (cos. 131)
    - b. P. Licinius Crassus (cos. 97) (1)
    - c. Others should have followed their example
      - 1) M'. Aquilius (2)
      - 2) M. Antonius (3)
    - d. Greek examples rare
      - 1) Themistocles
      - 2) Theombrotus of Ambracia upon reading Plato's *Phaedo* (4)
  - 2. Aris' wife
    - a. Will hardly have read Pythagoras or Plato (5)
    - b. Given her age and ugliness is unlikely to have inflamed Scaurus' passion (6)
    - c. Two accounts of her death prevail in Sardinia (7)
      - 1) Committed suicide upon hearing of Aris' plan to marry Bostar's mother in Rome (8)
      - 2) Murdered by Aris' freedman (10)
- F. Comparison of families involved in this trial (13)

IV. Digression: the testimony of the Sardinian witnesses

- A. The preceding charges refuted because not solely resting upon testimony of witnesses (14)
- B. In the case of an unknown witness one must weigh the facts (15)
- C. An argument appropriate to the facts (16)
  - 1. Is immutable
  - 2. Is not invented but adopted by an orator
  - 3. C. could accept defeat by such an argument
- D. If confronted by bands of Sardinians, C. would flee for refuge (17)
  - 1. To the protection and clemency of the audience
  - 2. To the jurors' oath
  - 3. To the justice of the Roman people
- E. If claims are supported (18)
  - 1. By account books, I will pay close attention and prepare my defence

2. By witness testimony, let them be at least known persons; I will consider how to deal with each
3. By witnesses of a single nation unsupported by documents, I will use a blanket denial (19–20)

V. Division (*divisio*) (21–2)
   A. Type of accusation
   B. The Sardinians
   C. Scaurus
   D. Grain supply

VI. Argumentation/refutation
   A. Type of accusation
      1. Triarius' failure to conduct an onsite investigation
         (a) Did he think Scaurus as easily crushed as Q. Titius Mutto? (23)
         (b) Contrast C.'s procedure
            (1) In Verres' case (24)
            (2) In representing the Reatines (27)
         (c) His clients did not want Triarius to know the true state of opinion in Sardinia (28)
         (d) Triarius' single witness in the first session (29)
      2. The trial politically motivated
         (a) Consul Ap. Claudius is an enemy of Scaurus (31)
            (1) That is nothing disgraceful (32)
            (2) The predecessor envied his successor (33)
         (b) He wanted to eliminate his brother Gaius' opponent in the consular elections
         (c) But his brother has withdrawn (35)
         (d) But he still nurtures a sense of grievance
         (e) A misapprehension of the Sardinians may be at play (36)
   B. The Sardinian witnesses
      1. Their credibility is destroyed by (38)
         (a) Their unanimity
         (b) Their greed, excited by promise of rewards
         (c) Their propensity to lie
      2. C. not averse to Sardinians (39)
         (a) His feeling for them as human beings
         (b) His brother's recent service there

3. Albucius and Megabocchus were convicted by Sardinian testimony, but the circumstances were different (40)
4. Their antecedents (42)
   (a) The deceitful Phoenicians
   (b) The treaty-breaking Carthaginians
   (c) Sardinia colonized by their rejected citizens
5. There are exceptions to the general pattern (43)
6. Sardinia is the only province that lacks a free community that is a friend to the Roman people (44)
   (a) North Africa has Utica (45a)
   (b) Further Spain [lacuna]
   (c) Gaul (45c)

C. Scaurus (45f–o)
   1. The Sardinians should value this family as highly as the rest of the world does (Amm. 22.15.24)
   2. He had inherited the feud with Dolabella (45h)
   3. He had no motive to plunder a poor province like Sardinia (45d)
   4. As aedile he produced splendid games (sch. Bob. *Sest.* 116)
   5. His house
      (a) No sign of laziness or greed (45i)
      (b) Quotation from prosecutor's summation (45n)
   6. Comparison of Scaurus and his family with the Sardinians (45o)

D. The grain supply [lost in lacuna]

VII. Peroration
   A. Visible buildings reminiscent of the family's achievements (46)
      1. The senate house: M. Scaurus sen.
      2. Temple of Castor and Pollux: L. Caecilius Metellus Delmaticus, the defendant's maternal grandfather
      3. Capitol with dedications by the defendant and his father (47)
      4. Temple of Vesta, from which the Palladium was rescued by L. Caecilius Metellus (cos. 251) as pontifex maximus (48)
   B. Contrasting appearance of father and son (the latter clothed in squalid raiment) (49)
   C. Apostrophe of the elder Scaurus (50)

1. Exordium (F 1)

The exordium aims to secure the listener's goodwill and attention and make the hearer amenable to the advocate's teaching (*docilis*): Quint. *Inst.* 4.1.5. C. chooses to open with a portrait of his client as an innocuous man with the modest goal of maintaining his family's good standing; he continues the picture later in the speech (45h and i).

(F 1) M. Scaurus had . . . eager to do Augustine (*RLM* p. 150) quotes this passage as the beginning of the speech. The defence of Sulla begins similarly ('I should above all have wished, jurors, that P. Sulla beforehand had been able to retain the lustre of his public standing and after suffering misfortune had been able to pluck some fruit of his moderation'). Both begin with the same word 'above all' (*maxime*), refer to his client's public standing (*dignitas*) and hint at dangers to the hopes of C. or his client. In Sulla's case the public standing has already been compromised (sc. by conviction for electoral malfeasance in campaigning for the consulate of 65: *TLRR* 201) so the hopes are more modest. Cf. also *Caec.* 23 'Caecina had above all to hope, assessors, that he have no dispute . . . ' Here C. already hints that Scaurus' prosecution is the result not of his own rapaciousness and arrogance but rather the enmity and offence taken by a powerful person. In 28 he will claim that there is no enmity against Scaurus among the populace of Sardinia. Finally in 31–7 he makes it clear that Appius Claudius is the hand behind the prosecution and dissects the underlying motives. The Latin sentence concludes with the standing of Scaurus' 'line, his family, and his name'; this seems to have been the point developed in the sequel (as well as in the peroration); cf. Grillius *RLM* p. 603: ' . . . he begins with the point which he thinks is honourable in the case. He does this in the speech for Scaurus since Scaurus' person or his family's distinction has an element of honourable standing, whereas the charge of extortion has an element of disgrace. What does Tullius do? He begins by praising his client's virtue or calling his ancestors to mind . . . ' Comparable in this respect is *Flac.*, which alludes to the services of his client's family, namely P. Valerius Publicola, in liberating Rome in 509 (§§1, 25; cf. Loutsch 1994, 521) and to his client's military service under his father and paternal uncle (Milan fr. sub fin. and fr. sch. Bob. vii respectively); the peroration includes a reference to his ancient line (106; similarly *Font.* 41).

2. Digression: M. Aemilius Scaurus sen. (F 2–5)

The prosecutor P. Valerius Triarius justified scheduling the trial before the consular elections on the grounds that Scaurus would otherwise follow the example of his father, buy the consulate with the moneys extorted in his province, and escape accountability by holding office and then accepting another province (Asc. p. 19C); the implicit assumption is that the consul-elect is immune from prosecution; this was probably because of the prestige of the office; cf. above 96 n. 48. This was, in fact, a weakness in the system that was combated by a senatorial decree of 53 and a *lex Pompeia* of 52 stipulating a five-year interval between magistracy and promagistracy; cf. above 99. In any case Triarius' argument gave C. an opening for discussing the career of and litigations engaged in by the elder Scaurus, whom he greatly admired in his youth (cf. *Off.* 1.76: 'Neither did M. Scaurus seem to me when I was a boy to yield first place to C. Marius . . .'); he is also invoked in the peroration (46, 49–50). For the order of fragments cf. on F 5.

(F 2) He also underwent . . . conducting the prosecution This and the following three fragments, all pertaining to the elder Scaurus, are cited in this order by Asc. (21–2C); see on F 5. The earliest trial in the extant enumeration, this is dated with a query to 103 (*TLRR* 68). The use of 'also' suggests that Asconius' excerpts may have omitted one or more earlier trials. The known prosecution for extortion of Scaurus by M. Junius Brutus (*Font.* 38; *orat.* no. 43, frs. 6–7) is agreed to have been earlier, either in 114 after his command as consul the previous year against Gallic and Ligurian tribes (*MRR* i. 531) or prior to his consulate if the suggestion of Marshall 1977, 416–17, is right that it furnished a close parallel to the scenario sketched by Triarius for the present case (see above). Asconius explains that Cn. Domitius acted out of anger at Scaurus' refusal to coopt him into the college of augurs and that the charge was failure properly to conduct rites in honour of the Penates at Lavinium; he demanded a fine as penalty (p. 21C). On the state sacrifice to the Penates in Lavinium made by the consuls, including participation by the pontifical college, shortly after entering office cf. Wissowa 1912, 164 and n. 6 and 518 and n. 2. It is unclear when Scaurus' alleged ceremonial flaw occurred. Suetonius, *Nero* 2.1, apparently refers to the same incident in recounting that as a result of his failure to be elected to succeed his father in a

priesthood (and perhaps the failure of his prosecution of Scaurus) Domitius carried a law transferring the election of priests from the colleges to seventeen of the thirty-five tribes; cf. Rotondi 1912, 329. It seems likely, as Geer 1929 argues, that Asconius has confused augurate and pontificate (Domitius' grandfather was coopted to the pontificate in 172: Rüpke 2008: 97 and §1476); for a different view cf. Marshall 1985, 129–32. Gruen 1964, 107, raises the possibility of 'an attack on Scaurus and the Metelli in retaliation for the trials of Albucius and Eburnus' (cf. *TLRR* 62 and 67). Connected with our trial is the anecdote that a slave of Scaurus visited the prosecutor in secret and offered to supply damning evidence against his master; Domitius, however, had him seized and returned to Scaurus (*Deiot.* 31; V. Max. 6.5.5; Plut. *Cap. util.* 91D, confusing prosecutor and defendant; Dio 27 fr. 92). Scaurus was acquitted by a vote of thirty-two tribes to three, albeit the tribes voting for acquittal were closely divided (Ascon. p. 21C). Cf. Münzer, *RE* 5.1 1325.36 ff.

(F 3) He was prosecuted . . . to fear them The prosecutor Q. Servilius Caepio was the son of the homonymous commander defeated by the Cimbri at Arausio (modern Orange) in 105. This trial has as its background the struggle over the composition of juries: the younger Caepio, seeking to maintain the equestrian domination challenged by the reformer M. Livius Drusus, became alienated from the senate and hence launched this prosecution of Scaurus, the leader of the senate (*princeps senatus*: cf. 46n.); cf. Münzer, *RE* s.v. Servilius 50; Scaurus, however, filed a counter-suit, which he contrived to bring to trial first (*TLRR* 96–7); cf. Münzer 1999, 276. Asconius ad loc. states that Caepio conducted his prosecution 'on account of the ill-will of the Asiatic embassy'. Scaurus' participation in such an embassy is, however, otherwise unattested, though the charge that he accepted a bribe from Mithridates (V. Max. 3.7.8) has been taken as corroboration. Alexander 1981 and *TLRR* 96 argues that Asconius' phrase actually refers to Rutilius' mission in Asia mentioned in our passage; but it is unclear how that could have been a factor in the prosecution of Scaurus. In any case, the conviction in 92 (or possibly 94) of P. Rutilius Rufus for extortion as legate in Asia was a miscarriage of justice dictated by the interests of the tax-farmers at a time when the jury courts were controlled by their fellow equites; cf. *Font.* 38 with n. ('how many finally did . . . fornication and lust'); *TLRR* 94; Morstein-Marx 1995, 146. Both Rutilius and Scaurus were tried

under the *lex Servilia Glauciae* against extortion; cf. the General Introduction.

(F 4) That guardian of the free commonwealth . . . tribune of the plebs 'Guardian of the free commonwealth' renders *custos . . . rei publicae*; cf. *Red. pop.* 21, where the phrase occurs in the plural; ibid. 9 (of C. Marius) 'guardian of the state (*civitatis*) and of your (pl.) rule (*imperium*)'; *Dom.* 102 (of himself as viewed by the senate) 'guardian of the homeland (*patria*)'; *Mil.* 65 (of Milo) 'guardian of me and of the homeland'. In the Latin text the phrase is juxtaposed with 'treason' (*proditio*) for jarring effect. 'The same man' will refer to Caepio (see previous n.). A native of Sucro in Spain, Q. Varius experienced a meteoric career in Roman politics. As tribune of the plebs in 90 he carried, probably early in his term, the law that bore his name, which was directed against 'those by whose aid or counsel they [sc. the Italian allies] had taken up arms against the Roman people' (Asc. p. 22C; cf. Rotondi 1912, 339–40). It was directed in the first instance against associates of M. Livius Drusus. Two fragments of Caepio's prosecution speech are preserved (*orat.* no. 85, fr. 6 and 7). Perhaps to influence opinion ahead of the trial, Varius 'harassed' Scaurus by summoning him before a *contio* and charging him with aiding the enemy; the reply of the elderly *princeps senatus*, fully conscious of his dignity, is preserved (*orat.* no. 43 fr. 11): 'The Spaniard Q. Varius asserts that M. Scaurus the *princeps senatus* summoned the allies to arms; M. Scaurus the *princeps senatus* denies it; there is no witness; which of the two, citizens, is it fitting for you to believe?'; similarly with reference to bribe-taking V. Max. 3.7.8. It is presumed that, since the outcome of the trial is unreported, either Scaurus was acquitted or the trial was suspended; cf. *TLRR* 100; Gruen 1965, 62–3; Badian 1969, 467. The following year Varius was prosecuted under his own law, convicted, and sent into exile; cf. *TLRR* 109; Badian 1969, 461–5; Gundel, *RE* s.v. Varius 7.

(F 5) I did not merely . . . consistent application This fragment, cited by Asconius (22C) after F 4, is introduced with the words 'He says again about M. Scaurus' father'. One might query whether C. did not establish his general relation to the elder Scaurus before enumerating the court cases involving him, i.e. whether in the speech this fragment did not precede 2–4. 'Without the backing of a fortune': literally 'without the defence (*praesidio*) of a fortune'. The elder Scaurus knew whereof he spoke: though the Aemilii Scauri were patrician, the family was impoverished, his father having been a *carbonarius*,

i.e. the owner of a charcoal-business (*Vir. ill.* 72); cf. Wiseman 1971, 84 and 198; he himself was initially in doubt whether to follow a public career or become a banker (*Vir. ill.* 72); hence Asconius' observation that 'Scaurus had to work just like a new man' (23C). In view of this fact as well as the elder Scaurus' contact with his grandfather (*Leg.* 2.36) the young C. was evidently encouraged to look to him as a model for building a political career; cf. Nicolet 1967; see further van der Blom 2010: 217–22.

3. Preliminary Refutation of Charges: Deaths of Bostar and of Aris' Wife (F 6–13)

The state of preservation leaves it unclear whether this speech lacked a narration (*narratio*) prior to the refutation or simply combined the two; cf. Berger 1978, 48 and 210 n. 3. Prosecutions for extortion under the Julian Law included charges of cruelty (*saevitia*) as well as seizure of funds (*pecunia capta*); cf. Henderson 1951, 75; Lintott 1981, 207; under the earlier *lex Servilia Glauciae* charges of immorality were entertained as well (*Font.* 38; *TLRR* 94). Murdering Bostar and driving Aris' wife to suicide were the most sensational charges and were evidently attested by Triarius' one witness in the first session (Valerius, probably the Roman name of Aris; see 10n.); hence C. deals with them early on. The prosecution evidently claimed that Bostar was poisoned while he shared a meal with Scaurus (F 9). Though C.'s refutation of the charge can no longer be reconstructed in detail, he appears to have challenged the prosecution's theory as to the motive and means; cf. F 8 and 9. On the other hand, C.'s refutation of the charge regarding Aris' wife was based upon several probabilities: the unlikelihood that she would, given her appearance and advanced age, have been an object of Scaurus' desire (6); the fact that Aris had motive for having her put to death (8); and the fact that Scaurus figured as the cause of her death in neither of the accounts commonly believed in Sardinia (9–12); for the argument see further Williams 1995, 163–6.

(F 6) Since the prosecution . . . variety of type The rhetorician Severianus (*RLM* p. 357) quotes these strictures together with the precept that the strong points should be placed first and last, the weaker ones buried in the middle. C. criticizes the prosecution case as 'heaped up' (*congesta*) in 'a kind of pile' (*acervo quodam*) and thus implies carelessness and lack of analysis and organization; for a similar

critique of opponents cf. *Planc.* 83: 'You have, one way or another, frequently piled up these points against me'; *Mil.* 64: 'Immortal gods! How he sustained the points that were piled up against him . . . !' Cf. also his damning judgment of his adversary Erucius at *S.Rosc.* 72: 'If you were delivering this prosecution before the very buyers of the goods . . . , nonetheless you should have come more carefully prepared'. On C.'s carefully calibrated assessment of the three opposing counsel in *Cael.* cf. Austin 1960, 154–7; Gotoff 1986. 'Variety' (*varietas*) originally referred only to colour; cf. *Fin.* 2.10; it will prove to be missing from the prosecution case not merely for lack of organizational skill; cf. the complaint about the witnesses at 19: 'a single colour, a single voice, a single people'.

(F 7) Now he said . . . dinner was removed Another quotation from Severianus (*RLM* p. 360), this time illustrating how the opponent's argument can be weakened or exaggerated by paraphrase; cf. Quint. *Inst.* 5.13.28. Bostar is topicalized by initial placement in the Latin sentence. The name itself is Semitic and was borne by several Carthaginian commanders; this man is attested only in connection with our speech; he is not expected to be known to the jurors (qualified as 'a certain': *quendam*); cf. Niese, *RE* s.v. It is possible that Bostar was fleeing Scaurus' arrival, but in the absence of full context the relation of ideas remains uncertain.

(F 8) If finally . . . except upon Bostar's death The fragment is quoted by the grammarian Arusianus (7.488.18) as an example of the doubling of a preposition (*in*, which appears both on its own and as a verbal prefix (*invado*); cf. on 45f). 'Finally' (*denique*) suggests that this is the climactic point in a series of hypotheses put forward by the prosecution. Triarius has evidently claimed that Scaurus committed the murder in order to seize Bostar's property. 'Appropriate' renders *invado in* ('seize possession of': *OLD* s.v. 6a), often so used; cf. *S.Rosc.* 6, 23, etc. The emphatic 'by no means' (*nullo modo*) is colloquial; cf. Hofmann 2003, 209. 'Those goods' (*illa bona*): the anaphoric pronominal adjective shows that the property in question has been previously defined.

(F 9) By Hercules . . . nor angry with him Quoted by Asconius (23C). The colloquial interjection 'by Hercules' (*mehercule*), introduced by C. in his later work, adds liveliness; it is short for 'so may Hercules help me' ((*ita*) *me Hercules* (*iuvet*)) and was normally used only by men; cf. Hofmann 2003: 137–8; *OLD* s.v. *mehercule*; the direct address to the jurors likewise calls attention to the following assertion.

L. Hostilius Tubulus was a byword for corruption in the late Republic. As praetor in charge of the murder court (*quaestio inter sicarios*) in 142 (*MRR i.* 475), he so flagrantly accepted bribes from those with pending cases that the following year P. Scaevola (cos. 133) as tribune of the plebs carried a plebiscite calling for an extraordinary court to handle the charge and when the court was constituted under the presidency of the consul Cn. Servilius Caepio, the accused went immediately into exile (*MRR* i. 477; *TLRR* 5); according to Asc. p. 23C, he was called back from exile but took poison rather than comply. The satirist Lucilius targeted him among other rogues (fr. 1138–41 W. = Cic. *ND* 1.63). Cf. Münzer, *RE* s.v. Hostilius 26 and on the unusual summons from exile Kelly 2006, 47–54. C. invokes the comparison with a notorious criminal to show that the prosecution's claims fall well short of plausibility. The digression on the causes of sudden death (attested by Martianus Capella, *Rhet.* 5.441) is assumed by editors to have occurred in this place; cf. the digression on quick-acting poison at *Cael.* 58–60.

(F 10) than what he had . . . defend the mother This and the next item are the first fragments preserved in the Ambrosian codex. The first sentence comprised a comparison ('than': *quam*) of the sale of goods with some other circumstance; perhaps the aim was to show that Scaurus was so well situated that the charge of murdering Bostar for his property was absurd (so Beier); or perhaps the speed was the focus, e.g. 'The goods were disposed of so quickly that no sooner had he (sc. Bostar) been buried than what he had was offered for sale' with the rapid sequence of events suggesting involvement of a family member. 'Come' (*age*) is a colloquial marker for a command (cf. Hofmann 2003, 149), to which urgency is added by the suffix *-dum* (cf. *OLD* s.v.). The address of Triarius without first name is common among adversaries before the bar; cf. Adams 1978, 145–6. Quint. *Inst.* 7.2.9–10 cites our speech as an example of *anticategoria* (turning the tables on the accuser); C. also used the technique in the early defences of Sextus Roscius and Lucius Varenus (F 9 Cr.). Indeed, an alternative suspect was virtually *de rigueur* for a successful defence on charges of murder; cf. Stroh 1975, 59; Riggsby 1999*a*, 38 and ch. 3.

(F 11) that you were afraid . . . unless 'Insolvent' is based on Mai's insertion of the negative (*non*); the transmitted infinitives in the clauses of fearing will likewise need to be emended to finite forms (*fuisses* for *fuisse*, *voluisset* for *voluisse*). 'Advertised for sale'; cf. *OLD* s.v. *proscribo* 2a. It is unclear who is being addressed (Bostar's

mother?), who the 'defendant' is (if it were Scaurus, one would expect C. to refer to him with the deictic pronoun *hic*) and why the goods have been advertised for sale.

(F 12) since Aris refused . . . clandestinely Quoted by Priscian (2.219.7) for the proper name as a rare example of the termination -*is* with lengthened *i* in Latin. Aris is a Sardinian first mentioned here; he will also figure in the intrigue described at 8–12; he is not otherwise known (an *RE* article is lacking). What did Aris refuse to give up? If C. is summarizing the prosecution case, then the reference will be to Aris' wife (sc. to Scaurus); the alternative explanation that Aris refused to surrender the dowry (sc. to his wife) fails to convince since by the time of Aris' departure no divorce had occurred; cf. 8; Gaumitz 1879, 284. Aris did, in fact, flee to Rome (9–10); hence Sigonius conjectured 'was constrained' (*est . . . coactus*) for 'attempted' (*est . . . conatus*); this seems likely to be correct unless our passage refers to some prior occasion.

(F 13) they ransom themselves . . . sought Quoted by Servius on Virgil, *G.* 1.58. The reference is to beavers (*castores*), whose name the Romans derived from *castrare* ('castrate') in the belief that their testicles provided medicinal benefits; cf. Maltby 1991, 113. According to ancient folklore, they castrated themselves to elude capture; cf. Juv. 12.34–6; Apul. *Met.* 1.9. In fact, however, beaver gall is secreted by special glands located at the bottom of the abdominal cavity in both sexes; it could not be extracted without killing the animal; cf. M. Wellmann, *RE* 3.1 400.23 ff. (s.v. Biber). The analogue in C.'s narrative will presumably be Aris' wife, left behind at his departure.

(1) We have heard . . . seen the following Quoted by Asconius (23C); for the fragment quoted at 24C see Fragments of Uncertain Location 1. Here C. is arguing the heroic stature of Roman suicides or quasi-suicides and the rarity of suicide among the Greeks. He thus aims to make it appear very unlikely that, as alleged by the prosecution, Aris' wife committed suicide to escape Scaurus' advances. Examples of suicide from early Roman history ('those matters'—the anaphoric pronoun *illa* inserted by Manutius) have been lost prior to this point, including the case of a kinsman of P. Crassus (see the n. after next); on C.'s use of historical examples in general cf. *Font.* 23n. The Romans drew a sharp distinction between events they had merely heard of from their fathers or the like and ones that took place in their own lifetime; cf. Morstein-Marx 2004, 107–16.

P. Crassus . . . into the hands of his enemies 'Of the same line and name' marks the transition from an earlier bearer of the name (see next n.). In 87 P. Licinius Crassus (cos. 97) took a leading part in the defence of Rome from the attack of Cinna and Marius. When the city fell, he committed suicide; one of his sons died with him at the hands of Fimbria; the other son, Marcus, escaped and lived to become the 'triumvir'; cf. Münzer, *RE* 13.1 287.64 ff. (Licinius 61); Marshall 1976, 92–3; Ward 1977, 53–7; Lovano 2002, 48 and n. 85.

(2) Though he enjoyed . . . disgrace of his old age 'The elder Crassus' will be P. Licinius Crassus Mucianus, who as consul in 131 was dispatched with an army to complete the incorporation of Pergamum into the Roman Empire in the face of an uprising led by the pretender Aristonicus; he laid siege to Aristonicus' headquarters at Leucae and continued operations as proconsul in 130 (*MRR* i. 500 and 503); when departing for home he was defeated in a surprise attack and while retreating north was captured by Aristonicus' Thracian mercenaries; rather than suffer further indignities, he provoked one of his captors to kill him; cf. Münzer, *RE* 13.1 334.5 ff., esp. 335.61 ff. (Licinius 71); Marshall 1976, 95. As consul in 101 Manius Aquilius was charged with putting down the slave revolt led by Athenion in Sicily, which had already raged for three years; he continued operations for two more years as a promagistrate (*MRR* i. 570–1 and 577 and ii. 2). He succeeded in defeating the slave band in battle and its leader in single combat, albeit himself severely wounded. His fortunes changed, however, when in 89 he was assigned as a legate to collaborate with C. Cassius, governor of Asia (*MRR* ii. 34–5), in restoring Nicomedes of Bithynia and Ariobarzanes of Cappadocia, both of whom had been driven out by Mithridates. In the ensuing war he suffered devastating defeat and withdrew first to Pergamum and then to Mytilene, whose inhabitants surrendered him to the king, who, after parading him through the cities of Asia, put him to death by pouring molten gold into his mouth; cf. Klebs, *RE* 2.1 324.56 ff. (Aquilius 11); Morstein-Marx 1995, 252–9; less likely the identification with Manius Aquilius (cos. 130) proposed by Marshall 1976, 95–6. 'The same honours' will refer to the holding of the consulship by all three men. After 'was unable to imitate' text begins in codex T. 'The glory of his courageous exploits' renders *laudem virtu]tis suae rerumque gestarum*, partly a conjectural supplement.

Tell me: . . . the second Crassus? M. Antonius, the orator immortalized as a principal speaker in *On the Orator*, was consul in 99 (*MRR ii.* 1) and had thus been endowed with 'supreme command'; cf. 37n. Amid the reprisals following the fall of Rome to Marius and Cinna in 87, Antonius' hiding place was betrayed by a careless slave: he was beheaded by the tribune P. Annius, and Marius had his head placed on the rostra; cf. von Rohden, *RE* 1.2 2590.33 ff. (Antonius 28); Lovano 2002, 48 and n. 83. The brothers L. and C. Julius Caesar Strabo likewise fell victim to Marian revenge in 87; the former sought refuge at the estate in Tarquinii of one Sextilius, whom he had successfully defended in court (*TLRR* 112), but was nonetheless betrayed; cf. Diehl, *RE* 10.1 428.53 ff. (Iulius 135); Lovano 2002, 48 and n. 84.

(3) In all the monuments... punished himself with death? Some sort of derogation of the Greeks is expected, especially before the bar, prior to the citation of Greek examples. Their acknowledged literary stature but inferior martial skills made C.'s line of criticism ('more embellished in words than facts') obvious (all the Roman suicides C. discusses are in a military context). Though C. cited plays before the bar when it suited his purpose (cf. e.g. *S.Rosc.* 46–7, *Cael.* 18, 36–8), here he dismisses them as fiction; both Livius Andronicus and Ennius had treated the saga of Ajax (*Trag.* pp. 2–3 and 19–20 = fr. X–XIII J. respectively). After the Persian War Themistocles lived for a time in the Peloponnese, but Spartan pressure forced him to flee to Persia, where Artaxerxes gave him refuge and assigned him Lampsacus, Magnesia on the Meander, Myus, Percote, and Palaescepsis as his fiefdom. He died of illness in Magnesia, but there was an early legend (Ar. *Eq.* 83–4), contradicted by Thuc. 1.138.4–5, that he committed suicide, allegedly because of a conflict between his promise to aid the Great King in a new war against the Greeks and his loyalty to his homeland. Cf. Kahrstedt, *RE* 5A2 1694.55 ff.; Podlecki 1975, 43; Lenardon 1978, 194–200; on C.'s use of him as an exemplum cf. Berthold 1965.

(4) But the Greeklings... to the place of its origin The diminutive ('Greekling', *Graeculus*) is ordinarily used in a 'contemptuous or disparaging sense'; cf. *OLD* s.v. a; for C.'s use of the term cf. Hanssen 1951, 184–91, especially 185. C. mentions the case again at *Tusc.* 1.84 with indication of his source: 'There is an epigram of Callimachus against Theombrotus of Ambracia, who, he said, although no adversity had befallen him, cast himself into the sea upon reading Plato's book.' Callimachus' extant epigram (23) shows that C. misremembered the name (the subsequent Latin tradition, except for Ov. *Ib.*

491–2, who does not mention the name, perpetuates the error: Lact. *Inst.* 3.18.10, Aug. *CD* 1.22; Epigr. Bob. 63; cf. Lundström 1960, 66–73; Spina 1989, 22–31): 'Farewell, Sun, Cleombrotus of Ambracia/leapt from a high wall to Hades/though he had seen no evil worthy of death, but had/unrolled Plato's one work about the soul'; for full collection of testimonies cf. Riginos 1976, 180–3, who argues that Callimachus invented the anecdote (cf. C.'s 'invent many tales'). After 'as I see written' 'among the Greeks' is transmitted, but this is surely a gloss on the previous 'among whom' and is accordingly omitted here. 'I believe' is added to avoid the appearance of expert knowledge before the bar; cf. Fragments of Uncertain Location 1n. C. summarizes the theory of the Forms set out by Plato, *Phaedo* 64b–67a; cf. Miles 2001.

(5) Now surely that Sardinian . . . than her chastity A *reductio ad absurdum* of Triarius' claim that Aris' wife committed suicide: she will hardly have been moved by reading Pythagoras or Plato; the implicit assumption, made explicit at 45d and o with a sneer at their native dress, is that the Sardinians stand on a much lower level of culture. Pythagoras is lumped together with Plato even though the doctrine of the soul C. attributes to Pythagoras at *ND* 1.27 is more akin to the Stoic world-soul than the Platonic conception, to say nothing of the metempsychosis often attributed to Pythagoras; cf. Dyck 2003 ad loc. C. also cites Pythagoras' prohibition of suicide at *Sen.* 73. Though he assumes that Pythagoras left writings, that point was disputed in antiquity; cf. D.L. 8.6; Riedweg 1997. C.'s source will be the prohibition of suicide at *Phaedo* 61d ff. In general, C. viewed Plato's dialogues as an amalgam of Socratic and Pythagorean teachings; cf. *Rep.* 1.16; Powell 1988 on *Sen.* 73. The phrase 'compact of nature' (*foedus naturae*) was probably coined by Lucretius (1.586, etc.), whom C. had been reading this year (*Q.fr.* 2.10(14).3 from early February); it occurs elsewhere in prose only at Col. 1 pr. 8; cf. *TLL* s.v. *foedus* 1006.29 ff.; Courtney 1961, 156. 'Law of nature' is also applied to the prohibition of suicide; C. will reflect more deeply on the subject at *Leg.* 1.18, 23, and 42. 'He tossed out': C. appears to have pioneered the use of the verb *iacio* of utterances, thus augmenting Latin's meagre store of verbs of speaking: cf. *OLD* s.v. 7–8; *TLL* s. v. 41.39 ff. 'Chastity' renders *pudicitia*; cf. *OLD* s.v.; Kaster 2005, 25 and 159 n. 42; for the underlying values ibid. 35–8.

(6) But he instantly retreated . . . love affair? If Triarius did so, he failed to evade C.'s sneer. In general C.'s humour did not spare

physical deformity or ugliness; cf. Corbeill 1996, 42. Possibly exaggerating her age, C. represents being 'witty' (*salsa*; cf. *OLD* s.v. *salsus* 3b) as her only possible attraction.

(7) So you may not . . . even more easily The discovery of arguments (*inventio*) was the first of the five 'parts' of rhetoric (e.g. Quint. *Inst.* 3.3.1) and a point of pride for orators but not one touted in court; hence here C. pretends to be sticking closely to the 'facts' learnt from his client, in this case public opinion in Sardinia about the cause of Aris' wife's death; similarly 16 'not invented but taken by the speaker'. Our lemma marks the end (in mid-sentence) of text preserved in codex T.

(8) as I said a little bit earlier . . . to marry her Here codex A's text begins. C. digresses with background to the two opinions, to which he returns in 9. Kreyssig's 'as I said a little bit earlier' is adopted as a minimal insertion that yields sense (*<ut paulo an>te dixi*). Aris is likely to be the subject (surely clarified in the preceding lacuna); the lost matter preceding will also have made it clear that Bostar's mother is the woman so unflatteringly described ('lustful and reprobate'). 'Repulsiveness' (*foeditas*) varies 'ugliness' (*deformitas*: 6) as the description of Aris' wife. Valerius Aris was presumably a Roman citizen (cf. 10n.); his return of the dowry not needed for support of the woman or of any children of the marriage would thus be expected; cf. R. Leonhard, *RE* 5.2 1589.65 ff. (s.v. *dos*).

(9) In this connection . . . than to endure it After the digression of 8 C. returns to the two views mentioned in 7. The prior view is qualified as 'in accord with the state and nature of things', but it will turn out that the second view is no less so and is the one C. has destined for detailed narration (10–12); it will then serve as the launching pad for his general reflections (13) since it presents Aris and Bostar's mother in a worse light. The 'nature of things' (*natura rerum* 'natural course of events, the way things happen': *OLD* s.v. *natura* 6a) is a criterion for judging an account, and to fall foul of it as a litigator is to court disaster; cf. the criticism of Erucius at *S.Rosc.* 45: 'your lack of arguments is such that you think that you must speak not only against us but even against the nature of things'. In this sentence as transmitted Aris' wife is said both to have been influenced by and to have acted out of 'distress' (*dolore*): 'upset by the distress (*dolore*) of the adultery . . . flared up with a woman's rage (*dolore*)'; but surely there was a gradation building to a climax; therefore Busche's conjecture 'disgrace' (*dedecore*) is adopted in the prior instance; that

would give further point to the description of the relation between Aris and Bostar's mother as 'infamous and notorious' (8); 'already' (*iam*) is also added to differentiate stages; it can easily have dropped out by saltation after 'wife' (*uxorem*). 'Adultery' renders *paelicatus*, literally 'the fact of there being a mistress'. C. prefers to leave the point vague, but 'pretending to flee in fear' presumably refers to Aris' fear of Scaurus for refusing to give him his wife; cf. on F 12. 'With his beloved' renders *cum illa sua*, literally 'with that woman of his'; similarly *Phil.* 2.69 'he bade his mistress (*illam suam*) have her own property' (ironically using the formula for divorce); *Fam.* 9.19(194).1 'I am surprised that he did not go . . . to his mistress (*suam*)'; similarly the application of erotic language to Verres' relation to Syracuse at *Ver.* 2.2.56: 'Verres calls to mind his beloved (*illam suam*) Syracuse'. 'A relationship' = *consuetudo* 'amorous association, sexual intercourse': *OLD* s.v. 5b. 'They would even be joined in matrimony': the weak link in the theory: how does she know this, and how would it be possible without a divorce? 'She flared up with a woman's rage' resembles the description of Cluentia's reaction to her mother's adultery with her husband Melinus: 'she was tormented by that common rage of women' (*Clu.* 13).

(10) The other view . . . died by hanging The greater credibility may result from the gap in the prior version (see last n.) and also from the timing of the death (see next n.). 'That witness': *iste* is anaphoric, possibly with an undertone of contempt: *OLD* s.v. 3; he was previously mentioned at F 12 and 9. He is now revealed to be one of the witnesses against Scaurus; he will presumably have blamed him for the death of his wife and perhaps also the death of Bostar, his second wife's son by a previous marriage. Is he perhaps the same witness referred to in 29? If so, one must assume that C. has chosen to refer to him only as 'Aris', rather than by his Roman name, in order to alienate the jury from him (contrariwise at *Arch.* 1 he first refers to his client by his Roman name, A. Licinius, to establish him in the mind of the jurors as Roman). C. will launch an attack on the credibility of Sardinian witnesses generally at 38. 'Guest-friend of yours': the connection may go back to 77, when the prosecutor's father, L. Valerius Triarius, was in Sardinia either as propraetor or as a legate *pro praetore*; cf. *MRR* ii. 91 and iii. 214–15; H. Volkmann, *RE* 8A1 233.12 ff. (Valerius 363); Brennan 2000, 404–5. The emphasis on the connection in this context, where a terrible crime is imputed to Aris, is evidently to embarrass the prosecutor, with whose family

C. had close ties: he would later incorporate C. Valerius Triarius, the prosecutor's brother, as a speaker in *Fin.* and act as guardian to his children; cf. ibid. 234.11 ff. (Valerius 365). In narrating Aris' (supposed) instructions to his freedman C. uses euphemism ('squeeze the neck': *collum oblidere*) and diminutives ('little fingers': *digitulis*, 'a bit of rope': *resticula*) to imitate the wheedling tone he imagines was used; cf. Hanssen 1951, 213.

(11) This suspicion prevailed... bent on suicide Nora is the oldest known Phoenician settlement on Sardinia with pottery finds dating to the eighth century; it was continuously occupied through the Roman period, but the ancient city is now largely under water; cf. Dyson and Rowland 2007, ch. 6. Our passage provides rare literary evidence for cult practice in Roman Sardinia. The cemetery is situated outside the city, as was the norm in Graeco-Roman antiquity (cf. Burkert 1985, 191–2; Toynbee 1971, 48–9), and sacrifices are offered there to the divinized ancestors (*di parentes*). In Rome the Parentalia were celebrated yearly for nine days beginning on 13 February; cf. Wissowa 1912, 232 ff.; Scullard 1981, 74–5. Archaeological finds confirm the existence of altars in Sardinian cemeteries where food and drink could have been offered; cf. Dyson and Rowland 2007, 126. Here it becomes clear that the freedman has testified to the suicide of Aris' wife, so this is a second example of *anticategoria* in this speech; cf. F 10n. C. reasons that the solitude created by the holiday would allow the murder to be carried out with minimal risk of detection (cf. *Clu.* 167: poisoning would not be attempted at a crowded wedding feast), whereas the lack of witnesses would be of no concern to a person bent on suicide.

(12) The suspicion received... married Bostar's mother C. likes to use a tight sequence of events to argue for an underlying plan; cf. *S.Rosc.*, where the fact that Mallius Glaucia brought word of the elder Roscius' death to T. Roscius Capito overnight is used to suggest that Capito was the mastermind and Glaucia the agent in the murder (§§19, 96–9). But neither in that case nor in ours is a causal connection necessarily established. If (according to the alternative explanation) Aris' wife had committed suicide, Aris' freedman would have known that this information was significant and that he could anticipate a reward for prompt reporting; and the news would have enabled Aris to marry Bostar's mother whether or not he was responsible for the death.

(13) There you have it! To what families... casting your votes! C.'s early rhetorical training was probably based upon *progymnasmata*

('preliminary exercises'), which included comparisons; cf. Frazel 2009, ch. 1. Here he makes the whole preceding narrative come down to a comparison of two families, that of the prosecution witness Aris, now married to Bostar's mother, condemned as 'foul', 'polluted', and 'disgraceful' with emphatic anaphora ('how': *quam*), and that of the defendant, the Aemilii Scauri; cf. the comparison of two houses, that of Clodia, witness for the prosecution, and that of the defence witness L. Lucceius at *Cael.* 55. 'There you have it!' renders the colloquial interjection *em*, often, as here, followed by an exclamation; it is a syncopated form of *eme* < *emo* 'take'; cf. Hofmann 2003, 146–8; *OLD* s.v. c; often used in comedy, it is rare in C. (but cf. *Sest.* 59; *Fam.* 13.15(317).1). 'Surrender' is Heinrich's supplement for the transmitted 'give' (*<de>datis*); the word may suggest surrender to the enemy of Roman commanders who made unauthorized peace treaties; cf. examples at *Off.* 3.109. The use of the pronominal adjective *hic* makes it clear that 'this family' is his client's family. For balance the defendant, too, receives emphatic threefold qualification with anaphora ('concerning what man, what family, what name': *de quo . . . de quo . . . de quo . . .*).

You see . . . every crime and disgrace The 'crime of mothers against children' was Bostar's murder, allegedly by his mother (cf. F 7 and 10), though the extant text fails to explain the motive and means (to clear the way for her marriage to Aris? cf. *Clu.* 27–8: Oppianicus' alleged murder of two sons to enable him to marry Sassia; similarly *Cat.* 1.14; Sal. *Cat.* 15.2). The crime 'of husbands against their wives' was Aris' alleged hand in his wife's murder; cf. 10–12. 'The two principal charges' are the murder of Bostar and the claim that Scaurus' unwanted sexual advances precipitated the suicide of Aris' wife. 'Shaped' renders *formata*, Klotz's conjecture for the transmitted ghost-word *famata*. The prosecution consists of several groups, the 'authors of the charges', namely Aris and Bostar's mother, who are said to be 'fouled with every crime and disgrace', and those who are 'ignorant or spiteful': the 'ignorant' will cover the main accuser, Triarius, from whom the facts have allegedly been concealed by the Sardinian witnesses (28), the 'spiteful' (*invidi*) Appius Claudius, Scaurus' predecessor as governor of Sardinia; see further 31–7, especially 33n. on 'envy' (*invidia*).

4. Digression: Charges Based on Arguments or Documents vs. Charges Based on Testimony (14–20)

This passage forms a transition to the main argumentative section of the speech and prepares the reader/listener for the procedure C. will follow. He claims that he has successfully refuted the preceding charges because they were based on probabilities as well as witnesses (14) and that charges of extortion based upon financial records (*tabulae*) would have to be taken very seriously (18) but that for charges levelled by unknown Sardinian witnesses a point-by-point refutation is unnecessary, a blanket denial suffices.

(14) By now, jurors, . . . cleared away, refuted, broken? C. rounds off the topic of 'these charges' (i.e. Scaurus' alleged role in the murder of Bostar and the suicide of Aris' wife) with two questions posed in such a form as to elicit a negative reply, the prior one introduced with the particle *num* ('surely no . . . '), the latter one with the simple negative (*non*). 'Charge' renders *crimen*, at this period not yet a 'crime'; cf. *OLD* s.v. 1 and 4. On 'suspicion' (*suspicio*) cf. *Font.* F 2n. 'Clear away' renders *perpurgo*, used literally of cleaning or purifying thoroughly; the metaphorical sense is already attested at *Mur.* 54 ('that third topic, cleared away by the previous speakers . . . '); cf. *OLD* s.v. 1 and 3; *TLL* s.v. 1 and 2a. 'Break' (*frango*) is likewise a physical act metaphorically applied to arguments: ibid. s.v. 9a.

How did this happen? . . . weigh it on his own Here C. begins to take the argument in a new direction by defining why one portion of Triarius' case was susceptible of refutation and contrasting that with the remaining portion. 'Refute' renders *diluo*, literally 'dissolve', the metaphorical use of arguments as early as *Inv.* 1.22; cf. *OLD* s.v. 1 and 4; *TLL* s.v. IA and B2b. For the basis of C.'s refutation cf. F 6–13n. 'Weigh' (*pondero*) begins as a physical process transferred to the mental sphere ('appraise, assess'): *OLD* s.v.; similarly *pendeo* ('depends', literally 'hangs'). The evidence of witnesses was a standard topic of rhetorical training, which provided a repertory of arguments for prosecution and defence; cf. *Rhet. Her.* 2.10; Quint. *Inst.* 5.7; Schmitz 1985, 1–18.

(15) Nor, jurors, . . . the facts themselves C. draws a sharp distinction between known and unknown witnesses and, since the Sardinian witnesses in this case will not be personally known to the jury, focuses on the latter. The procedure C. advocates is essentially the same one

he has followed in refuting the previous testimony. 'Inference' (*coniectura*) was perhaps originally a term used in the interpretation of dreams (cf. *OLD* and *TLL* s.v.); on the need for drawing inferences (from behaviour or the like) when faced with unknown witnesses see *Flac.* 6; similarly *Font.* 23. With 'suspicion' he appropriates the prosecutor's typical tool (cf. *Ver.* 2.5.65; *Font.* F 2n.) for purposes of the defence.

Not only an African . . . master of his own will The first reference (in the extant text) to the nation that is bringing charges is already prejudicial: an 'African' (*Afer*) can be an inhabitant of the northern coast of Africa west of Egypt; here, however, it is clearly used as a racial term for a person of Carthaginian blood; cf. *OLD* s.v.; 42 and 45a; C. then allows 'Sardinian' as a concession (*sane* 'to be sure'; not rendered in the translation) to their preferred designation. The Sardinians are implicitly crude and unscrupulous in contrast to 'someone more elegant and scrupulous'; but even the latter can be influenced in various ways, so a fortiori the Sardinians can likewise; similarly at *Flac.* 23 he complains that the Greeks of Asia Minor who have testified against his client are a 'people by no means scrupulous in pronouncing testimony'; cf. the similar attack on the credibility of Gallic witnesses at *Font.* 27–32; for racial stereotyping in this speech see further on 38 and 42. The 'licence to lie' recurs at 38 as the Sardinians' notion of what differentiates free and slave; see ad loc. The person so described is 'master of his own will' in that his will is not bound by external facts, i.e. he has no scruples about lying; cf. *OLD* s.v. *dominus* 3d.

(16) The argument . . . by the truth 'The argument appropriate to the matter': cf. Pl. *Phaedr.* 277b, where knowing the truth about the subject is the first requirement of artful speech. C. similarly privileges argument over the testimony of witnesses at *Cael.* 22: 'I shall draw you away from witnesses and not allow the veracity of this court . . . to be subject to the will of witnesses, which can easily be moulded, effortlessly bent and twisted. I shall litigate with arguments . . . ' 'Footprint' is the literal meaning of *vestigium*; it comes to be applied metaphorically to any 'trace' left behind; so here it is a guide to 'nature' in contrast to a speaker's artificial creation; cf. *OLD* s.v. A 'mark' (*nota*) is a sign by which one recognizes something: *OLD* s.v. 1d; the 'mark of the truth' is a concept in epistemology; cf. *Luc.* 58: 'presentations . . . that will have no credibility once the mark of the true and false has been removed'; *Luc.* 84: 'you will nonetheless not

pass judgment by that mark by which you say you must'. 'Not invented but taken': cf. 7, where C. was at pains to dispel the impression that he had 'invented' his case.

(17) Would you confront me . . . the roar of Africans? C. complains that the prosecution is not using the tactics proper to a court of law ('to hem me in with charges': cf. *Clu.* 53 'the case was pressed by witnesses'; 14n.) but is applying quasi-military pressure. The word rendered as 'line', *agmen*, is 'an army on the march' or 'column' of soldiers: *OLD* s.v. 5a; 'band' (*caterva*) is often used of non-Roman and thus less well organized troops: *OLD* s.v. 2; C. will revert to martial imagery in 20. 'Roar' (*fremitus*) is the high-volume, inarticulate sound of animals or crowds of people; C. had applied it to hostile foreign witnesses at *Flac.* 23 ('I deny that what you call decrees are testimonies but (I assert that they are) the roar of needy persons'); cf. *OLD* s. v.; 'the roar of Africans' may be meant to suggest lions.

I will not be able . . . this line and name In contrast to the previous arguments, which C. was able to refute since Triarius gave him 'something . . . about which to dispute' (14), he claims that he cannot dispute the witnesses' testimony. Was this because they were too numerous? Similarly in his defence of Verres Hortensius decided not to interrogate the prosecution witnesses (*Ver.* 2.5.155); C. hints at a similar policy at *Font.* 22. Instead C. takes refuge in the 'good faith'/'protection' (*fides*) of the jurors (sc. because they are bound by their oath (*ius iurandum*), which is also mentioned separately); cf. Freyburger 1986, 213–17; Mommsen 1899, 219 and 395. In general, the Romans took their oaths very seriously and fulfilled them conscientiously in good and bad times; see further Latte 1968, 375–9. 'Clemency' renders *mansuetudo*, originally 'tameness' (of animals); cf. *OLD* s.v.; it contrasts with the 'cruelty' ascribed to the prosecution's witnesses (13); cf. *Ver.* 2.5.115, where C. contrasts *clementia* and *mansuetudo* with cruelty. The theme of *mansuetudo* is often sounded either separately or in combination with pity (*misericordia*) in the peroration; cf. *Mur.* 90; *Sul.* 92–3; *Rab. post.* 46. The defendant's family receives the predicate 'leading' (*princeps*), originally referring to the 'first' in a given endeavour or field and hence 'preeminent'; it comes to be a title, as in the phrase *princeps senatus* applied to the elder Scaurus (cf. 46n.), and was later adopted by Augustus and his successors to emphasize the non-military character of their position (as opposed to *imperator* 'commander'); cf. *OLD* s. vv. The status of the Aemilii Scauri is ascribed to the 'fairness' (*aequitas*) of the Roman people (sc. in electing them to offices); the 'divine power' (*numen*) of the gods also helps explain the family's success.

(18) 'He demanded...extracted' C. interposes in direct speech a summary of the prosecutor's argument, an example of C.'s use of the techniques of popular oratory. These points amount to the essence of the typical extortion case; cf. *RS* p. 65 §3 (the Gracchan extortion law): 'if anything] has been removed, seized, commandeered, procured or appropriated'; *Ver.* 2.1.10: 'will I not prove to these jurors that C. Verres took money contrary to law?'; Venturini 1979, ch. 5; Alexander 2002, 107. Triarius seems to have taken a leaf from the *Verrines*, where similar behaviour is ascribed to Verres; cf. e.g. *Ver.* 2.4.44 'no one has been found so mad as to snatch that silver, so distinguished and so hallowed, no one so bold as to lay claim to it, no one so impudent as to demand that he sell it'.

If you teach us...my defence The advantage claimed for account books (*tabulae*: *OLD* s.v. 7a) is that their preparation involves a chronological sequence (*series*) and system (*ordo*: *OLD* s.v. 15a) for organizing data; cf. Thilo 1980, 177–8 and 180.

If in the end...contend with each C. establishes a hierarchy of witnesses with 'good and approved men' at the top; cf. *Off.* 3.18 and 73 for the behaviour of such men as a criterion or object of inquiry. The distinction between known and unknown witnesses is resumed from 15; since the Sardinian witnesses are necessarily unknown at Rome, C. claims that it is justified to deal with them not individually but by blanket rejection of their testimony; cf. Quint. *Inst.* 5.7.5.

(19) But if all the witnesses...what am I to do? 'Colour' is used 'as an indication of race or birth': *OLD* s.v. *color* 3e, citing our passage; C. thus adumbrates the racial argument of 42. 'A single voice' is amplified at 38 with the claim of a conspiracy and is repeated at 41. Supporting arguments would give C. something to argue against (cf. 14), as would documents (*litterae*), though C. is careful to add that they can be fabricated (*OLD* s.v. *fingo* 9a). 'Where...am I to turn?' alludes to the famous dilemma of C. Gracchus (*orat.* no. 48, fr. 61): 'Where should I take my wretched self? Where should I turn? To the Capitol? But it is awash in my brother's blood. Home? To see my wretched mother abject and lamenting?'; the passage is also imitated by C. at *Mur.* 88 and elsewhere; cf. Bonnet 1906, 42–3.

Am I to argue...an unknown person? C. gives a sample of what a dispute with such a witness would look like. C.'s objections will be met in each case with an assertion on the other side that cannot be checked ('Who will know it? Who will judge?'). *Flac.* 23 argues similarly: 'With what argument am I to refute the statement of the man who says "we gave," nothing more? . . . What am I to say against an unknown person?' Similarly *Flac.* 40.

(20) Therefore I shall not deal . . . with a single onslaught Here C. makes it clear that he is going to handle the Sardinians' testimony as a single category and not individual points; contrast *Leg.* 1.36–7, where he explains that he is going to go over the matter previously discussed 'point by point and distinctly' (*articulatim distincteque*). 'Collusion' renders *conspiratio*, also alleged at 37; thereafter it will be varied with the stronger synonym 'conspiracy' (*coniuratio*: 38, 40). 'Forced out' (*expresso*) and 'compelled' (*coacto*) imply threats, made explicit at 37. With 'onslaught' (*impetus*), used three times here, 'battle line' (*acies*), and 'lay low' (*prosterno*) C. returns to the martial imagery of 17; see ad loc.

5. Division (*divisio*) of the Case (21–2)

The taxes Sardinia paid in kind were one of Rome's major sources of grain (cf. Rickman 1980, 106–7; Garnsey 1988, 182). In view of the recent shortage (cf. 39n.; Introduction sec. 3), the prosecution was clearly expecting charges of mishandling the grain supply to strike a chord with the jury; hence Triarius' care to include this point in all witness testimony (21). C. placed similar emphasis on the topic in prosecuting Verres: 'Now we are broaching the matter of grain, which excels the other charges in the scale and type [reading *genere* with Sydow] of wrong-doing . . . It has escaped none of you, jurors, that all the utility and advantage of the province of Sicily . . . consists above all in the grain supply; in other matters we are aided by that province, but in this we are nurtured and sustained' (*Ver.* 2.3.10–11). Here C. assures the jurors, primed to hear about this topic, that he will deal with it but only after he has discussed some other matters, namely the 'type of accusation', the Sardinians, and Scaurus. These three interposed topics will all turn out to be ways of defusing the testimony of the Sardinians about Scaurus and his handling of the grain supply; for a similar strategy of foregrounding minor arguments and postponing the expected point until he has won over the jurors cf. Stroh 1975, 146, apropos of *Q.Rosc*; similarly the handling of murder charges in *Clu.*

(21) The single most . . . agreement of them all In his defences C. often seeks to isolate the principal charge; cf. e.g. *Font.* 19: 'Learn now about the charge of a duty on wine, which they [sc. the prosecutors] claim to be the most invidious and principal one'. 'Interrogated all the Sardinians': when? At 29 C. says that Triarius produced only one witness in the first session (*actio*). Stroh 1975, 47–8 n. 74, presumes that, to speed up proceedings (cf. Introduction sec. 5a), Triarius, like Cicero in the first session of Verres' trial, had witness testimony essentially substitute for his connected speech (sc. in this, the second session); hence C. can now refer here to what the prosecutor asked 'all the Sardinians'; on the other hand, Lintott 2008: 20 and n. 33 thinks that the orator had access to the content of testimony reproduced on the exterior of groups of sealed tablets that had to be submitted (similarly Powell 2010, 29) so that C. could have known this information without the evidence having as yet been introduced in court; C. does, however, speak of the testimony having been read out (38). 'And the charge': here the Latin has a relative pronoun (*quod*, literally 'which') referring to the entire previous assertion about the grain supply; in the MSS it is followed by *genus* ('kind'), which was rightly deleted by Gaumitz 1879, 285; it was probably either a variant reading for 'charge' in the next sentence or a marginal note that crept into the text (there will be reference to the *genus* of the prosecution in 22 and 23). For 'charge' (*crimen*) cf. 14n. The 'agreement' of the Sardinian witnesses becomes suspect when described as a 'compact' (*foedus*); C. dilates on the point at 38.

Before I touch upon . . . any terrors for me 'Lay . . . the foundations of our . . . defence': The metaphor from building appears as early as *Clu.* 30: 'to use this as the beginning and foundation of the defence'; cf. *Mur.* 14: 'the foundations of the defence have been laid'; *Cael.* 5: 'I believe I have laid the foundations of my defence'. A frequent topic of C.'s defences is that he (or his client) does not fear or need not fear some aspect of the prosecution case, be it the charge, the supporting testimony, or the authority of the accuser; cf. *Mil.* 67 (similarly 72): 'We no longer fear this charge regarding Clodius, but we dread your suspicions, Pompey'; cf. *Mur.* 58; *Flac.* 35 and 38; *Cael.* 23 and 50.

(22) I shall speak first . . . about the grain supply Here C. offers a clear division (*divisio*) of the topics to be dealt with in the remainder of the speech: (1) the type of accusation, (2) the Sardinians, (3) Scaurus, (4) the grain supply. Under the type of accusation he will criticize Triarius for inadequate preparation and haste in assembling

and presenting his case and discuss Ap. Claudius' relation to the prosecution (23–37). 'The Sardinians' will be an attack on the general character of the Sardinian witnesses based upon their racial background and history (38–45f). In the scanty remains of the discussion of Scaurus C. portrays him as a mild man pursuing no feuds except an inherited one, dilates on his splendid aedileship and defends him against charges of luxurious living (45h ff.). Nothing survives of his reply to charges about the grain supply.

6. The Type of Accusation I: Triarius' Failure to Conduct an Onsite Investigation (23–30)

What C. meant by the 'type of accusation' (*genus accusationis*: 22) was not *prima facie* clear. He offers, in fact, a two-pronged critique: the case was hastily cobbled together (23–30), and its motive was not to right wrongs done to the Sardinians but to reap political gain (31–7).

(23) What manner . . . crush my client? Asc. (19C) states that the prosecutors were granted thirty days each to conduct investigations in Sardinia and Corsica but declined to carry them out on the grounds that the case had to be tried before the elections so as to prevent Scaurus from buying victory with his ill-gotten gains and then enriching himself in another province after the end of his term of office (cf. F 2–5n.; Introduction sec. 5b). C. ignores this explanation and suggests that Triarius' failure to visit the province was the result of overconfidence.

When I was a boy . . . in the Cattle Market L. Aelius was perhaps a freedman of the philologist L. Aelius Stilo, an eques of Lanuvium who taught both C. and Varro; cf. Suet. *Gram.* 3 = *gram.* 53, no. 10; Klebs, *RE* s.v. Aelius 7; Kaster 1995, 68–70; for freedmen acting thus on behalf of their patrons cf. Treggiari 1969, 80 and n. 8. If the name is correctly restored (praenomen and nomen are reversed in T and badly corrupted in A), the defendant was Q. Titius Mutto, possibly to be identified with the moneyer Q. Titius who issued coins in 90 (*RRC* no. 341) and the man attacked by Lucilius (fr. 1067 W.); cf. Wiseman 1964, 131 = 1987, 24 and 1971 §437; F. Münzer, *RE* s.v. Titius 33; *MRR* iii. 206; the case is missing from *TLRR*; a Q. Mutto is also mentioned by C. (apparently as a reprobate) in his defence of Fundanius (F 1 Crawford). The epithets assigned to the litigants show clearly, as often, where C.'s sympathies lie; cf. e.g. *Cat.* 1.3. 'Disreputable' (*sordidus*) is used by C. of various persons of whom he disapproves, whether for lowly birth or low character; possibly he has in mind the sense of *mutto* (= penis); cf. *OLD* s.vv. The text must be defective, with the words 'with . . . as investigator' (*quaesitore*) having dropped out (cf. the similar expression at Asc. 34C *quaesitore A. Torquato*), since the official, not the opposing litigant, will have posed the question. Aelius' quip is an example of utter self-assurance both for the late hour and the venue chosen for the investigation. The place known as the Cattle Market (Forum Boarium), though no longer used as such in C.'s time, occupied the area adjacent to the Tiber between the base of the Aventine and that of the Capitoline; a communications hub, it was the site of Rome's two earliest bridges, the departure point of a ferry and three gates in the Servian wall; it was thus frequented by merchants and travellers and a fertile source of gossip; cf. Richardson 1992 s.v. Forum Boarium; Coarelli 1988; id. *LTUR* s.v.

(24) Did you suppose . . . M. Aemilius Scaurus? An indignant question. In the Latin 'you' is juxtaposed with 'in the case of M. Aemilius Scaurus' for contrast; and his client is given full dignity with all three names (cf. Adams, 1978, 145), identical also with the name of his father, the famous leader of the senate (see on F 2 and 5; 46).

He says . . . in the province itself C. gives Triarius an explanation in direct speech, another example of C.'s use of techniques of popular oratory; cf. 18. C. cites his own experience in prosecuting Verres to counter the claim that on-the-spot research was unnecessary since the Sardinians brought their information to Rome. He depicts his Sicilian clients as having qualities that inspire trust ('prudent by nature, practised by experience, deeply educated') in contrast with the Sardinians, who will be portrayed beginning at 38 as utterly lacking culture and credibility. Somewhat similar is the contrast of the Sicilians' testimony against Verres with the present case at *Flac.* 17–18. The repetition in diverse function (polyptoton) of the word 'province' drives home the point.

(25) Should I not . . . fields themselves? 'The arable-farmers' (*aratores*): those who occupied land subject to tribute of a tithe of the year's crop (*ager decumanus*) payable to the *publicani*; this comprised all the grain-land of Sicily, not just the public land of the Roman people, such as the *ager Leontinus*; cf. *Ver.* 2.3.13. For the 'complaints and wrongs of the arable-farmers' cf. *Ver.* 2.3.122: 'I assert that the

arable-farmers were ejected, the lands subject to tribute were harrassed and emptied by Verres, the province was ravaged and laid waste'; similarly 47 and 66. C. implies that his onsite investigation was inevitable, but it was to a degree imposed upon him by the refusal of the current governor L. Metellus (*MRR* ii. 128–9; cf. 33n.) and some communities, such as Leontini (cf. *Ver.* 2.3.109–10 and 122), to cooperate; cf. Pritchard 1971; Dilke 1980; Brennan 2000, 492–3; Alexander 2002, 49–50; Dubouloz 2007.

I traversed... the ploughshare 'I traversed' (*peragravi*) will have been geminated, as regularly when C. adds 'I say' (cf. e.g. 49), though it is transmitted only once (an example of haplography); similar error at *Phil.* 5.33. C. conducted his investigation in Sicily for approximately fifty to fifty-five days from the beginning of the intercalary month to the beginning of April 70; he may have visited Agrigentum towards the end of the intercalary month; cf. Marinone 2004, 66 and n. 4. C.'s complaint of the rigours of the season ('the harshest winter') is likely to be much exaggerated. Located 4 km from the sea on the south coast of Sicily, Agrigentum is bounded by the two small rivers Hypsas (modern Drago) and Akragas (modern S. Biagio) and steep mountains on the north and east. A deep valley (Valle della Croce) divides the city into two unequal parts; cf. Hülsen, *RE* 1.1 1187.68 ff. (s.v. Akragas). C. calls the Leontine Plain the 'head (*caput*) of the grain supply' (*Ver.* 2.3.47) and the Leontines the 'leaders (*principes*) of the grain supply' (ibid. 109); he would later complain that Mark Antony gave 2,000 *iugera* of this choice land to Sex. Clodius, his teacher in rhetoric: *Phil.* 2.43 and 101, 3.22; more vaguely 8.26; Plin. *Nat.* 18.95 also praises the fertility of the soil; wheat grew wild there (Diod. 5.2.4). The wrongs done the Leontine arable-farmers form a major topic of *Ver.* 2.3 (110 ff.), though the town of Leontini offered C. no support (ibid. 109). 'Practically' (*paene*) softens the bold personification; 'the place itself and the lake' are similarly personified in 27. 'Ploughshare' renders *stiva*, which is 'the shaft of a plough-handle' or 'stilt': *OLD* s.v.

(26) And so that case... touching my argument 'Extracted' (*expressa*) implies obtaining something in spite of countervailing pressure (see n. before last and 20n.); cf. *Cael.* 66; *OLD* s.v. *exprimo* 4. 'Vividness' was taught by traditional rhetoric under the stylistic virtue 'ornament'; cf. Quint. *Inst.* 8.3.61 ff. as well as 9.2.40; Lausberg 1998, §810; it was clearly a goal of his presentation; cf. *Div. Caec.* 38; *Ver.* 1.7 and 2.3.47 and 58; Innocenti 1994; Frazel 2009, 204–5.

It seemed to me . . . in my bedchamber 'Justifiable' or 'acceptable' is a rendering of *probabilis* used of arguments; cf. *OLD* s.v. 2a. 'True' (*verum*) is suspect; possibly it is a gloss on *probabile*; one expects something like *aptum* ('appropriate'). The subjugation of Sardinia was completed by 227; though much of Sicily came under Roman control by the end of the First Punic War (241), the whole island was not organized as a province until Syracuse fell to M. Claudius Marcellus (211) and M. Valerius Laevinus completed pacification of the island in 210 (Livy 26.40); nonetheless Sardinia receives no such commendation ('most faithful and ancient'); similarly *Ver.* 2.2.2 and 2.3.64; cf. 44n. 'In my bedchamber (*cubiculum*)': it was not abnormal for a Roman to receive individual clients in his bedchamber, but it was to transact business with a public dimension there; cf. Sen. *Ira* 3.8.6; Riggsby 1997, 41 and 47–8.

(27) Recently when the Reatini . . . taught me that case Reate (modern Rieti) was a prefecture located on the Velinus (modern Velino) river in the Sabine country. The patron–client relation existed as early as C.'s consular year, when the prefecture placed some of its young men at his disposal as a private guard; cf. *Cat.* 3.5. The area is amply irrigated by that river as well as its tributaries the Himella (modern Salto) and Tolenus (modern Turano). The limey waters tended to stagnate with entailed flooding of the Rosea Plain to the south; hence as early as 272 M'. Curius Dentatus as censor cut the 'channels' (*cuniculi*) C. mentions to provide drainage to the Nar river (cf. *MRR* i. 198); thereby the Rosea Plain remained moist but free of floods; on the term *cuniculi* and its application to water channels cf. *OLD* s.v. and Puchstein, *RE* s.v.; on Etrusco-Roman hydraulic engineering see Grewe in Oleson 2008, 325–33. The regulation of the waterflow was, however, an apple of discord between the Reatines and the neighbouring Interamnates. If the drainage was insufficient, the Reatines complained of flooding; an excessive outflow could, however, flood Interamna. The dispute to which C. alludes was to be heard by the consuls and ten assessors, as he notes in describing his visit to the site in a letter of 27 July, where he also refers to Scaurus' case as imminent (*Att.* 4.15(90).5 and 9); a dispute recurred in AD 14 pitting Reate against Rome (Tac. *An.* 1.79.3); C. seems to have pleaded the Reatines' case with success since in the later dispute the channel is open and the Reatines object to a plan to block it; cf. Shackleton Bailey ad loc.; Weiss, *RE* 1A1 345.67 ff. (s.v. Reate); G. Radke, *RE* 8A1 625.33 ff. (s.v. Velinus). Here C. twice uses the

word *fides* of his relation to the Reatines; he states first that they are 'under my protection' (*in fide mea*), then that only by autopsy of the site could he satisfy 'my pledge' (*fidei meae*) (sc. to provide satisfactory advocacy); cf. Freyburger 1986, 149 ff., especially (on our passage) 161. 'The place (*locus*) itself and the lake (*lacus*)', a pun; cf. *Ver.* 2.4.107; the place is personified, like the Leontine Plain in 25.

(28) Nor would you . . . enmity against Scaurus In saying that Triarius would not have done otherwise, C. makes the benevolent assumption that the rival counsel was equally committed to conscientious fulfilment of his pledge; see the previous n. and, on C.'s ties to the family, 10n. 'Those Sardinians of yours': 'those' implies contempt or dislike, as often; cf. *OLD* s.v. *iste* 3. 'Far different from what was reported to you' continues the portrayal of Triarius as 'ignorant'; cf. 13n. In fact, however, the timing of the trial was probably a strategy devised by Triarius to forestall Scaurus' election as consul, which, it was thought, would prejudice the outcome; cf. Introduction 5a. The text of T breaks off in the middle of the word 'people' and does not resume until 'or' in the middle of 31.

(29) by <whose> breath . . . a single witness produced A's text resumes here in mid-sentence. The breath by which Aetna burns is, as Beier saw, that of Typhon, according to myth buried by Zeus but still occasionally belching fire; cf. O. Touchefeu-Meynier, *LIMC* s.v. Typhon. The comparison is between the case prior to the compulsory adjournment (*comperendinatio*) as presented by C. in prosecuting Verres and by Triarius here (on the procedure cf. 4; *Font.* 37n.). C. paints a striking contrast: in order to forestall the defence plan of delaying until the following year with a more favourable constellation of magistrates, C. reduced his initial prosecution speech to a one-hour summary of evidence followed by a long parade of witnesses, here hyperbolically indicated ('with the testimony of the whole of Sicily'), whereas Triarius produced but a single witness by that point; for the strategies and timetable in Verres' case see *Ver.* 1.30 ff.; Cowles 1917, appendix; Habermehl, *RE* 8A2 1628.7 ff. (Verres 1); Gelzer 1969, 42–3.

But what a witness . . . manifest perjury? C. uses the exclamation 'immortal gods!' more than 100 times to call attention to an extraordinary fact. 'Unknown': cf. 18, where C. stipulates of witnesses 'let them only be known'; in 19 he elaborates: 'What eloquence can refute . . . the impudence of an unknown person?' 'Insignificant' renders *levis*, literally 'light'; such a witness is one 'lacking authority' and hence shading towards 'unreliable', as opposed to *gravis*, literally 'heavy', hence 'venerable, august', the epithet applied to the elder Scaurus' leadership of the senate (46); cf. *OLD* s.v. *levis* 12 and 15 and *gravis* 13a; he thus prepares the ground for the blanket denial of the 'authority' (*auctoritas*) of the prosecution witnesses at 38. 'Session' renders *actio*, one of 'two or more processes in a trial' (*OLD* s.v. 6b), in this case the one prior to the compulsory adjournment; see previous n. The witness has, as was often the case, taken the gentile name of the man who brokered the grant of citizenship, L. Valerius Triarius; cf. H. Solin, *OCD*[3] s.v. names, personal, Roman 9; Badian 1958, 253–5. For the elder Triarius' position in Sardinia in 77 cf. 10n. C. already complained of the perjury of the Sardinian witnesses at 20. If it was committed in court testimony, perjury was originally punished by the perpetrator's being hurled from the Tarpeian rock (*Lex XII* 8.12); cf. Latte, *RE* 15.1 354.2 ff. and 355.49 ff. (s.v. Meineid); there is no evidence for trials on this charge in the late Republic; cf. *TLRR* Index of Procedures.

(30) But if the omen of your name . . . but for salvation 'The omen of your name': the Ambrosian scholiast explains that C. alludes to the ancestral custom of the consuls in levying troops to see that men with the names Valerius and Statorius were enrolled first as an omen that the army would 'be strong' (*valere*) and 'stand its ground' (*stare*). He pretends that such considerations have led the prosecutor to call Valerius as his first witness; cf. Corbeill 1996, 73. The 'your' prior to 'name' is plural, pointing to the homonymy. 'Not for destruction': *vale* 'farewell' was a formula for 'taking leave of the dead' (cf. *OLD* s.v. *valeo* 3c) and so could be interpreted as an ill omen for Scaurus, but C. insists that, like the ancestors, he will interpret the name as a good omen (sc. for his client). For another joke about an omen for the defendant cf. *Ver.* 2.4.7: 'none of these [sc. statues], I say, did he [sc. Verres] leave except a very old wooden one of Good Fortune; he refused to have her in his house'.

But all that speed and haste . . . the consular elections This sentence begins by summarizing the criticisms developed since 23 of Triarius' conduct of the case, namely the hasty preparation and inadequate evidence of the first session, and draws the conclusion that the case has been put together for the sake of the consular elections. 'Trial' (*iudicium*) occurs twice in this sentence in different cases (polyptoton) and juxtaposed to underline the paradox. 'The consular elections', held in abeyance until as late in the sentence as possible, will form the next topic.

7. Type of Accusation II: the True Motive (31–7)

The prosecutor's haste, C. suggests, is explicable only if the real goal is to convict the defendant prior to the consular elections, in which he is canvassing; conviction would, of course, make him ineligible for office. C. depicts this as a strategy developed by the current consul Ap. Claudius Pulcher to benefit the candidature of his brother Gaius, since both he and Scaurus are patricians and the office is open to only one patrician at a time. In the consular elections for 53 Scaurus faced competition from the plebeians Cn. Domitius Calvinus and C. Mummius as well as his fellow patrician M. Valerius Messalla Rufus, with the further complication of C. Claudius Pulcher's possible candidature. The result was 'one of the most corrupt races that the Romans had ever seen'; delayed by scandals and disorders, the winners, Domitius and Valerius, did not enter office until July 53; see Gruen 1974, 148–9; Tatum 1999, 231 (source of the quoted words); *MRR* ii. 227–8.

(31–4) In this context . . . fear or disgrace In his defences C. must sometimes neutralize the (real or imagined) opposition of a major political figure, such as that of Sulla in *S.Rosc.* or Pompey in *Mil.* Here C. describes first his own relation to the consul Appius Claudius (31 through the first sentence of 32) and then Appius' relation to the prosecution (second sentence of 32 through 34).

(31) In this context . . . firm reconciliation Ap. Claudius is the new topic, his name pushed to the earliest possible point in the Latin sentence. Appius was the eldest of three sons of a homonymous father (cos. 79; *RE* s.v. Claudius 296) and the Caecilia Metella (*RE* s.v. Caecilius 135) who gave refuge to C.'s client Sextus Roscius; there were also three daughters, including Clodia Metelli, the presumed 'Lesbia' of Catullus' poems and lightning-rod for C.'s invective in *Cael.*; on the possibility that she was a half-sister to her brothers cf. Tatum 1999, 34–5. Appius supported his brother P. Clodius' moves against C. in 58 and was the following year the sole praetor to oppose C.'s recall from exile: *MRR* ii. 200; cf. Spielvogel 1997, 70, on his brothers' support as a constant in P. Clodius' career. Upon C.'s return, Pompey, whose elder son had married Appius' daughter, took pains to reconcile the two, a step in the process of assimilating C. to

the dominant coalition; cf. *Fam.* 1.9(20).4 and 19 with Shackleton Bailey's n.; *Fam.* 3.10(73).8 and 10; *Q.fr.* 2.11(15).2–3; Münzer, *RE* 3.2 2850.45–50; Constans 1921, 15–25; Johannemann 1935, 67–8; Gruen 1974, 353; Spielvogel 1993, 158 and 167–8. There would be further tensions in C.'s relation to Appius: Appius avoided meeting his successor when C. took over from him as governor of Cilicia: *Fam.* 3 with Constans 1921, 53–92; then, in the first half of 50, C.'s prospective son-in-law Dolabella twice prosecuted Appius: *TLRR* 344 and 345 (at *Fam.* 3.12(75).2 C. claims, disingenuously, that the engagement was entered into without his knowedge). Friendship (*amicitia*) was an important element in Roman politics of the time (cf. Brunt 1988, ch. 7) and abjuring friendship correspondingly tricky; at *Off.* 1.120 C. recommends proceeding cautiously.

For that role . . . an easy reconciliation C. alludes to Appius' 'role' (*partes*) with an anaphoric pronominal adjective (*eae*); it was by now known to the audience if only through his brother Publius' speech; cf. 37n. The following argument assumes that Appius is the prime mover behind the prosecution. C. ascribes alternative motives: (1) he was genuinely moved by 'a sense of grievance' (*dolor*) and 'suspicion' (*suspicio*; see on 14) or (2) he neglected his victim through (*a*) lack of awareness or (*b*) the assumption that they could be easily reconciled. The conjunction rendered 'either . . . or' (*aut . . . aut*) is commonly used to set off mutually exclusive alternatives; here, however, the force is weaker.

(32) I will say so much . . . bitter towards him When he feels he has to criticize a third party in the course of a defence, C. may, as here, seek to limit the damage in advance by saying that he goes no further than the case demands; cf. e.g. *S.Rosc.* 83, *Cael.* 31–2.

What disgrace . . . never dishonour For liveliness the signal-word *quid?* introduces each question, though here it is only rendered once ('tell me'); similar repetition e.g. at *Ver.* 2.4.127–8. Appius' grandfather, also an Ap. Claudius Pulcher (*RE* s.v. Claudius 295), was defeated by the younger Scipio Africanus in the canvassing for censor in 142, an early example of the new personality-driven electoral politics cutting through tradtional patron–client ties; cf. Plut. *Aem. Paul.* 38.3; Astin 1967, 111–13; hence the enmity; for C.'s relations with Appius cf. 31n. 'Disgrace' (*turpitudo*) is physical, applied originally to 'unsightly appearance' and hence developing to something morally shameful, whereas 'dishonour' (*dedecus*) denotes the absence of *decus* ('esteem, honour, glory'); cf. *OLD* s.vv.

(33) The predecessor envied . . . quite widespread Ap. Claudius governed Sardinia in 56 as a promagistrate (propraetor with query: *MRR* ii. 547) and was succeeded the following year by Scaurus (as proconsul): *MRR* ii. 210 and 217–18. Power and its exercise inevitably attract 'envy' (*invidia*; in our text the corresponding verb *invidere*; cf. the reference to 'envious persons' (*invidi*) at 13) even if it is properly exercised; cf. Pöschl 1983, 14, and on *invidia* in general Kaster 2005, ch. 4. The successor could have considerable influence on the predecessor's image. Thus C., who in 50 succeeded Appius as governor of Cilicia, forbade an embassy to Rome to praise his predecessor's administration (*Fam.* 3.8(70).2 ff.) or the erection of a monument in his honour (*Fam.* 3.7(71).2–3). Verres' successor as governor of Sicily, L. Caecilius Metellus, at first repealed some of his decisions but then reversed course, forbidding destruction of his statues, demanding commendations of Verres' administration from Sicilian communities, threatening communities that sent envoys to testify against him, etc.; cf. *Ver.* 2.2.12, 62–4, 139, and 160–4; Habermehl, *RE* 8A2 1626.64 ff. s.v Verres 1; Alexander 2002, 49–50.

Indeed this everyday circumstance . . . C. Claudius 'Culture' renders *humanitas*; it recurs in 44 as a factor that can overcome a bad inborn character; it is used in a broad sense and distinguishes the human from the beast; cf. *OLD* s.v. 2. For Appius' 'wisdom' (*sapientia*) cf. *Fam.* 3.8(70).3, where he is called 'wise' (*sapiens*). These qualities would, according to C., have made Appius proof against the all-too-human tendency to denigrate his successor but for the political considerations sketched in the sequel. C. now finally specifies what he had in mind under 'consular elections' (30), namely the expected candidature in 54 of C. Claudius Pulcher, the second of the three sons; cf. Münzer, *RE* s.v. Claudius 303. As praetor in 56 (*MRR* ii. 208) he had joined the youngest brother, P. Clodius, to prevent the removal from the Capitol of the tablet inscribed with the law that precipitated C.'s exile; cf. Dio 39.21; Tatum 1999, 220–1. He governed Asia from 55 to 53 (*MRR* ii. 218, 224 and 229) and after his return was prosecuted for extortion and convicted by October 51 (*TLRR* 336); he went into exile and never attained the consulate.

(34) Whether the latter . . . and in other matters The Claudii Pulchri were patrician, but in 59 P. Clodius had transferred to the plebs in order to stand for the tribunate; cf. *Dom.* 34–41, where C. details his objections to Clodius' adoption by the 20-year-old P. Fonteius; Mommsen 1887–8, i. 487; Lintott 1999, 121–8; Tatum 1999, ch. 4.

As tribune, he then carried the legislation that drove C. into exile; cf. Rotondi 1912, 394–5; Tatum 1999, ch. 5. C. has his tongue firmly in his cheek as he speaks of Gaius contemplating a transfer to the plebs to enhance his electoral chances and of Appius 'remembering' his brother's previous elections as a patrician that would complicate any such transfer. Asc. 26C notes the raillery and points out that Gaius, unlike Appius, had not been reconciled with C. On the consulate being open to only one patrician at a time cf. Mommsen 1864–79, i. 125, and 1887–8, ii. 79–80; Lintott 1999, 36 and 104–5. By the late Republic patrician status was no longer a general requirement for membership of the board of pontiffs (see below), but it remained a requirement for four priesthoods: the flaminates of Jupiter, Mars, and Quirinus and the post of *rex sacrorum* ('king of sacred rites', the successor in ritual function of the kings of Rome); cf. Kübler, *RE* 18.4 2226.66 ff. (s.v. *patres/patricii*); it was also a prerequisite for membership of the Salii, a religious confraternity at Rome and some other Italian cities: ibid.; Mommsen, 1887–8, ii. 32; cf. in general Wissowa 1912, 555–9; Latte 1960, 115–16; Beard *et al.* 1998, ii. 5.4. Although patrician status was no longer a requirement for the pontificate, about half the places in the college were reserved for plebeians, so the position is analogous to that of the consulate (cf. Taylor 1942, 386–7 and 407). Gaius was praetor in 56 and must previously have been quaestor; Broughton, *MRR* ii. 547, and Rüpke 2008, no. 1228, date his Salian priesthood prior to his father's death in 76; Gaius had thus competed as a patrician in at least three elections.

Therefore he did not want . . . fear or disgrace Appius' influence would, of course, be at its apex during his consulate (if he were charged with overseeing the elections, he could also help a candidate in specific ways; cf. Rilinger 1976, 143–51); hence he is keen to see his brother stand this year; similarly as praetor in 57 he had aided Publius' election as aedile. Thus Appius feels he must either intimidate Scaurus (sc. so that he will abandon his candidature) or discredit him.

(35) Would I not think . . . almost beyond all others? 'Highest office' (*honor amplissimus*) is a fairly common combination in C. (cf. e.g. *Flac.* 45, *Brut.* 54); here the prospective consulship of C. Claudius is meant. During C.'s exile, his brother Quintus was ceaselessly active in the cause of his restoration; indeed on 23 January 57, when supporting a motion for his brother's recall, he was attacked by a mob of Clodius' followers and left for dead; cf. *Sest.* 76; Plut. *Cic.* 33.4;

Münzer, *RE* 7A2, 1293.46 ff. The relations of the brothers were never closer than during and in the years immediately following the exile; hence this warm acknowledgement of fraternal love; for similar public appreciations of Quintus cf. *Red. sen.* 1 and 37; *Red. pop.* 5 and 7; for the relations of the brothers see further Bradley 1991, ch. 8. For Quintus' service in Sardinia see 39n.; for his career in general Wiseman 1987, 34–40; McDermott 1971; Münzer, *RE* s.v. Tullius 31.

'But his brother is no longer canvassing' An imaginary objector quoted in direct speech, a feature of popular rhetoric; cf. 18n.; C. counters strongly. Gaius withdrew from the campaign evidently alleging that he was detained in Asia by pressing business (see below). Appius and his colleague had, in fact, entered into a secret agreement with the consular candidates C. Memmius and Cn. Domitius Calvinus, as was later disclosed: *Att.* 4.17(91).2; cf. Courtney 1961, 154.

Tell me, then . . . so easily healed? C. enumerates factors that might detain a provincial governor and personifies the province itself as a 'suppliant' (*supplex*). The businessmen, tax-farmers, and citizens will all be Romans who might fear a change to the detriment of their interests if the governor left the province prematurely to canvass at Rome; 'all allies' are also mentioned but clearly carry less weight. C. ostensibly takes at face value C. Claudius' claim that he is sacrificing his personal ambitions to serve the interests of others, but in light of his later conviction for extortion (see 32n.) his continuation in office was probably rather motivated by a desire to maximize profits. C. adds a reason that might prompt a lawsuit, namely the wounding (*exulcero* 'make raw or sore', here used metaphorically; cf. *OLD* s.v. 1–2) of feelings; but whose feelings were wounded? The only clue in context is the reference to Appius' offence at his successor (33), though the shift from Gaius to Appius seems abrupt.

(36) And yet . . . the fact itself C. here raises an alternative possibility: not so much the wishes of the Claudii as the misperception of the Sardinians, derogated as 'barbarians', may underlie the case. Greek *barbaros* was formed to mimic what seemed to them the unintelligible babblings of speakers of foreign languages and soon came to have strongly negative connotations; cf. Dihle 1994, 47–51; as early as Plautus the Romans adopted the word to designate non-Greek foreigners, likewise with a negative valence; cf. LSJ and *OLD* s.vv.; see further Riggsby 2006, 67–9 (typical structure and deployment of ethnography by Roman authors) and 215–16 (comparison of Greek and Roman concepts); Balsdon 1979, ch. 4. The negative ethnic

stereotype of the Sardinians will be elaborated at 38 and 42–5. C. makes a similar point, however, about the common people of Rome at *Q.Rosc.* 29: 'The common people are this way: they judge few things based on fact, many based on opinion'.

The Sardinians are convinced . . . Scaurus' reputation C. has chosen to express this idea in the impersonal passive with the agent unspecified (*persuasum est Sardis*). It is a fair question how they could have come by this conviction if not through Appius or his agents, and C. abandons the pretence that Appius is not involved in the sentence after next.

They are also led on . . . on this point 'The hope of benefits and rewards' corresponds to the fifth of the six methods of influence indicated at *Off.* 2.22 ('captured by hope of largesse and promises'); see further on *Font.* 25 ('Those jurors . . . self-interest or enmity'). C. leaves it perhaps deliberately vague whether he speaks of rewards provided by law or extralegal inducements promised by Appius Claudius; cf. Alexander 1985, 29–30. No doubt the Sardinians' expectations are naïve ('they think that a consul can do anything'; cf. on *Font.* 27 ('A greater gain . . . is practically bound up')), but C. immediately implies a basis in promises actually made; the point receives emphasis through alliteration (*putant posse, praesertim . . . pollicentem*). In view of his ostensible wish to maintain friendship with Appius (32), he closes off discussion advisedly: giving or inducing others to give false testimony was a criminal offence; cf. Mommsen 1899, 431 and n. 9, 668 n. 1, 635 nn. 2 and 3, and 675 nn. 3 and 4; Robinson 1995, 102. Cf. *Flac.* 13, where C. breaks off a topic ostensibly out of regard for the feelings of the prosecutor Laelius.

(37) And yet . . . toward my own brother C. now claims that he has treated Appius no differently in this speech than if he were his brother. He clarifies that he does not mean that he has spoken in the manner of Appius' actual brother, Publius, also one of Scaurus' advocates, who has said a lot (*multa*)—probably a barb aimed at Publius' long-windedness as well as his criticism of Appius; cf. Constans 1921, 23; on Publius' participation see further Introduction 5b. Rather, C. has spoken as he has always behaved toward his own brother Quintus.

Therefore, jurors, . . . hope and threats By referring again to the 'type' (*genus*) of prosecution C. signals the conclusion of the first segment of his quadripartite case (cf. 21–2). He contrasts two styles of prosecution, each described with four adverbs, the first set emphatically denied with anaphora of 'nothing' (*nihil*), the other affirmed and then elaborated by nouns in the instrumental ablative ('collusion . . . threats'). The 'speed' and 'haste' of the prosecution were criticized in 30 after the discussion of Triarius' failure to visit Sardinia in contrast to C.'s own procedure in several cases and his calling of merely one witness in the first session of the trial; cf. ad loc. The claim of 'collusion' (*conspiratio*) was already raised at 20 and will be intensified by the still stronger claim of 'conspiracy' (*coniuratio*) in the sequel (38, 40). 'Command' (*imperium*) inheres in the office of consul and implies the right to control troops; cf. Bleicken 1981. 'Hope' (sc. of rewards) has already been mentioned as a tool of the prosecution (36); see also 38. Only here are 'threats' explicitly mentioned, though they are implied by some of the language in 20; see ad loc.; similarly *Flac.* 19: 'Let us deeply scrutinize the nature and manner of the charges: now you will find nothing except hope, terror, and threats.' A cretic plus trochee, one of C.'s favourite clausular rhythms, rounds off the impressive period.

8. The Sardinian Witnesses (38–45c)

A personal interest in the outcome could be held to invalidate the testimony of witnesses (cf. 36n.), a common argument in extortion cases (cf. Quint. *Inst.* 5.7.5), but here C. goes further, claiming a conspiracy of the Sardinian witnesses against his client (cf. Greenidge 1901, 482 n. 5) as well as the untrustworthiness of Sardinian testimony in general.

(38) I come now to the witnesses. Transitional formula, common in C.'s oratory of all periods (cf. e.g. *S.Rosc.* 79, 83, 124), to the second major part of the case described at 22 as 'about the Sardinians'.

I shall teach . . . license to tell lies A tricolon adducing three points to undermine the credibility of the prosecution's Sardinian witnesses: their suspect unanimity, their greed, and their propensity to lie.

I shall teach . . . semblance of witnesses The discrediting of the prosecution's witnesses is a major task of the defence. At 14–17 C. contrasted two types of pleadings, those dependent on argumentation and those dependent on witnesses; the points raised prior to that passage were of the former type, which he claimed as superior; see on 14. 'Credibility' (*fides*) is the quality of witnesses par excellence; it can also refer to the 'loyalty' or 'reliability' of a foreign people in relations with Rome; cf. Vasaly 1993, 196–7. 'Authority' (*auctoritas*) implies that the testimony has weight with the jury; cf. *OLD* s.v. 8d; cf. the punning gibe at *Flac.* 53: 'let them cease to suppose that there is authority (*auctoritas*) in that testimony of which no one has been found to be the author (*auctor*)'. C. reinforces the point by denying the Sardinians not merely status as authentic witnesses but even the appearance or semblance (*imago*: cf. *OLD* s.v. 8; *species*: *OLD* s.v. 6) of witnesses.

In the first place . . . read out What were read out in court (*recitata*) were the witnesses' depositions. 'Conspiratorial pact': *compromisso . . . et coniuratione* by hendiadys. With *compromissum* ('pact') C. reaches for a metaphor from Roman private law: it was an agreement, insured by a deposit of money, of several parties to abide by the decision of an arbiter; cf. *OLD* and Berger 1953 s.v.; Buckland 1963, 532. With the allegation of 'conspiracy' (*coniuratio*) C. goes beyond the 'collusion' (*conspiratio*) previously alleged (20, 37) to a potential danger to the state; cf. also 40. The word was laden with sinister connotations since the senate's decree suppressing the Bacchanalia, seen as a threat to the Roman state, in 186 (*CIL* i^2. 581); cf. Livy 39.8 ff.; Beard *et al.* 1998, i. 91–6 with literature. C. deployed the term in 63 to brand Catiline and his followers as enemies of the state; cf. Dyck 2008*a* on *Cat.* 1.1.5–9.

in the second place . . . promise of rewards 'Self-interest' is often alleged to vitiate witness testimony; cf. n. on 38–45c and *Font.* 21n.; for the particulars 36n. Similarly in his defence of Verres Hortensius argued that the witness Artemo of Centuripae was in league with the prosecutor; cf. *Ver.* 2.2.156; Ayers 1950, 43.

finally by the people . . . license to tell lies Vanitas ('mendacity') was criticized by C. as a vice potentially inhering in retail trade (*Off.* 1.150). The charge of mendaciousness was a standard one against witnesses (*Part.* 49). Similarly C. describes the Sardinians as a 'mendacious people' (*vanissima . . . gens*) at 45o. The allusion to characteristics of the people (*natio*) of Sardinia, following upon the reference to the behaviour of 'barbarians' (35), further advances the argument from ethnic stereotypes that was adumbrated at 15 and 17 and dominates the following chapters; cf. Vasaly 1993, 194–7. The Sardinians' general reputation at Rome may be gauged by the quasi-proverbial iambic verse cited at *Fam.* 7.24(260).2 and Fest. p. 428 L: 'Sardinians are for sale, one more worthless than the next' (evidently, as Lintott observes *per litt.*, a joke advertisement of a slave-dealer); the poet C. Licinius Calvus turned the idea against a Sardinian enemy: 'The disgusting person of the Sardinian Tigellius is for sale' (fr. 36 H. = 3 Bl. and C.); cf. Otto 1890: 308–9; Balsdon 1979, 64. According to *Phil.* 6.19 Romans differ from other peoples in that freedom is proper to them; cf. Cowan 2008. The propensity of slaves to lie was an entrenched stereotype in ancient thought; cf. Wiedemann 1981, 54.16; Bradley 1994, 124–5 and n. 27, 143–4 and n. 20; hence the rule that their testimony was admissible in court only if taken under torture: Greenidge 1901, 479–81 and 491–3; Buckland 1908, 86–91; Robinson 1981, 223–7; Bradley 1994, 165–70.

(39) Not that I say . . . complaints A verb is clearly required but has been omitted by A; editors supply it in various forms; I read *nego* 'I deny' for *ego* 'I' (Beier already suggested *ego nego*) and follow Beier's change of *numquam* 'never' to *umquam* 'ever'; the *n* will have been omitted in copying and falsely reinserted. This claim and the following argument are meant to enhance C.'s credibility since, as Riggsby 1999*b*, 429, notes, 'a transparently universal argument is unpersuasive'; C. nonetheless contrives to get as much mileage as possible from it.

I am neither . . . toward the Sardinians C. recognizes that he would be unfeeling (*inhumanus*) to deny the Sardinians as human beings any claim to be heard. At *Off.* 1.30 he acknowledges the difficulty of putting into practice the famous verse of Terence's Chremes 'I am a human being; I hold nothing human alien to me' (*Hau.* 77). At *Phil.* 8.18 he denies that any citizen regarded the Massiliotes' troubles as alien to himself.

especially since my brother . . . on Pompey's orders For some five months in 57–6 Quintus Cicero served in Sardinia as one of fifteen legates whom Pompey, charged with a special five-year *cura annonae* ('supervision of the grain supply'), dispatched to critical areas to expedite grain shipments to Rome: *MRR* ii. 211 and 213; Garnsey 1988, 201 and 215–17. The work appears to have consisted above all in agreeing multi-year supply contracts so as to ensure continuity; cf. Rickman 1980, 56–7. As Wiseman 1987, 37, observes, this appears to have been a payback for Pompey's support for C.'s recall from exile (Marcus had been asked but declined: *Att.* 4.2(74).6; cf. Johannemann 1935, 56), and Quintus aimed to dispatch it 'as quickly and painlessly as possible'; cf. also Thomasson 1991, 19 and n. 99.

He consulted their interests . . . esteemed by them C. points to an exchange ('in turn': *vicissim*) whereby his brother's good faith (*fides*) and humanity (*humanitas*) are balanced by the Sicilians' favourable attitude towards him. C. speaks of the *humanitas* in this sense of Quintus as governor of Asia at *Q.fr.* 1.1(1).3, 25, 37, and 38; for a different sense cf. 33n. Similarly, he had occasion to praise Quintus' 'fairness' (*aequitas*) and 'foresight' (*prudentia*) as governor at *Flac.* 49. 'Loved and esteemed': cf. the similar description of the attitude of the colonists and original inhabitants of Pompeii towards P. Sulla at *Sul.* 62.

(40) Let this refuge... Gauls, Africans, Spaniards The word for 'refuge' (*perfugium*) was a favourite of C.'s but virtually died out with him, being replaced by *refugium*. The verb 'be kept open' (*patet*) is emphasized by placement at the head of two successive clauses. 'Conspiracy' (*coniuratio*) is again invoked as a danger to fair process (cf. 37, 38), this time reinforced by the likewise ominous 'intrigue' (*insidiae*). C. is being ostensibly even-handed in the application of this principle, but even here the Sardinians are subtly undercut by being placed on the same level with peoples who were more remote and more recently conquered.

T. Albucius... authentic records The philhellene T. Albucius governed Sardinia as propraetor probably in 104 (cf. *MRR* i. 560) and was prosecuted by C. Julius Caesar Strabo (cur. aed. 90) after his return (at *Div. Caec.* 63 C. sees an analogy between C. Julius and himself in that the former also was the provincials' preferred prosecutor). Upon conviction Albucius went into exile to Athens. Cf. *TLRR* 67; Klebs, *RE* s.v. Albucius 2. C. Megabocchus is not otherwise known; cf. Münzer, *RE* 15.1 121.25; *TLRR* 294; Wiseman 1971, no. 542. Shackleton Bailey ad loc. suspects that the Megabocchus mentioned at *Att.* 2.7(27).3 may have been the son of the convicted governor. For 'variety' cf. F 6n. For the prosecution's failure to present financial records cf. 18.

(41) Now there is a single... held out by others The record of previous convictions on testimony from the given province was evidently a standard topic in extortion cases; cf. *Ver.* 2.2.155: 'especially since quite a number who were praetors there were convicted from that province, only two acquitted'. Contrasting the present case with the previous convictions based upon the testimony of 'fair witnesses' (40), C. continues his argument that the Sardinians who have testified in this trial are not independent witnesses but participants in a conspiracy ('a single voice, a single sentiment') fuelled by bribery; the specifics ('promises and rewards') are repeated from 38; cf. also 36 'hope of advantages and rewards'.

'But the Sardinians . . . free men For the use of an imaginary interlocutor cf. 30n. C. sets up three pairs of predicates as prerequisite for a successful prosecution based on Sardinian testimony and suggests that they are missing from the present case. Each pair is essentially a single quality presented in positive and negative terms, with the order reversed for the final set. 'Uncorrupted, voluntarily, not at someone's instigation': similar is the claim at *Flac.* Milan fr. that 'Asia' (i.e. the Asiatic witnesses) has not come 'uncorrupted or spontaneously' but 'impelled, solicited, stirred up, constrained' by others; cf. also *Flac.* 26. 'Under no obligation to anyone' renders *soluti*, which can refer to being free from debt (*OLD* s.v. *solvo* 14b), an oblique reference to the 'rewards' (*praemia*) alleged at 36 and 38.

If they should . . . the reputation of their race? What has just been said about the past and possible future credibility of Sardinian witnesses is in tension with the general point about 'the people themselves' (38), which C. does not propose to abandon (indeed it is destined for elaboration in the sequel). He reconciles the positions by stating that such success should be treated as a paradox—a source of joy and wonderment. Again the possible future success is contrasted with the present case, which lacks those prerequisites ('with all these qualities lacking'); hence a different attitude is called for on the Sardinians' part, expressed as a rhetorical question ('will they not . . . ?'); for their reputation cf. 38n.

(42) All records . . . utterly untrustworthy The Phoenicians were a Semitic people settled along the Eastern Mediterranean coast between Tell Sukas in Syria and Akko in Galilee. Establishing a string of trading posts between their homeland and Spain, they dominated the Mediterranean sea-lanes and trade from the eleventh to the eighth century; cf. J.-F. Salles, *OCD* s.v. Perhaps C. has in mind the tales told by the disguised Odysseus upon his return to Ithaca that prominently feature deceitful Phoenicians; cf. *Od.* 14.288 ff. and 15.415 ff. At *Rep.* 3 fr. inc. sed. 5 C. echoes criticism of the Phoenicians by Greek moralists for promoting a taste for luxuries; he goes still further ibid. 2.9, claiming that their maritime activity amounted to piracy; cf. Isaac 2004, 325–6.

The Carthaginians, descended from them The ancient tradition going back to the fourth-century Greek historian Timaeus (*FGrH* 566 F 60 and 82) is that Carthage was founded in 814/813 BC by settlers from Tyre.

have shown . . . degenerated not at all 'Carthaginians'' (*Carthaginiensium*) limits 'many rebellions' in A; but *Poeni* 'Carthaginians' stands in the previous clause; therefore Mueller rightly deleted *Carthaginiensium* as an unwanted gloss. 'Degenerate' (*degenero*) usually implies deviation for the worse from standards of one's forebears; cf. *Flac.* 25: 'L. Flaccus not only did not degenerate from this uninterrupted and well attested virtue of his ancestors . . . ' But here C. ironically finds that the Carthaginians uphold the (already base) standards of their Phoenician ancestors; contrast *Agr.* 2.95, attributing the Carthaginian character to environment, not heredity. 'Treaty-breaking Carthaginians' (*Poeni foedifragi*), cited by C. at *Off.* 1.38, looks like the beginning of a hexameter; it seems likely to be an Ennian tag; cf. Skutsch 1985, 781–2; it had quasi-proverbial status at Rome; cf. Otto 1890, 291; Freyburger 1986, 224. The Elder Cato, too, played variations on that theme (cf. *Hist.* p. 81, fr. 84). C. may have in mind above all Hannibal's attack on Saguntum on the basis of the Roman view that Saguntum was theirs, having been carved out as an exception in the treaty which defined the Ebro River as the limit of the two powers' spheres of influence in Spain (cf. Livy 21.2.7, *contra* Polyb. 2.13.7 with Walbank 1957–79 ad loc.). As seems to be the case with the treaty-breaking, 'rebellions' probably looks to relations with Rome; C. may be glancing at the Third Punic War, declared by the Carthaginian senate after Rome sent a strong force to support Utica (cf. 45 'Utica testifies' n.).

The Sardinians . . . rejected by them C. oversimplifies Sardinia's complex ethnic composition (see 43n.). As early as 2000 BC the island was inhabited by a population that built massive stone towers (*nuraghi*), about 8,000 of which have been discovered. Phoenicians settled there from around the ninth century. The Carthaginians annexed the island to their empire *c.*500, the Romans beginning in 238; cf. Rowland 2001; Dyson and Rowland 2007. 'Settle' (*deduco*) was the term used for establishing a regular colony of Roman citizens; cf. *OLD* s.v. 9; C. does not want to grant the Carthaginian settlers on Sardinia so much dignity but paints the island as a kind of detention-centre set up to receive the mother country's human refuse. That C. could still plausibly depict the island in such terms suggests a certain success of the Sardinians in maintaining a Punic cultural identity in spite of the assimilation of some local elites to the Roman rulers (cf. 43); cf. van Dommelen 1998, especially 44–5.

(43) So when there was no soundness . . . so many infusions? 'This race' evidently refers to the Phoenicians, who had led off the

exposition (42); their colonists, the Carthaginians, settled in Africa and intermarried with local tribes there (cf. 17 'by the roar of the Africans', 42 'of mixed African blood'); the Carthaginian colonists will, in turn, have intermarried with the indigenous populace of Sardinia (see the previous n.), though C. makes no specific mention of this. 'In its unadulterated state' renders *pura*, Heinrich's conjecture for the transmitted *plena* ('full'); if the transmitted text is retained, it is advisable to insert, with Clark, *pestilentiae* immediately preceding so that it becomes a race 'full of plague'. 'Become foul' or 'sour' (*coacesco*) is used of wine that goes off: *OLD* s.v.; 'infusion' (*transfusio*, literally 'pouring from one container to another': ibid. s.v.) continues the metaphor of liquids.

(43–4) In this connection . . . a few C. mentions his Sardinian guest-friend Cn. Domitius Sincaius only here (cf. Münzer, *RE* s.v. Domitius 82); though the transmitted name is unparalleled, a Sincius is attested at *CIL* v. 2511; cf. Schulze 1904, 266. This man, like L. Cornelius Balbus (*Balb.* 6), had been granted Roman citizenship by Pompey (according to sch. Bob. ad loc.; it is not known which Domitius lent his name); such ties facilitated the romanization of local elites. As van Dommelen 1998, 43, remarks apropos of Sardinia, it was Roman policy to maintain local elites in power, and those who cooperated could retain their patronage networks. Cf. in general Badian 1958, 154–67; Dahlheim 1977, 303–13; Balsdon 1979, 89–91. Rickman 1980, 57 and 107, suspects that Sincaius was rewarded for expediting grain shipments to Rome during the shortage; he compares the incentives offered by the Emperor Claudius for placing ships in the service of the grain supply (Suet. *Cl.* 18–19). The name of a group of Sardinians who likewise received citizenship from Pompey has been lost; at *Balb.* 24 C. confirms that 'many' from Sardinia and some other provinces have received Roman citizenship. That group together with Sincaius provided testimonials (*laudationes*) for Scaurus; see above p. 97 n. 54; in general *Font.* 45n. 'Sound men' renders *boni*; cf. Shackleton Bailey 1986, 23 n. 37: 'solid, substantial citizens and supporters of the existing order'. 'I trust there are a few' is more dubious than affirming; cf. *OLD* s.v. *quidam* 4b '(pl.) a certain number, some few'.

(44) When I speak . . . line itself and their people In Latin litotes is used for emphasis ('I certainly make exceptions' *neque . . . neminem excipio*). Here C. does not go into the theory of definition (as he could have done; cf. *Top.* 26–34 with Reinhardt 2003 ad loc.); he merely wants to establish that exceptional individuals such as Sincaius do not

invalidate the overall type (*genus*) that he posits. He accounts for the exceptions through 'character' (*mores*) and 'culture' (*humanitas*; see 33n.) but does not explain exactly how these qualities defeat vice (he uses a form of the verb *vinco*).

The facts themselves show clearly... or free? The denial of credibility (*fides*) brings the argument back to the starting point (38). 'Partnership' (*societas*) is any sort of sharing and is used in 45a of participation in a war. 'Bond' is *coniunctio*, literally a 'yoking together' of two parties. 'Our nation' is *nomen nostrum*, literally 'our name', often so used: *OLD* s.v. *nomen* 19. As 'proof' of this assertion C. raises a rhetorical question highlighting what he suggests is a unique deficiency of Sardinia. The Bobbio scholiast explains: 'some communities are subject to tribute, some free; those subjugated in war are subject to tribute; those that enter into friendship of their own accord are free'. This is the general rule; the Sicilian town Panhormus, though conquered, was free, however, perhaps because it was resettled by Roman colonists; cf. Kienast 1965, 484 n. 8. Cf. in general Mommsen 1887–8, iii. 655 ff.; Badian 1958, 33–47. For the application of 'friend' and 'friendship' in interstate relations cf. in general Williams 2008. The status of Sardinian communities was thus determined by their stubborn resistance to Roman conquest almost 200 years previously (on which cf. Dyson and Rowland 2007, 129; Huss 1985, 266–7), which seems a very dubious basis for inferring current attitudes towards Rome; Dyson 1985, 263, perhaps takes our passage too much at face value without considering its polemical thrust. Contrast C.'s characterization of Sicily as the 'most faithful and ancient province' (26) even though the conquest of the whole island was more recent; see ad loc.; in the *Verrines* it was, of course, in the interest of the case to play down the extent of Sicilian opposition to Roman rule; cf. Pritchard 1975, 42. The position in Sardinia changed when in June 46 the inhabitants of Carialis were granted Roman citizenship and their city status as a *municipium* by Caesar; cf. Motzo 1936.

(45a) Africa herself... Utica testifies C. follows up by comparing various provinces which, in contrast to Sardinia, have communities that are free or 'friends' of the Roman people. The first example is 'Africa', which can be used geographically of the continent but is also the name of the province Rome established on Carthaginian territory after her defeat and destruction. For the genetic connection with Sardinia cf. 42n.; Moscati 1967. Under 'loyal kingdoms'

C. understands in the first instance Numidia under Masinissa and his successors, though he converted to the Roman cause only in 206 after fighting the Romans for five years in Spain. More surprising than the attitude of the 'loyal kingdoms' of Africa—and therefore emphasized—is anti-war sentiment 'in the province', as C. anachronistically describes what was then Carthaginian territory. In winter 150/149 Utica defected from Carthage, contributing to the outbreak of the Third Punic War and ensuring her later status as a 'free community' and provincial capital; cf. detailed narrative by Harris, *CAH* viii. 142–62; Huss 1985, ch. 19.

By the death of the Scipios Further Spain ... MS A terminates after the first three letters of the word 'death' (*int<eritu>*, restored by Beier). C. refers to the death of the brothers Cn. Cornelius Scipio Calvus (cos. 222) and P. Cornelius Scipio (cos. 218) within one month, probably in 211, during the struggle with the Carthaginians in Spain; cf. Richardson 1986, 35–42. In the following lacuna C. evidently detailed that, while all other communities of Spain defected from Rome, Gades (modern Cadiz) alone remained loyal, receiving and fostering the leaderless Roman army (sch. Ambr. ad loc.). In defending Balbus two years previously, C. had dilated on the preferential position enjoyed by Gades (*Balb.* 4–35).

(45b) poor in resources, its populace untrustworthy These words are quoted out of context by the grammarian Arusianus. The reference will presumably be to Sardinia; the epithet 'untrustworthy' (*fallax*) was assigned to the Sardinians' Phoenician ancestors at 42.

(45c) (peoples) have been found ... *brothers of the Roman people* The fragment is quoted in the scholium to Lucan 1.427: 'And the Arverni: Cicero says of them in the speech for Scaurus: "(peoples) have been found of such type as to be called brothers of the Roman people"'. Lucan himself (1.427–8) says that the 'Arverni dared to invent (*fingere*) that they were brothers to Latium/from the blood of the Trojan people'; Sidonius Apollinaris (*Ep.* 7.7.2) depends on Lucan's formulation. Elsewhere it is the Aedui who are called 'brothers of the Roman people'; cf. *Att.* 1.19(19).2; *Fam.* 7.10(33).4; Caes. *Gal.* 1.33.2 etc. Hirschfeld 1913, 194, plausibly suspects that, since Caesar's war in Gaul was a current topic, C. contented himself in our passage with the general statement that even in Gaul there were tribes so friendly as to be called brothers of the Roman people; the scholiast then wrongly connected the remark with the Arverni, rather than the Aedui. Similar claim at *Ver.* 2.4.72 (similarly 5.125): 'the people of

Segesta consider themselves joined with the Roman people . . . even by blood relationship'.

9. Scaurus (45f–o)

As was usual in criminal prosecution, Triarius no doubt included a discussion of Scaurus' previous life (*vita ante acta*) to establish a propensity and/or need to commit the alleged crimes; cf. Alexander 2002, 107. C. continues from F 1 his depiction of Scaurus as mild and disinclined to pursue vendettas (45h) and seeks to counter suggestions of cupidity and laziness (45i) and a luxurious lifestyle (45l and n).

(45f) when this name . . . throughout all nations The fragment is quoted by the grammarian Arusianus for the use of the preposition *per* ('throughout') even though the verb itself (*pervagatum* 'spread') contains it; cf. on F 8. Presumably 'this name' is that of the Aemilii Scauri. In the vicinity of this fragment evidently belongs the testimony of Ammianus 22.15.24 that C. exhorted the Sardinians to follow the authority of the rest of the world in their view of 'the noble family'.

(45h) When, out of many . . . but inherited Quoted by Asconius 26C as pronounced after two-thirds of the speech. For the proverbial expression 'one out of many' cf. Otto 1890, 358. For Caepio's prosecution of the elder Scaurus in late 92 or early 91 for extortion see F 3n.; nothing more is known about the family connection between Caepio and Cn. Cornelius Dolabella. C.'s client prosecuted Dolabella in 78 for extortion in Cilicia during the previous two years (*MRR* ii. 80 and 84) and forced him into exile; cf. *TLRR* 135; Münzer, *RE* s.v. Cornelius 135. This is an example of 'precocious prosecution' (cf. Cic. *Off.* 2.47 and 49) since Scaurus was probably only 18 if he held the quaestorship at the minimum age (30) in 66; cf. Henderson 1958, 205 n. 10; dating according to *MRR* ii. 153 (with a query). C. presents this case as an exception to Scaurus' general mildness (cf. F 1) and excuses it on grounds that it was inherited; on the heritability of enemies cf. Hinard 1980; Epstein 1987, 43–6.

(45d) What the devil is that reason? This fragment is quoted by Eugraphius on Ter. *Hau.* 4.3.38 to illustrate the use of *malum* ('the devil'), added parenthetically to questions for emphasis; cf. *OLD* s.v. 8; cf. *Ver.* 2.1.54 and 2.2.43; *Q.Rosc.* 56; *Phil.* 1.15 and 10.18.

If there is a close connection with the following fragment, 'reason' (*ratio*) will be used in the sense 'ground, motive' (cf. *OLD* s.v. 8a), namely for extorting money. For an example of such a question in context see e.g. *Ver.* 2.4.7 ('What is this case of mine?') and *Font.* 4.

Would the sheepskin coat . . . failed to move? The Romans were by this time familiar with purple vestments as a mark of royalty in the Hellenistic courts; cf. Reinhold 1970, 33–6. Scaurus' dealings with royalty occurred during his service with Pompey in Asia (66–1), including service as a promagistrate in Syria *c.*65–61 (proquaestor 65–64, proquaestor pro praetore 63–61 according to *MRR* ii. 528). During this time he had to choose between Hyrcanus and Aristobulus as successor to the Maccabean throne and deal with the interference of Aretas III, king of Nabataea, whom he depicted on bended knee on some of the coins he struck as aedile in 58: *RRC* no. 422.1a. Contrary to C.'s claim, however, Scaurus proved only too bribable; cf. Joseph. *AJ* 14.29–33 and 37 and *BJ* 1.123–30; Henderson 1958, 196–8. The 'sheepskin coat' (*mastruca*) was the native dress of the Sardinians, the name itself apparently borrowed from their language; cf. *OLD* s.v.; similarly in 45o he speaks of 'witnesses covered in skins', using their dress to portray the Sardinians as provincial and uncouth; cf. his contemptuous dismissal of T. Albucius' battle as governor of Sardinia with 'petty bandits dressed in sheepskin' (*cum mastrucatis latrunculis*: *Prov.* 15); cf. also *Font.* 33 with n.

(45i) especially since the proximity . . . idleness or greed Quoted by Asconius 26C as part of C.'s defence of Scaurus' magnificent house, which Triarius had no doubt invoked to stir up envy and suggest that Scaurus perpetrated extortion in order to maintain a luxurious lifestyle. Asconius goes on to explain that the house was located on the Palatine as one descends from the Sacred Way and passes through the next street on the left (27C). Scaurus bought and demolished the neighbouring house that had been built by Cn. Octavius (cos. 165) in order to enlarge his own: Cic. *Off.* 1.138–41; this passage, with its praise of 'moderation' (*mediocritas*) and comparison of the electoral success of Octavius and failure and ultimate disgrace and disaster of Scaurus, suggests that the latter had overstepped the bounds. The house was notable for accommodating in its atrium the colossal marble columns that had adorned the temporary theatre Scaurus had built for his aedileship (58: *MRR* ii. 195), which accommodated 80,000 spectators (double the capacity of Pompey's later theatre); cf. Plin. *Nat.* 36.115; von Hesberg 2005, 40; at 11 metres the height

of the columns was comparable to that of public buildings, such as the market basilica in Pompeii; cf. Plin. *Nat.* 36.6 and 114; von Hesberg 2005, 33 and 35 with literature. In this context C. took the opportunity to praise the magnificence of his client's aedileship (sch. Bob. on *Sest.* 116), a point also emphasized in Scaurus' own defence speech (Asc. 20C = *orat.* 140, no. 5); the prosecutor no doubt claimed that Scaurus meant to recoup his losses as aedile by pursuing rapacious policies in Sardinia. The house was later sold to P. Clodius for 14.8 million sesterces (Plin. *Nat.* 36.103); in Asconius' day it was in the hands of C. Caecina Largus, cos. with Claudius AD 42 (Asc. 27C). On Scaurus' wealth and his use of it cf. in general Shatzman 1975, 290–2. According to C. the 'proximity' (sc. to the Forum, senate house, etc.) ensures that Scaurus means to take an active part in public affairs and not succumb to the laziness that afflicted some aristocrats of the time; cf. Livius Drusus' directions to his architect to build his house on the Palatine in such a way that everything he did would be visible to all (Vel. 2.14.3; Plut. *Mor.* 800f) and C.'s claim that his own house was 'within the field of vision of practically the entire city' (*Dom.* 100); on the other hand, C. privately excoriated the 'gentlemen of the fishponds' (*piscinarii*) for neglecting their civic duties: *Att.* 1.18(18).6; 1.19(19).6; 1.20(20).3; 2.1.(21).7. In addition, the populousness of the area, so C. claims, protects his client against any suspicion of greed, though the purchase and demolition of the neighbouring house might suggest otherwise; see above. By contrast, C. Gracchus gave expression to his political views by moving out of his house on the Palatine to live near the Forum among the poor (Plut. *CG* 33.1). On the general theme of 'the house and the wider community' in C.'s speeches cf. Treggiari 1999, 41–5.

(45l) Further I, who have Alban columns, transported them by panniers Quintilian 5.13.40 quotes the fragment as an example of the use of humour to disarm a cutting remark. As Quintilian makes clear, C. pretends that the objection was that Scaurus had his columns transported by wagons rather than panniers. Perhaps Triarius took a leaf from Cicero's Verrine prosecution, since C. emphasizes that the statues Verres plundered at Aspendos were removed 'by wagons' (*plaustris*) (*Ver.* 2.1.53). Panniers were a developed form of animal portage but limited to the carrying-capacity of a single animal; the invention of the yoke made possible the transport of much heavier loads by teams of asses, steers, mules, or—for the heaviest loads—oxen; see further Raepsaet in Oleson 2008, 588–98. Besides the mode

of transport, there is also an implied contrast of C.'s columns made of locally quarried marble with the imported marble of his client's columns; cf. Plin. *Nat.* 36.6, who speaks of 'Lucullan marble', perhaps to be identified with 'Africano' marble named for its dark colour rather than its provenance, which has been identified as Teos; cf. Gnoli 1971, 148–9; Ballance 1966.

(45n) Did you have no house?... your own fortunes Through 'you were in want' is cited by C. himself *Orat.* 223, Quint. *Inst.* 9.2.15 and 4.122 and various later rhetoricians and grammarians, the remainder by C. at *Orat.* 224. The passage is probably continuous and quotes words Triarius addressed to Scaurus, perhaps in the peroration when he had already established the basis in evidence and argument and so he can now proceed 'by suggestion' (*per suggestionem* according to the terminology of some rhetoricians noted by Quintilian in the former passage; cf. Lausberg 1998, §772). Triarius answers his own questions (as Quint. points out); cf. the set of questions and answers at *Q.Rosc.* 22. From 'you have run' to 'at other people's property' the Latin shows an elegant chiastic arrangement of verb, subject-qualifier, and preposition plus object. Though it is not attested elsewhere, 'to run into columns' is assumed to be a proverbial description of insanity (cf. Otto 1890, 89), here wittily applied in the literal sense (with a pun on *incurro*, which can also mean 'attack'; cf. *OLD* s.v. 1 and 3; at *Mil.* 76 it is applied to Clodius' attacks on all and sundry). 'You have raged insanely' (*insanus insanisti*) is an example of *figura etymologica*. 'Other people's property' renders Burchard's *aliena* for transmitted *alienos*, which yields no sense. Possibly the 'sunken, dark, prostrate house' refers to that of Bostar, the description making it an implausible object of Scaurus' envy. For the claim of the governor's loss of perspective cf. *Ver.* 2.3.52 (similarly 65): 'you... neglected such infamy accruing to yourself, such risk to your head and your fortunes'.

(45o) Although you could not escape... witnesses covered with skins? Quoted by Asconius 27C. The antecedent of 'these points' (*haec*) remains unclear. The memory of Scaurus' father was a major asset and hence emphasized both by C. (cf. F 5 with n.) and the defendant himself (cf. Asc. 20C). The grandfather referred to is, as Asconius explains, his maternal grandfather L. Metellus; see the n. after next. For the Sardinians as 'mendacious' (*vanus*) cf. 38n. (*vanitas*); for their characterization as 'unreliable' (*levis*) cf. 29n. For

their native dress cf. 45d n. C. draws a stark contrast between defendant and accusers as early as 13.

10. Peroration (46–50)

It was a standard part of Roman judicial 'theatre' for the defendant and family to dress in squalid clothing in order to appeal to the jurors' pity in the peroration; cf. e.g. *Flac.* 106; *Sest.* 144–5; Winterbottom 2004, 220–1; Bablitz 2007, 84. C. does not omit this point (cf. 49n.) but goes beyond it to present Scaurus' family as deeply embedded in the leading institutions of the Roman state and the buildings that embody them.

(46) On whatever point... headship of his father This and the following lemma, quoted by Asconius 27–8C, are a notable example of C.'s ability to lend his case an aura of objectivity by exploiting monuments visible to the jurors; cf. Pöschl 1983, 34; Vasaly 1993, 38. For the use of 'supply' (*suppedito*) metaphorically of arguments and the like cf. *Off.* 1.104: 'Our Campus (sc. Martius) and the pursuit of hunting supply honourable examples of recreation'. A venerable building on the north side of the Comitium, the senate house was thought to have been built by the king Tullus Hostilius; it was restored and enlarged by Sulla beginning in 81 but would be incinerated during the funeral rites for P. Clodius less than two years from the date of our trial; cf. Richardson 1992 and Coarelli, *LTUR* s.v. Curia Hostilia. 'Headship' (*principatus*) refers to the tenure of Scaurus *père* as leader of the senate (*princeps senatus*); a potentially influential figure, he was a consular appointed by the censors or consuls and was the first called upon to express an opinion in senatorial debate. He was, if possible, to be an ex-censor from one of the greater families (*maiores gentes*) of the patricians; Scaurus was evidently chosen, even though he was not an ex-censor, for lack of a candidate so qualified; cf. Suolahti 1972, 208 and 217–18; cf. also Ryan 1998, 171–224 (known *principes senatus*, especially 189–91, on Scaurus) and 225–46 (method of appointment); O'Brien Moore, *RE* Supp. 6, 699.22 ff.

My client's grandfather... and imploring them T's text resumes in the middle of the verb 'to have established' (*consti*]*tuisse*). The reference is to Scaurus' maternal grandfather L. Caecilius Metellus Delmaticus, cos. 119 (*MRR* i. 525). He owed his second cognomen to his triumph over the Dalmatians (117). He was pontifex maximus by 114, since in that year he adjudicated the charges of unchastity (*incestum*) levelled against three of the Vestal Virgins (Rüpke 2008, 110 and no. 982; *TLRR* 38–40); in view of popular discontent with the acquittals, two of the cases were retried by a special tribunal the following year with resulting convictions (*TLRR* 41–2). The temple 'in your (pl.) field of vision' is that of Castor and Pollux in the Forum, which he rebuilt with the spoils of his Dalmatian victory; cf. Orlin 1997, 134, who argues that the spoils were used for dedications, not reconstruction; Nielsen, *LTUR* s.v. Castor, aedes, templum; Richardson 1992 s.v. Castor, aedes; Rüpke 2007, 43, and 2008, no. 982; Münzer, *RE* s.v. Caecilius 91. According to Roman legend the temple was vowed by the dictator A. Postumius during the battle on Lake Regillus (496) because the giant figures of the divine twins were seen leading the Romans to victory; their temple was also the centre of a healing cult (hence 'they themselves have often supported by their aid many who were in difficulties and imploring them'); they can thus be appropriately appealed to as saviours; cf. Wissowa 1912, 268–71; Orlin 1997, 22 and 30.

(47) The renowned Capitolium . . . M. Scaurus before . . . With 'before' T's text breaks off; a lacuna of seven lines of 17 to 21 letters each follows. Located between the Forum and the Campus Martius, the Capitoline was the smallest of Rome's seven hills and was dominated by the temple to Jupiter, Juno Regina, and Minerva begun by the Tarquins and completed in the early days of the Republic; it was the centre of Roman official cult; see further Wissowa 1912, 38–43; Latte 1960, 149–54; Richardson 1992 s.v. Capitolinus Mons; Tagliamonte and Reussner, *LTUR* s.v. Capitolium; Tagliamonte and De Angeli, *LTUR* s.v. Iuppiter Optimus Maximus Capitolinus, aedes, templum; Beard *et al.* 1998, ii. 1.9b. C. is careful to link his client with his father as benefactors of the cult.

of that illustrious L. Metellus . . . and our empire Another L. Caecilius Metellus, a remote ancestor (cos. 251), became pontifex maximus in 243; cf. Rüpke 2008, 76 and no. 978. He rescued the Palladium from the burning temple of Vesta in 241, whereby he is said to have lost his sight with resulting grant of the privilege of riding to senate meetings in a chariot (Plin. *Nat.* 7.141). Since, however, he is also attested as dictator for the purpose of holding elections in 224 (*fast. Cap.*, Plin. *Nat.* 7.141), the mode of transport must have been granted for some other disability; cf. Münzer, *RE* s.v. Caecilius 72; Rüpke

2007, 41–2. The Palladium was an ancient statue of a goddess armed with shield and spear often thought to have fallen from heaven and to possess magic properties. The oldest saga is of the Trojan Palladium, believed to be a talisman of the city's safety, the theft of which by Odysseus and Diomedes cleared the way for the fall of Troy. Various Greek and Italian cities as well as New Troy claimed to have a Palladium, often identified with the original Trojan one. For C. the Roman Palladium had a similar talismanic function ('a pledge of the safety of us and our empire'). In dramatizing Metellus' action Ovid makes it clear that the Roman Palladium was, in fact, considered identical with the Trojan (*Fast.* 6.417 ff.); similarly D.H. *Ant.* 2.66.5; Servius on *Aen.* 7.188 mentions it beside Priam's sceptre and Iliona's veil among the 'seven pledges that maintain the Roman empire'. Cf. L. Ziehen, *RE* 18.3 171.60 ff., especially 182.24 ff. (s.v. Palladion); Wissowa 1912, 159 n. 5; Faraone 1992, 6–7; P. Demargne, *LIMC* 2.1 965 ff. The Palladium was kept, along with the sacred fire, the Penates, and the sacred phallus, in the *penus*, the inaccessible inner room of the temple of Vesta. These sacred objects had to be rescued from fire and carried to safety a number of times in the course of Roman history; cf. C. Koch, *RE* 8A2 1724.25 ff. and 1729.66 ff. (s.v. Vesta).

(47–8) If only he could briefly . . . from these flames After these words T shows a gap of seven lines. 'If only he could briefly rise up': orators frequently use the idea of someone rising from the dead (*exsisto*) to make an emphatic point; so most famously *Cael.* 33–4, an excoriation of of Clodia put in the mouth of her ancestor Ap. Claudius Caecus; see further Dufallo 2007, 16–22; other examples at *OLD* s.v. *exsisto* 1b. The verb 'snatch' (*eripio*) is repeated from the previous sentence to reinforce the parallelism. 'This' (*hic*) and 'that' (*ille*) are used to distinguish the present situation from the historical incident invoked as a parallel. 'Flames' renders *flamma*, used here, as often by C., metaphorically of 'a highly dangerous situation'; cf. *OLD* s.v. 3c. 'Scion' = *stirps*, literally 'stem' but common in figurative use of a child or descendant; cf. *OLD* s.v. 1 and 5b.

(49) but I also see you . . . as god is my witness For C.'s gemination of verbs ('I see . . . I see') cf. 25 above and *Font.* 25n. C. claims that the image of the apostrophized *princeps senatus* is not a mere mental impression ('I do not merely contemplate you in thought'; cf. *Mil.* 79 'form in your thought the image of this stipulation of mine'); similar emphasis on the visual element at *S.Rosc.* 98: 'Do you not seem to see with your eyes these things that you have heard, jurors?'

On C.'s art of 'making people who are absent from the court appear as though they are actually present' cf. Axer 1989, 302. The defendant appears in squalid raiment ('the sordid raiment of your son'), a routine appeal to pity in the peroration; see above on 46–50. C. 'prompts' the jurors to react in a certain way ('not without great mental anguish and pain'). Asc. 20C confirms that Scaurus, in fact, moved the jurors 'with his squalor and tears and the memory of his lavish aedileship and the people's favour and especially the memory of his father's authority'. T breaks off after the oath 'as god is my witness' (*me dius <fidius>*); seven lines are lost before text resumes.

... even if perchance he had not known him ... first citizen of the community C. is evidently still discussing the image (*species*) of the elder Scaurus (in contrast to the sight presented by his son).

(50) How am I now to address you? ... Therefore whatever way ... you ... C. embraces the Platonic dualism delineated at 4, which enables him to portray the elder Scaurus as still a vital force in the community. 'But you ... are active in the hearts and on the lips of all' is reminiscent of the last line of Ennius' epitaph 'I fly alive on the lips of all' (*varia* fr. 17 V.^{2}), cited by C. at *Tusc.* 1.34 and *Sen.* 73 (see Powell 1988 ad loc.); cf. also *Ver.* 2.2.56: 'it [sc. a large payment made on the governor's orders] began to be on everyone's lips and in their conversation'. After this fragment seven lines are lost in T. In this vicinity C. will have mentioned the wounds his client received in the service of the state (attested by Quint. *Inst.* 6.1.21), another standard topic of the peroration; cf. *Rab. perd.* 36; Winterbottom 2004, 220.

Fragments of Uncertain Location

(1) This, I say ... investigated by others This fragment is quoted out of context in a passage of Asconius (24C) the authenticity of which has been challenged by Madvig 1828, 78–81, on grounds that it deals with a grammatical point, rather than content; he does not, however, question the authenticity of the Ciceronian fragment; cf. also Marshall 1985, 141. It was *de rigueur* for an advocate to deny any sort of expert knowledge before the bar; cf. *S.Rosc.* 46, *Ver.* 2.4.5, *Sest.* 48, etc. This fragment has been thought to bear on the piece of folklore cited in F 13, after which recent editors place it; but C. would perhaps not take his witticism so seriously. Gaumitz 1879, 284, refers it to the Greek lore cited at 2–5, but that material does not appear to be lacunose.

(2) in general terms The fragment is quoted out of context by the grammarian Charisius (1.224.31); its placement thus remains unclear.

Unplaced Testimony

The grammarian Pompeius (5.144K) states that in our speech C. distinguished between the *Sardi* as persons of Sardinian descent and the *Sardinienses* who took up residence there (Hollis 2007: 80 compares *Hispanus/Hispaniensis*); this testimony is sometimes connected with 42 (Olechowska 1984 ad loc.; Riggsby 1999*a*, 132); but the argument there is not lacunose, and so much of the speech is lost that it remains uncertain exactly how C. accommodated the point. Riggsby (1999*a*, 132) suspects that C. is drawing distinctions of credibility between different segments of the population.

APPENDIX 1

Chronological Table

149	*Lex Calpurnia* establishes the extortion court
123	*Lex Acilia* transfers juries to the equites and modifies procedure
by 115	Birth of M. Fonteius
106	Birth of Cicero; *lex Servilia* restores a role for senators on juries
104 or 101	*Lex Servilia Glauciae* sharpens extortion law; juries again transferred to equites
*c.*97	Birth of M. Aemilius Scaurus
91 or 90	Murder of Fonteius' father at Asculum; beginning of Social War
89	Scaurus becomes Sulla's stepson upon the latter's marriage to Metella
before 87	Fonteius moneyer
84?	Fonteius urban quaestor
83	Fonteius legate in Spain
82	*Lex Cornelia* restores the juries to the senators
78	Scaurus prosecutes Cn. Cornelius Dolabella
77/76?	Fonteius legate in Macedonia
75	Fonteius praetor; Cicero quaestor in Lilybaeum (Sicily)
74–72?	Fonteius governor of Transalpine Gaul
73–71	C. Verres governor of Sicily
70	Cicero prosecutes Verres for extortion; *lex Aurelia* divides juries among three classes
69	Fonteius prosecuted for extortion
66?	Scaurus Pompey's quaestor in Asia
65–61	Scaurus promagistrate in Syria and Palestine
59	*Lex Iulia* further sharpens extortion law
58	Scaurus aedile
56	Scaurus praetor
55	Scaurus governor of Sardinia
54	Scaurus prosecuted for extortion and acquitted, defeated in consular elections
52	Scaurus convicted of electoral misconduct (*ambitus*) and exiled

APPENDIX 2

The Text

In the defence of Fonteius the following are the variants of the text translated here from A. C. Clark's Oxford Classical Text:

Clark	Dyck
9 arbitrabuntur	arbitrabantur
13 praecipuis populi Romani praemiis	populi Romani copiis praemiisque
17 videatis eos oppugnare quibus victoribus	videant eos oppugnari sine quibus
18 nominibus	hominibus
19 Elesiodulis	Elesioduni
21 tenere ad unam quamque rem sapientiam iudicis videte	ad unam quamque rem sapientiam iudicis valere existimatis videte
36 volunt	ut velint
42 fuit enim maior talium tum	fuit enim maior olim talium

In the defence of Scaurus the following are the variants of this translation from the text edited by E. Olechowska (Bibliotheca Teubneriana):

Olechowska	Dyck
F 11 fuisse . . . voluisse	fuisset . . . voluisset
2]tis	laudem virtu]tis
4	{apud Graecos}
8 te dixi	<ut paulo an>te dixi
9 paelicatus dolore	iam paelicatus dedecore
13 <in>famata	formata
21	{genus}
posita	<bene> posita
23 a quo	<quaesitore . . . > a quo
25	<peragravi>[2]
39 neque †ego . . . numquam	neque nego . . . umquam
40 coniurationi	coniurationi via
42 Carthaginiensium	{Carthaginiensium}
43 plena	pura
45n alienos	aliena
49 me dius	me dius <fidius>
50 at	et

APPENDIX 3

On Behalf of M. Aemilius Scaurus: Comparison of Fragment Numbers

Olechowska	Dyck
1	1
2	2
3	3
4	4
5	5
6	6
7	7
8	8
9	9
10	-
11	10
12	11
13	12
14	13
Dyck	Olechowska
1	1
2	2
3	3
4	4
5	5
6	6
7	7
8	8
9	9
10	11
11	12
12	13
13	14ß

Glossary of Political and Ethical Terms

The following are the major terms from the realms of politics/administration and ethics that are at play in the defences of Fonteius and Scaurus:

allies (*socii*) States having a treaty of alliance (*foedus*) or other recognized relation with Rome. They were autonomous in their internal affairs but obliged to supply troops under Roman command and subject to other burdens that varied with the terms of the treaty. The internal autonomy eroded as the powers of Rome's provincial governors grew. The Italian allies received Roman citizenship as a result of the Social War (91–87).

audacity (*audacia*) The recklessness that leads a person to cross the line to wrongdoing; cf. *S.Rosc.* 75; in some contexts C. uses the term with reference to action against the existing constitution; cf. Wirszubski 1961.

chastity (*pudicitia*) The physical state defended by an attitude of *pudor* (see 'modesty'); cf. Kaster 2005, 45.

command (*imperium*) The word could be use of a specific act but also of the power to command troops, a characteristic of the higher magistrates (dictator, master of the horse, consul, praetor); *imperium* also came to be used of the sphere in which the Roman state exercised command, i.e. its empire.

conscientious, conscientiousness (*religiosus*, *religio*) Originally *religio* was a feeling of inhibition in the face of divine power; in some contexts it can be 'regard for the cult of the gods'; later the constraints can be social; hence *religio* is sometimes rendered as 'sense of obligation'. In forensic contexts the constraint is often the oath the witness had to swear before testifying.

credibility or **faithfulness** (*fides*) This comes into play in forensic rhetoric as a quality of witness testimony since the witnesses were bound by oath, to which they were either faithful (*fideles*) or not. The jurors, too, were bound by oath (to render a true verdict), so their *fides*, too, is often appealed to by the litigators; see also 'pledge'.

culture (*humanitas*) The quality that distinguishes the human being from the beast; in some contexts best rendered 'humanity'.

duty (*portorium*) A fee for transport of goods beyond a certain point; so named because originally collected at harbours (*portus*); such charges were governed by a law of the censors; cf. de Laet 1949.

eques (pl. equites) A member of the class of citizens meeting a property qualification of 400,000 sesterces but not members of the senate. Originally the equites, as their name indicates, made up Rome's cavalry; they might be provided with a horse at public expense (*equites equo publico*) or an allowance for purchase of such (*equites equo privato*); later they frequently provided their horses privately. Since senators were excluded from large-scale commerce, the equites filled the vacuum; they also engaged in farming the taxes Rome imposed on many of its provincial subjects. Beginning with C. Gracchus' reform of 123 the equites made up the juries of Rome's courts; this continued, with some variations, until Sulla restored the juries to senatorial control (82); after the Aurelian Law (70), the juries were divided equally between the senators, the equites and the *tribuni aerarii*, a group satisfying the same property qualification as the equites. Cf. Brunt 1988, ch. 3.

fair, fairness (*aequus, aequitas*) *aequus* originally means 'level' and hence comes to mean 'balanced, impartial'. *aequitas* is the standard C. regularly appeals to in his forensic rhetoric and expects the jurors to embrace; at *Cat.* 4.2 he refers to 'the Forum, in which all fairness is contained'. Sometimes it is a principle in opposition to the 'letter of the law' (*summum ius*), on which cf. *Off.* 1.33.

faithfulness See 'credibility'.

good (*frugi*) A term of commendation, especially of slaves 'having merit, sober, thrifty', or the like. It was famously applied as a second cognomen to C. Calpurnius Piso (cos. 133), the man who carried the law establishing the first standing court at Rome (see 'standing courts').

good faith (*fides*) This is used of one's being able to be trusted to adhere to one's oath; see 'credibility'.

humanity (*humanitas*) See 'culture'.

juror (*iudex*) A member of the panel judging cases in the courts of Rome. The list (*album*) of eligible jurors was drawn up each year by the praetor. The jurors for a particular case were selected by lot with a right of rejection (*reiectio*) reserved for the litigants.

leader of the senate (*princeps senatus*) A consular (and frequently an ex-censor) appointed by the censors or consuls; as the first member called upon to speak on issues deliberated by the senate, he could exercise great influence; cf. Suolahti 1972; Ryan 1998, 171–224 and 225–46; O'Brien Moor, *RE* Supp. 6, 699.22 ff.

legate (*legatus*) Legates were men of senatorial rank appointed to assist provincial governors or military commanders; the appointment was usually made by the senate on recommendation of the responsible official. Caesar tended to appoint his own legates and expand their use at the expense of the military tribunes (see below).

lust (*libido*) Unbridled desire for any object; a weaker synonym is *cupido* 'desire'; *libido* may, but need not, refer to sexual desire.

military tribunes (*tribuni militum*) They were assigned six to a legion and were its most senior officers. The tribunes of the first four legions were elected, the rest appointed by the commander. They were ordinarily equites with five years of military experience.

modesty (*pudor*) The attitude that protects one from compromising one's chastity (*pudicitia*) and from social embarrassment generally; cf. Kaster 2005, ch. 2.

moneyers (*tresviri monetales* or *tresviri aere argento auro flando feriundo* 'the three men for smelting and striking bronze, silver, and gold') Minor urban magistrates elected annually from *c.*207 on to issue coinage at Rome as needed. Caesar increased their number to four (Suet. *Caes.* 41), but it was lowered to three again by Augustus; cf. *RRC* 598–603.

pledge (*fides*) In forensic contexts most frequently the pledge given by the advocate to provide his client with the best possible representation; see also 'credibility', 'protection'.

popularis Of persons 'claiming to speak for the interests of the (common) people'; of causes 'promoting the interests of the (common) people'; it was a tactic, rather than an ideology, and often pursued by junior politicians aiming to advance their careers; cf. Tatum 1999, 1–11; C. sometimes contrived to appropriate the term for himself or his policies; cf. Seager 1972.

praetor The praetors were originally two in number and the supreme magistrates of Rome (< *prae-ire* 'to go in advance', sc. in battle). In 367, however, the Licinian-Sextian Law added a third, patrician praetor, and the two original praetors became known as consuls (*consules*); the praetor also held *imperium* (see 'command') but a lesser (*minus*) one than theirs. The number of praetors was gradually raised so that they could handle the governing of overseas provinces and preside over the expanding number of standing courts; see entry below. Sulla then increased the total to eight praetors and provided that all should serve in the city and then be sent with proconsular *imperium* to govern provinces the following year.

protection (*fides*) A Roman under threat might call upon the 'protection of fellow citizens' (*quirito*); and a conquered enemy might seek the protection of the victorious commander; cf. *Off.* 1.35.

publicans (*publicani*) Farmers of taxes imposed by Rome upon public land (*ager publicus*) or at toll stations in the provinces; they were usually organized in companies of partners who provided capital and shared the risks and profits; they employed professional managers (*magistri*); see 'equites'; Badian 1972 and *OCD* s.v.

pure (*castus*) The term referred originally to ritual purity of persons or places and then, since sexual purity is thereby implied, sexual purity.

quaestor, quaestorship The lowest regular magistracy, filled by election by the tribal assembly; since Sulla's law, the candidates had to be at least 30 years of age and had to have held a military tribunate or lower magistracy. In the late Republic there were twenty quaestors, two at Rome (*quaestores urbani*) administering the treasury under the senate's supervision, the rest posted to the provinces, where they had judicial, financial, and military duties in support of their respective governors. From Sulla's time having held the quaestorship entitled one to membership of the senate.

regard for obligation or the cult of the gods See 'conscientious, conscientiousness'.

safety (*salus*) One's personal safety, mentioned in forensic rhetoric since that of the defendant was under threat in the trial. Salus was also from early times worshipped as a goddess at Rome and appealed to by those in difficulties; see Winkler 1995.

self-interested (*cupidus*) Term used in a broad sense, in these speeches especially of witnesses testifying for the prosecution.

sound men (*boni*) Term applied by Cicero with approbation to supporters of the existing order.

standing (*dignitas*) Literally 'worthiness', related to *dignus* 'worthy'. It involves one's rank in society and is a factor taken into account in assessing one's own behaviour and that of others; cf. Kaster 2005, 144–5.

standing courts (*quaestiones perpetuae*) Courts at Rome trying public offences; as the name implies, they were constituted every year. Cases were tried before juries of thirty or more members (see 'equites') normally presided over by a praetor. The first such court was the extortion court established in 149 by a law carried by C. Calpurnius Piso Frugi; others were later added for such crimes as embezzlement (*peculatus*), seditious violence (*vis*), improper electioneering (*ambitus*), etc.

surrender (*deditio*) As referred to here, the Roman practice of surrendering to the enemy a commander who made a peace treaty not authorized by the senate; C. Hostilius Mancinus was the most famous example; cf. Rosenstein 1986.

tribuni aerarii See 'eques'.

upright (*sanctus*) Beginning as 'secured by religious sanctions, sacrosanct' the word comes to refer to persons 'holy' or 'blessed' and then 'upright, virtuous' *OLD* s.v.

The following is a 'reverse glossary' that presents the Latin term followed in each case by the English translation(s) ordinarily used here:

aequitas: fairness

aequus: fair

audacia: audacity
boni: sound men
castus: pure
deditio: surrender
dignitas: standing
fides: credibility, faithfulness, good faith, pledge, protection
frugi: good
humanitas: culture, humanity
imperium: command
iudex: juror
legatus: legate
libido: lust or unbridled greed
portorium: duty transit dues
princeps senatus: leader of the senate
publicani: publicans
pudicitia: chastity
pudor: modesty
quaestiones perpetuae: standing courts
religio: conscientiousness, regard for obligation or the cult of the gods
religiosus: conscientious
salus: safety
sanctus: upright
socii: allies
tresviri monetales or *tresviri aere argento auro flando feriundo*: moneyers
tribuni militum: military tribunes

GLOSSARY OF RHETORICAL TERMS

The following are terms of grammar, rhetoric, prosody, and textual criticism used in the commentary.

anaphora Repetition of a word for emphasis at the head of successive clauses.

anticategoria 'Counter-accusation' a strategy of turning the tables on the prosecutor and claiming that he or his associates is, in fact, guilty of the crime.

apodosis The main clause of a conditional sentence.

argumentation (*argumentatio* or *probatio*) According to ancient theory, one of the major subdivisions of a forensic speech, placed after the narrative (*narratio*) or, if this is counted as separate, the division of topics (*divisio* or *partitio*) and before the refutation (*refutatio*) but sometimes combined with the latter; cf. Lausberg 1998, §262.

clausula Concluding rhythm of a clause or sentence; Cicero (and other prose authors) tended to favour clausulae of a certain prosodic shape.

cretic A unit of prosody comprising a heavy syllable followed by a light syllable and another heavy syllable, whereby a 'heavy' syllable contains a long vowel or diphthong or a short vowel followed by two consonants.

diaeresis 'Division'; the corresponding Latin term is *distributio*. The dividing up of a subject into its constituent parts in order to give it greater rhetorical weight; cf. Lausberg 1998, §675.

divisio The announcement of the subdivisions of the argumentation, sometimes treated as a separate 'part' of the speech; see 'argumentation'.

exordium In rhetorical theory the first 'part' of the speech, its aim being to render the listener attentive, teachable, and favourably disposed; cf. Lausberg 1998, §267.

figura etymologica A syntactic pattern whereby two cognate words appear in the same sentence.

gemination Doubling of a word for emphasis.

haplography Scribal error by which a word is skipped or truncated through confusion of the same or similar letters.

hendiadys A figure whereby two words are coordinated when one would be expected to modify the other.

hyperbole Exaggeration.

invention The first of the 'parts' of rhetoric the discovery of arguments, the means for which were much elaborated in rhetorical theory; cf. Lausberg 1998, §§260–442.

litotes An assertion made by negation of the opposite; understatement.

narrative (*narratio*) Account of the facts of the case; according to rhetorical theory, the 'part' of a forensic speech following the exordium and preceding the *divisio* (if this is considered a separate part) or otherwise the argumentation; see 'argumentation'.

parts of rhetoric Five in number according to ancient theory: invention, disposition, elocution, memory, and delivery; cf. Lausberg 1998, §255.

polyptoton Use of the same noun in different cases for emphasis.

progymnasmata 'Preliminary exercises' used in rhetorical schools to train pupils separately in the various types of argument that comprise a speech, such as comparison, panegyric, fictive speech (attributed to another person), etc.; cf. Lausberg 1998, §1106–38.

tricolon Sentence comprised of three parallel clauses.

trochee Prosodic unit consisting of a heavy syllable followed by a light syllable.

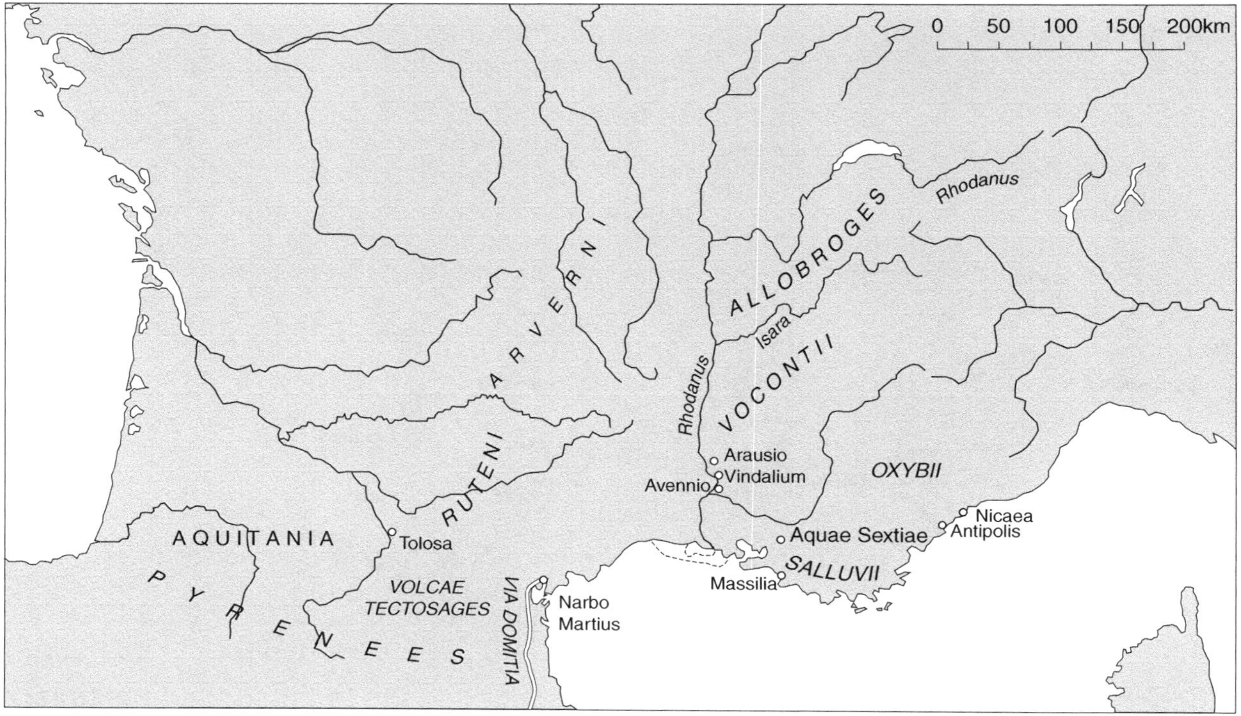

Map 1. Gaul in the 70s BC

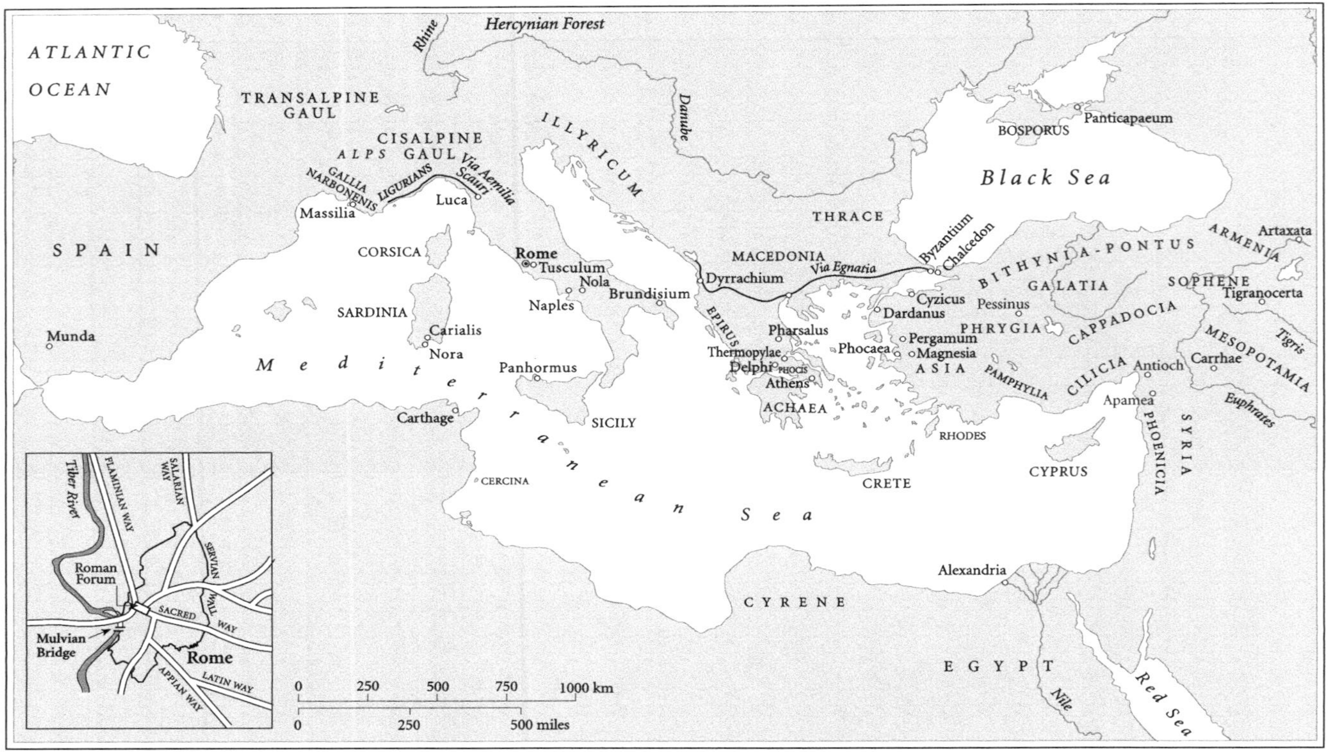

Map 2. The Roman World in the Late Republic

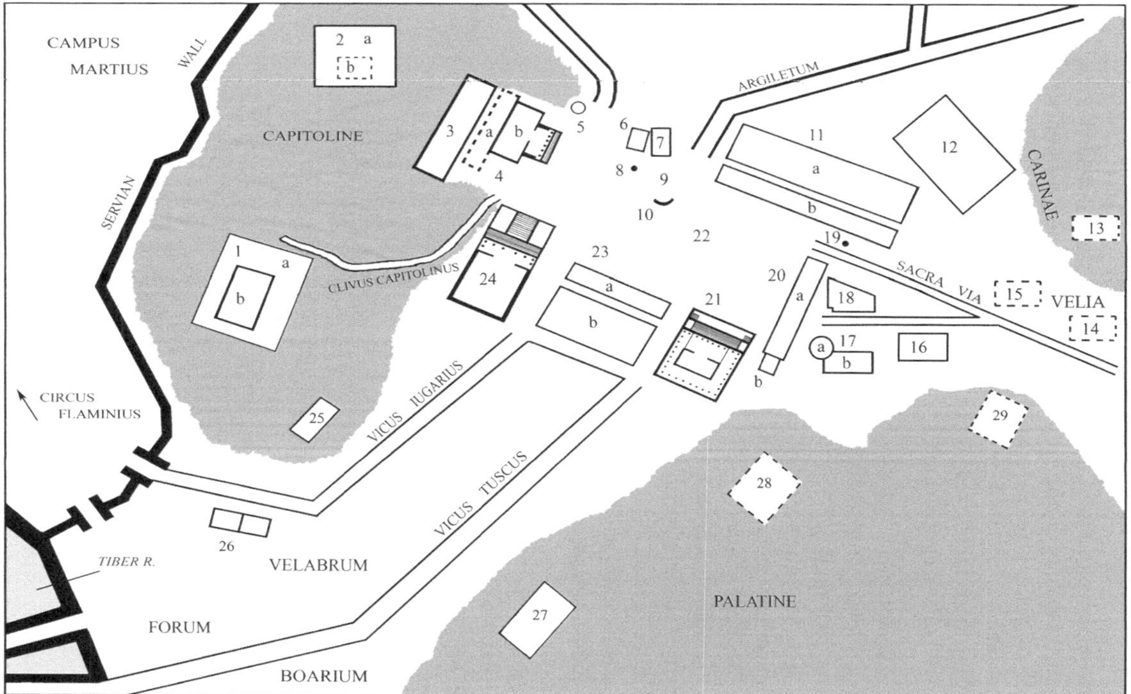

Map 3. Rome in the Late Republic

Rome in the Late Republic

The accompanying sketch-map represents the larger structures present in the centre of the city during the late Republic, whereby the basilica Sempronia (23b) is still in place, before being torn down to make way for the larger basilica Iulia ca. 54. Broken lines indicate structures whose location is uncertain; those mentioned in the text or commentary are noted by an asterisk (*) following the name.

1. a. Capitolium*
   b. Temple of Iuppiter Optimus Maximus*
2. a. *arx* (citadel)*
   b. *Temple* of Iuno Moneta (?)*
3. Tabularium (record depository)
4. a. Basilica Opimia (?)
   b. Temple of Concordia
5. carcer *Tullianum* (prison)
6. Basilica Porcia
7. Curia Hostilia (senate house)*
8. columna *Maenia*
9. Comitium*
10. Rostra
11. a. Basilica Fulvia / Paulli
    b. *tabernae novae* (shops)
12. Macellum (market)
13. Temple of Tellus (?)
14. Temple of Honos and Virtus (?)
15. Temple of the Penates (?)
16. domus *publica* (house of the *pontifex maximus*)
17. a. Temple of Vesta*
    b. Atrium of Vesta (dwelling of the Vestal Virgins)
18. Regia
19. Well-Head of Libo (?)
20. a. Basilica Aemilia
    b. *lacus Iuturnae* (sacred pool)
21. Temple of Castor and Pollux*
22. Forum*
23. a tabernae *veteres* (shops)
    b. Basilica Sempronia
24. Temple of Saturn and *aerarium* (treasury)*
25. Temple of Fides

26. Temples of Fortuna and Mater Matuta
27. Temple of the Magna Mater
28. Site of Cicero's house and the portico of Catulus on which Clodius built his shrine of Libertas (?)
29. Temple of Iuppiter Stator (?)

References

Achard, G. 1981. *Pratique rhétorique et idéologie politique dans les discours 'optimates' de Cicéron*. Mnemosyne Suppl. 68. Leiden.

Adams, J. N. 1978. 'Conventions of Naming in Cicero', *Classical Quarterly*, 72: 145–66.

Albrecht, M. von. 2003. *Cicero's Style*. Leiden and Boston.

Alexander, M. C. 1981. 'The *Legatio Asiatica* of Scaurus: Did it Take Place?', *Transactions of the American Philological Association* 111: 1–9.

—— 1982. 'Repetition of Prosecution and the Scope of Prosecutions in the Standing Criminal Courts of the Late Republic', *Classical Antiquity*, 1: 141–66.

—— 1985. '*Praemia* in the *Quaestiones* of the Late Republic', *Classical Philology*, 80: 20–32.

—— 2002. *The Case for the Prosecution in the Ciceronian Era*. Ann Arbor.

Astin, A. E. 1967. *Scipio Aemilianus*. Oxford.

Austin, R. G., ed. 1960. M. Tulli Ciceronis *Pro M. Caelio oratio*. 3rd edn. Oxford.

Axer, J. 1989. 'Tribunal–Stage–Arena: Modelling of the Communication Situation in M. Tullius Cicero's Judicial Speeches', *Rhetorica*, 7: 299–311.

Ayers, D. M. 1950. 'The Speeches of Cicero's Opponents: Studies in *Pro Roscio Amerino*, *In Verrem*, and *Pro Murena*'. Diss. Princeton.

Bablitz, L. 2007. *Actors and Audience in the Roman Courtroom*. London and New York.

Badian, E. 1958. *Foreign Clientelae*. Oxford.

—— 1964. *Studies in Greek and Roman History*. New York.

—— 1966. 'Notes on *Provincia Gallia* in the Late Republic' in R. Chevallier (ed.), *Mélanges d'archéologie et d'histoire offerts à André Piganiol*. Paris, ii. 901–18.

—— 1967. 'The Testament of Ptolemy Alexander', *Rheinisches Museum*, 110: 178–92.

—— 1969. 'Quaestiones Variae', *Historia*, 18: 447–91.

—— 1972. *Publicans and Sinners*. Ithaca, NY.

—— 1989. 'The *Scribae* of the Roman Republic', *Klio*, 71: 582–603.

—— 1993. 'The Legend of the Legate Who Lost his Luggage', *Historia*, 42: 203–10.

Ballance, M. H. 1966. 'The Origin of Africano', *Papers of the British School at Rome*, 34: 79–81.

Balsdon, J. P. V. D. 1938. 'The History of the Extortion Court at Rome, 123–70 B.C.', *Papers of the British School at Rome*, 14: 98–114.
——1979. *Romans and Aliens*. London.
Barlow, C. T. 1980. 'The Roman Government and the Roman Economy, 92–80 B.C.', *Transactions of the American Philological Association*, 101: 202–19.
Bates, R. L. 1986. '*Rex in Senatu*: A Political Biography of M. Aemilius Scaurus', *Proceedings of the American Philosophical Society*, 130: 251–88.
Beard, M. 2007. *The Roman Triumph*. Cambridge, Mass.
——and J. North. 1990. *Roman Priests: Religion and Power in the Ancient World*. Ithaca, NY.
——J. North, and S. Price. 1998. *Religions of Rome*. 2 vols. Cambridge.
Bellen, H. 1985. *Metus Gallicus—Metus Punicus: Zum Furchtmotiv in der römischen Republik*. Akademie der Wissenschaften und der Literatur Mainz Abhandlungen der geistes- und sozialwissenschaftlichen Klasse, 3. Stuttgart.
Berger, A. 1953. *Encyclopedic Dictionary of Roman Law*. Transactions of the American Philosophical Society NS 43/2. Philadelphia.
Berger, D. 1978. *Cicero als Erzähler*. Frankfurt am Main.
Berry, D. H. 2000, tr. Cicero. *Defence Speeches*. Oxford.
——and A. Erskine, eds. 2010. *Form and Function in Roman Oratory*. Cambridge.
Berthold, H. 1965. 'Die Gestalt des Themistokles bei M. Tullius Cicero', *Klio*, 43–5: 38–48.
Birks, P., A. Rodger, and J. S. Richardson. 1984. 'Further Aspects of the *Tabula Contrebiensis*', *Journal of Roman Studies*, 74: 45–73.
Bleicken, J. 1981. *Zum Begriff der römischen Amtsgewalt: Auspicium—potestas—imperium*. Nachrichten der Akademie der Wissenschaften, Philol.-hist. Klasse, 1981/9. Göttingen.
——1995. *Cicero und die Ritter*. Abhandlungen der Akademie der Wissenschaften. Philol.-hist. Klasse, 3/213. Göttingen.
Bloch, G. 1909. 'M. Aemilius Scaurus. Étude sur l'histoire des partis au VIIe siècle de Rome', *Mélanges d'histoire ancienne*, 25: 1–81.
Bonnet, M. 1906. 'Le Dilemme de C. Gracchus', *Revue des Études Anciennes*, 8: 40–6.
Bradley, K. R. 1991. *Discovering the Roman Family*. New York and Oxford.
——1994. *Slavery and Society at Rome*. Cambridge.
Brennan, C. 2000. *The Praetorship in the Roman Republic*. 2 vols. Oxford and New York.
Brinton, A. 1988. 'Cicero's Use of Historical Examples in Moral Argument', *Philosophy and Rhetoric*, 21: 169–84.
Brunt, P. A. 1965. '"Amicitia" in the Late Roman Republic', *Proceedings of the Cambridge Philological Society*, 11: 1–20.

——1971. *Italian Manpower 225 B.C.-A.D. 14*. London.

——1988. *The Fall of the Roman Republic and Related Essays*. Oxford.

Bücher, F. 2006. *Verargumentierte Geschichte: Exempla Romana im politischen Diskurs der späten römischen Republik*. Stuttgart.

Buckland, W. W. 1908. *The Roman Law of Slavery*. Cambridge.

——1963. *A Text-Book of Roman Law*. Cambridge.

Bulst, C. M. 1964. '"Cinnanum Tempus"', *Historia*, 13: 307–37.

Burkert, W. 1985. *Greek Religion, Archaic and Classical*, tr. J. Raffan. Oxford.

Campardou, J. 1949. 'Un milliaire de Cneus Domitius Ahenobarbus imperator découvert à Treilles (Aude)', *Gallia*, 7: 195–205.

Chandler, D. C. 1978. 'Quaestor Ostiensis', *Historia*, 27: 328–35.

Chevallier, R. 1976. *Roman Roads*, tr. N. H. Field. Berkeley-Los Angeles.

Christol, M. 2010. *Une histoire provinciale: La Gaule narbonnaise de la fin du IIe siècle av. J.-C. au IIIe siècle ap. J.-C.* Paris.

Citroni Marchetti, S. 1995. 'Lo spazio straniato: Percorsi psicologici e percezione del tribunale nelle orazioni di Cicerone "pro Fonteio", "pro Q. Roscio comoedo", "pro Cluentio". I', *Materiali e Discussioni per l'analisi dell'antichità*, 35: 9–57.

Clark, A. C., ed. 1907. *Q. Asconii Pediani orationum Ciceronis quinque enarratio*. Oxford.

Clemente, G. 1974. *I Romani nella Gallia meridionale (II–I sec. a.C.)*. Bologna.

Coarelli, F. 1988. *Il foro Boario dalle origine alla fine della Repubblica*. Rome.

Constans, L. A. 1921. *Un correspondant de Cicéron, Ap. Claudius Pulcher*. Paris.

Corbeill, A. 1996. *Controlling Laughter: Political Humor in the Late Roman Republic*. Princeton.

——2010. 'The Function of a Divinely Inspired Text in Cicero's *De haruspicum responsis*', in D. H. Berry and A. Erskine (eds.), *Form and Function in Roman Oratory*, Cambridge, 139–54.

Coskun, A. 2006. '*Quaestiones Fonteianae:* Staatsraison und Klientelpolitik im Kontext von Ciceros *Pro M. Fonteio oratio*', *Latomus*, 65: 354–63.

Cottier, M., *et al.*, eds. 2008. *The Customs Law of Asia*. Oxford.

Courtney, E. 1961. 'The Prosecution of Scaurus in 54 B.C.', *Philologus*, 105: 151–6.

Cowan, E. 2008. '*Libertas* in the *Philippics*', in T. Stevenson and M. Wilson (eds.), *Cicero's Philippics: History, Rhetoric and ideology*. Auckland, 140–52.

Cowles, F. H. 1917. *Gaius Verres: An Historical Study*. Ithaca, NY.

Craig, C. P. 1981. 'The *Accusator* as *Amicus*: An Original Roman Tactic of Ethical Argumentation', *Transactions of the American Philological Association*, 111: 31–7.

——1986. 'Cato's Stoicism and the Understanding of Cicero's Speech for Murena', *Transactions of the American Philological Association*, 116: 229–39.

Craig, C. P. 2004. 'Audience Expectations, Invective and Proof', in J. G. F. Powell and J. Paterson (eds.), *Cicero the Advocate*. Oxford, 187–213.

Crawford, J. W. 1984. *M. Tullius Cicero: The Lost and Unpublished Orations*. Göttingen.

Dahlheim, W. 1977. *Gewalt und Herrschaft: Das provinziale Herrschaftssystem der römischen Republik*. Berlin and New York.

D'Arms, J. H. 1972. 'Pro Murena 16 and Cicero's Use of Historical Exempla', *Phoenix*, 26: 82–4.

David, J.-M. 1995. 'Le Tribunal du préteur: Contraints symboliques et politiques sous la République et le début de l'Empire', *Klio*, 77: 371–85.

Diehl, H. 1988. *Sulla und seine Zeit im Urteil Ciceros*. Hildesheim.

Dihle, A. 1994. *Die Griechen und die Fremden*. Munich.

Dilke, O. A. W. 1980. 'Divided Loyalties in Eastern Sicily under Verres', *Ciceroniana*, NS 4: 43–51.

Doyle, M. W. 1986. *Empires*. Ithaca, NY, and London.

Dubouloz, J. 2007. 'Autorité romaine, fermiers de l'impot et contribuables en Sicile les années 70 av. J.-C.', in J. Dubouloz and S. Pittia (eds.), *La Sicile de Cicéron*. Besançon, 147–68.

Dufallo, B. 2007. *The Ghosts of the Past: Latin Literature, the Dead and Rome's Transition to a Principate*. Columbus, Ohio.

Duval, P.-M. 1949. 'A propos du milliaire de Cneus Ahenobarbus trouvé dans l'Aude en 1949', *Gallia*, 7: 207–31.

Dyck, A. R. 1996. *A Commentary on Cicero*, De officiis. Ann Arbor.

——1998. 'Narrative Obfuscation, Philosophical *Topoi* and Tragic Patterning in Cicero's *Pro Milone*', *Harvard Studies in Classical Philology*, 98: 219–41.

——2001. 'Dressing to Kill: Attire as a Proof and Means of Characterization in Cicero's Speeches', *Arethusa*, 34: 119–30.

——ed., comm. 2003. Cicero, *De natura deorum I*. Cambridge.

——2004. *A Commentary on Cicero*, De legibus. Ann Arbor.

——ed., comm. 2008*a*. Cicero, *Catilinarians*. Cambridge.

——2008*b*. 'Rivals into Partners: Hortensius and Cicero', *Historia*, 57: 142–73.

——ed., comm. 2010. Cicero, *Pro Sexto Roscio*. Cambridge.

——2011. 'Cicero's Abridgement of his Speeches for Publication', in M. Horster and C. Reitz (eds.), *Condensed Texts - Condensing Texts*. Wiesbaden, 369–74.

Dyson, S. L. 1985. *The Creation of the Roman Frontier*. Princeton.

——and R. J. Rowland, jr. 2007. *Shepherds, Sailors, and Conquerors: Archaeology and History in Sardinia from the Stone Age to the Middle Ages*. Philadelphia.

Earl, D. C. 1967. *The Moral and Political Tradition of Rome*. Ithaca, NY.

Ebel, C. 1975. 'Pompey's Organization of Transalpina', *Phoenix*, 29: 358–73.

—— 1976. *Transalpine Gaul: The Emergence of a Roman Province*. Leiden.

Epstein, D. F. 1987. *Personal Enmity in Roman Politics 218–43 BC*. London.

Faraone, C. A. 1992. *Talismans and Trojan Horses: Guardian Statues in Greek Myth and Ritual*. New York and Oxford.

Flacelière, R. 1977. 'Cicéron à Delphes?', *Études Delphiques à la mémoire de P. De La Coste-Messelière*. Paris, 159–60.

Flower, H. I. 1996. *Ancestor Masks and Aristocratic Power in Roman Culture*. Oxford.

Frank, T. 1933. *ESAR* i.

Frazel, T. D. 2009. *The Rhetoric of Cicero's 'In Verrem'*. Göttingen.

Freyburger, G. 1986. *Fides: Étude sémantique et religieuse depuis les origines jusqu'à l'époque augustéenne*. Paris.

Fugier, H. 1963. *Recherches sur l'expression du sacré dans la langue latine*. Paris.

Futrell, A. 1997. *Blood in the Arena: The Spectacle of Roman Power*. Austin, Tex.

Garnsey, P. 1988. *Famine and Food Supply in the Greco-Roman World: Responses to Risk and Crisis*. Cambridge.

Garuti, I., ed. 1967. M. T. Ciceronis *Pro M. Fonteio oratio*. Milan.

Gaumitz, H. 1879. *De M. Aemilii Scauri causa repetundarum et de Ciceronis pro Scauro oratione*. Diss. Leipzig = *Leipziger Studien zur classischen Philologie*, 2: 249–89.

Gayraud, M. 1981. *Narbonne antique*. Paris.

Geer, R. M. 1929. 'M. Aemilius Scaurus (Suetonius *Nero* ii. 1 and Asconius on Cicero *Pro Scauro* 1)', *Classical Philology*, 24: 292–4.

Gelzer, M. 1969. *Cicero, ein biographischer Versuch*. Wiesbaden.

—— 1984. *Pompeius: Lebensbild eines Römers*. 2nd edn., ed. L. Herrmann-Otto. Stuttgart.

Gnoli, F. 1971. *Marmora romana*. Rome.

Gotoff, H. C. 1986. 'Cicero's Analysis of the Prosecution Speeches in the *Pro Caelio*: An Exercise in Practical Criticism', *Classical Philology*, 81: 122–32.

Greenidge, A. H. J. 1901. *The Legal Procedure of Cicero's Time*. Oxford.

Grenier, A. 1937. 'La Gaule romaine', *ESAR* iii. 379–644.

Gruen, E. S. 1964. 'Politics and the Courts in 104 B.C.', *Transactions of the American Philological Association*, 95: 99–110.

—— 1965. 'The *lex Varia*', *Journal of Roman Studies*, 55: 59–73.

—— 1968. *Roman Politics and the Criminal Courts, 149–78 B.C.* Cambridge, Mass.

—— 1971. 'Pompey, Metellus Pius and the Trials of 70–69 B.C.: The Perils of Schematism', *American Journal of Philology*, 92: 1–16.

—— 1974. *The Last Generation of the Roman Republic*. Berkeley, Los Angeles, and London.

Hadas, M. 1930. *Sextus Pompey*. New York.

Hanssen, J. S. T. 1951. *Latin Diminutives: A Semantic Study*. Bergen.
Harris, W. V. 1979. *War and Imperialism in Republican Rome, 327–70 B.C.* Oxford.
Hartung, H.-J. 1974. 'Religio und sapientia iudicum: Einige grundsätzliche Bemerkungen zu einem Geschworenenspiegel in Ciceros Reden', *Hermes*, 102: 556–66.
Hassall, M., M. Crawford, and J. Reynolds. 1974. 'Rome and the Eastern Provinces at the End of the Second Century B.C.: The So-Called "Piracy Law" and the New Inscription from Cnidos', *Journal of Roman Studies*, 64: 195–220.
Hellegouarc'h, J. 1972. *Le Vocabulaire latin des relations et des partis politiques sous la République*. 2nd edn. Paris.
Henderson, C. 1958. 'The Career of the Younger M. Aemilius Scaurus', *Classical Journal*, 53: 194–206.
Henderson, M. I. 1951. 'The Process "de repetundis"', *Journal of Roman Studies*, 41: 71–88.
Hermon, E. 1993. *Rome et la Gaule transalpine avant César 125–59 av. J.-C.* Naples and Quebec.
—— 1995. 'Pouvoir et revenus en Transalpine au Ier siècle av. J.-C.: Un aspect du rapport centre-périphérie', *Revue des Études Anciennes*, 97: 565–74.
Hesberg, H. von. 2005. 'Die Häuser der Senatoren in Rom: Gesellschaftliche und politische Funktion', in W. Eck and M. Heil (eds.), *Senatores populi Romani: Realität und mediale Präsentation einer Führungsschicht*. Stuttgart, 19–46.
Hinard, F. 1980. '*Paternus inimicus*: Sur une expression de Cicéron', *Mélanges de littérature et d'épigraphie latines, d'histoire ancienne et d'archéologie: Hommages à la mémoire de Pierre Wuilleumier*. Paris, 197–210.
Hirschfeld, O. 1913. 'Die Haeduer und Arverner unter Römischer Herrschaft', in *Kleine Schriften*. Berlin, 186–208.
Hofmann, J. B. 2003. *La lingua d'uso latina*. 3rd edn., ed. L. Ricottilli. Bologna.
Hollis, A. S., ed. 2007. *Fragments of Roman Poetry c. 60 BC–AD 20*. Oxford.
Holst, H. 1925. *Die Wortspiele in Ciceros Reden*. Symbolae Osloenses Suppl. 1. Oslo.
Humbert, J. 1925. *Les Plaidoyers écrits et les plaidoiries réelles de Cicéron*. Paris.
Huss, W. 1985. *Geschichte der Karthager*. Munich.
Hutchinson, G. O. 2010. 'Deflected Addresses: Apostrophe and Speech (Sophocles, Aeschines, Plautus, Cicero, Virgil and Others)', *Classical Quarterly*, 60: 96–109.
Innocenti, B. 1994. 'Towards a Theory of Vivid Description as Practiced in Cicero's *Verrine* Orations', *Rhetorica*, 12: 355–81.

Isaac, B. 2004. *The Invention of Racism in Classical Antiquity*. Princeton and Oxford.

Itgenshorst, T. 2005. Tota illa pompa: *Der Triumph in der römischen Republik*. Göttingen.

Johannemann, R. 1935. *Cicero und Pompeius in ihren wechselseitigen Beziehungen bis zum Jahre 51 vor Christi Geburt*. Emsdetten.

John, C. 1876. 'Sallustius über Catilinas Candidatur im Jahr 688', *Rheinisches Museum*, 31: 401–31.

Jouanique, P. 1960. 'Sur l'interprétation du *Pro Fonteio*, 1, 1–2', *Revue des Études Latines*, 38: 107–12.

Kajanto, I. 1965. *The Latin Cognomina*. Helsinki.

Kaster, R. A., ed., tr., comm. 1995. C. Suetonius Tranquillus, *De grammaticis et rhetoribus*. Oxford.

——2005. *Emotion, Restraint and Community in Ancient Rome*. Oxford.

Kelly, G. P. 2006. *A History of Exile in the Roman Republic*. Cambridge.

Kienast, D. 1965. 'Rom und die Venus vom Eryx', *Hermes*, 93: 478–89.

Klodt, C. 1992. *Ciceros Rede Pro Rabirio Postumo. Einleitung und Kommentar*. Stuttgart.

——2007. Review of Siani-Davies 2001, *Gnomon*, 79: 597–605.

Kunkel, W., and R. Wittmann. 1995. *Staatsordnung und Staatspraxis der römischen Republik*. ii. *Die Magistratur*. Munich.

Labruna, L. 1976. *Il console sovversivo*. Naples.

Laet, S. de. 1949. *Portorium: Étude sur l'organisation douanière chez les Romains, surtout à l'époque du haut-empire*. Bruges.

Latte, K. 1960. *Römische Religionsgeschichte*. Munich.

——1968. *Kleine Schriften zu Religion, Recht, Literatur und Sprache der Griechen und Römer*, ed. O. Gigon, W. Buchwald, and W. Kunkel. Munich.

Laurence, R. 2001. 'Afterword: Travel and Empire', in C. Adams and R. Laurence (eds.), *Travel and Geography in the Roman Empire*. London and New York, 167–77.

Lausberg, H. 1998. *Handbook of Literary Rhetoric: A Foundation for Literary Study*, tr. M. T. Bliss, A. Jansen, D. E. Orton, ed. D. E. Orton and R. D. Anderson. Leiden.

Leigh, M. 1995. 'Wounding and Popular Rhetoric at Rome', *Bulletin of the Institute of Classical Studies*, 40: 195–215.

Lenardon, R. J. 1978. *The Saga of Themistocles*. London.

Levy, E. 1933. 'Von den römischen Anklägervergehen', *Zeitschrift der Savigny-Stiftung für Rechtsgeschichte*, 53: 151–233.

Lewis, R. G., tr., comm. 2006. Asconius, *Commentaries on Speeches of Cicero*. Oxford.

Lintott, A. W. 1981. 'The Leges de Repetundis and Associate Measures under the Republic', *Zeitschrift der Savigny-Stiftung für Rechtsgeschichte*, 98: 162–212.

Lintott, A. W. 1992. *Judicial Reform and Land Reform in the Roman Republic: A New Edition, with Translation and Commentary, of the Laws from Urbino*. Cambridge.
——1999. *The Constitution of the Roman Republic*. Oxford.
——2008. *Cicero as Evidence*. Oxford.
Loutsch, C. 1994. *L'Exorde dans les discours de Cicéron*. Brussels.
Lovano, M. 2002. *The Age of Cinna: Crucible of Late Republican Rome*. Stuttgart.
Lowe, E. A. 1934. *Codices Latini Antiquiores*, part 1. Oxford.
Lundström, S. 1960. 'Falsche Eigennamen in den Tuskulanen', *Eranos*, 58: 66–79.
McDermott, W. C. 1971. 'Q. Cicero', *Historia*, 20: 702–17.
MacKendrick, P. 1995. *The Speeches of Cicero*. London.
Madvig, I. N. 1828. *De Asconii Pediani aliorum veterum interpretum in Ciceronis orationes commentariis disputatio critica*. Copenhagen.
Mai, A., ed. 1814. *M. Tulii Ciceronis trium orationum pro Scauro, pro Tullio, pro Flacco partes ineditae*. Milan.
Maltby, R. 1991. *A Lexicon of Ancient Latin Etymologies*. Leeds.
Marinone, N. 2004. *Cronologia ciceroniana*. 2nd edn., ed. E. Malaspina. Rome and Bologna.
Marshall, B. A. 1976. 'Some Crassi in Cicero's *Pro Scauro*', *Latomus*, 35: 91–6.
——1977. 'Two Court Cases in the Late Second Century B.C.', *American Journal of Philology*, 98: 417–23.
——1985. *A Historical Commentary on Asconius*. Columbia, Ohio.
Marshall, P. K. 1979. 'The Learning of Servatus Lupus', *Mediaeval Studies*, 41: 514–23.
Meiggs, R. 1960. *Roman Ostia*. Oxford.
Meloni, P. 1949. 'Sei anni di lotte di Sardi e Corsi contro i Romani (236–231 a.C.)', *Studi Sardi*, 9: 121–41.
Meyer, H. D. 1957. *Cicero und das Reich*. Diss. Cologne.
Meyer, I. 2003. 'Zur Datierung von Ciceros Rede *de haruspicum responso*', *Göttinger Forum für Altertumswissenschaft*, 6: 97–109.
Miles, M. 2001. 'Plato on Suicide (Phaedo 60C–63C)', *Phoenix*, 55: 244–58.
Mommsen, T. 1864–79. *Römische Forschungen*. 2 vols. Berlin.
——1887–8. *Römisches Staatsrecht*. 3 vols in 5. Berlin.
——1899. *Römisches Strafrecht*. Leipzig.
Morstein-Marx, R. [as Kallet-Marx, R. M.] 1989. 'Asconius 14–15 Clark and the Date of Q. Mucius Scaevola's Command in Asia', *Classical Philology*, 84: 305–12.
——1995. *Hegemony to Empire: The Development of the Roman* Imperium *in the East from 148 to 62 BC*. Berkeley.

——2004. *Mass Oratory and Political Power in the Late Roman Republic.* Cambridge.

Moscati, S. 1967. 'Africa Ipsa Parens Illa Sardiniae', *Rivista di Filologia e di Istruzione Classica,* 95: 385–8.

Motzo, B. R. 1936. 'Cesare e la Sardegna', in *Sardegna romana.* Rome, 25–49.

Münzer, F. 1999 (orig. 1920). *Roman Aristocratic Parties and Families,* tr. T. Ridley. Baltimore and London.

Nicolet, C. 1966–74. *L'Ordre équestre à l'époque républicaine (312–43 av. J.-C.).* 2 vols. Paris.

——1967. 'Arpinum, Aemilius Scaurus et les Tulli Cicerones', *Revue des Études Latines,* 45: 276–304.

——2000. *Censeurs et publicains: Économie et fiscalité dans la Rome antique.* Paris.

Niebuhr, B. G., ed. 1820. *M. Tullii Ciceronis orationum pro M. Fonteio et pro C. Rabirio fragmenta.* Rome.

North, H. F. 2000. '*Lacrimae Virginis Vestalis*', in S. K. Dickison and J. P. Hallett (eds.), *Rome and her Monuments: Essays on the City and Literature of Rome in Honor of Katherine A. Geffcken.* Wauconda, 357–67.

Olechowska, E., ed. 1984. *M. Tullius Cicero,* fasc. 25a. *Pro M. Scauro oratio.* Leipzig.

Oleson, J. P., ed. 2008. *The Oxford Handbook of Engineering and Technology in the Ancient World.* Oxford.

Orlin, E. 1997. *Temples, Religion and Politics in the Roman Republic.* Leiden.

Osthoff, G. 1952. *Tumultus—Seditio: Untersuchungen zum römischen Staatsrecht und zur politischen Terminologie der Römer.* Diss. Cologne.

Otto, A. 1890. *Die Sprichwörter und sprichwörtlichen Redenarten der Römer.* Leipzig.

Parke, H. W., and D. E. W. Wormell. 1956. *The Delphic Oracle.* 2 vols. Oxford.

Paterson, J. 1978. '*Transalpinae Gentes*: Cicero, *De re publica* 3.16', *Classical Quarterly,* 28: 452–8.

Peyron, A., ed. 1824. *M. Tulli Ciceronis orationum pro Scauro, pro Tullio et in Clodium fragmenta inedita.* Stuttgart and Tübingen.

Piazza, M. P. 1987. 'La "lex Valeria" e le "tabulae dodrantariae et quadrantariae"', in *Studi in onore di Arnaldo Biscardi.* Milan, vi. 267–91.

Podlecki, A. J. 1975. *The Life of Themistocles.* Montreal and London.

Pöschl, V. 1983. *Literatur und geschichtliche Wirklichkeit: Kleine Schriften II,* ed. W.-L. Liebermann. Heidelberg.

Powell, J. G. F., ed., comm. 1988. Cicero, *Cato maior de senectute.* Cambridge.

——2010. 'Court Procedure and Rhetorical Strategy in Cicero', in D. H. Berry and A. Erskine (eds.), *Form and Function in Roman Oratory,* Cambridge, 21–36.

Powell, J. G. F. and J. Paterson, eds. 2004. *Cicero the Advocate*. Oxford.

Pritchard, R. T. 1971. 'Gaius Verres and the Sicilian Farmers', *Historia*, 20: 224–38.

—— 1975. '*Perpaucae Siciliae Civitates*: Notes on *Verr.* 2,3,6,13', *Historia*, 24: 33–47.

Radke, G. 1964. 'Römische Strassen in der Gallia Cisalpina und der Narbonensis', *Klio*, 42: 299–317.

Rambaud, M. 1980. 'Le Pro Fonteio et l'assimilation des Gaulois de la Transalpine', in *Mélanges de litérature et d'épigraphie latines d'histoire ancienne et d'archéologie: Hommage à la mémoire de Pierre Willeumier*. Paris, 301–16.

Rancoule, G. 1985. 'Observations sur la diffusion des importations italiques dans l'Aude aux IIe et Ier siècles avant J.-C.', *Revue archéologique de Narbonnaise*, 18: 263–75.

Rawson, E. 1977. 'More on the *Clientelae* of the Patrician Claudii', *Historia*, 26: 340–57 = *Roman Culture and Society*. Oxford, 1991, 227–44.

—— 1991. *Roman Culture and Society: Collected Papers*. Oxford.

Reeve, M. D. 1992. 'The Turin Palimpsest of Cicero', *Aevum*, 66: 87–94.

Reinhardt, T., ed., tr., comm. 2003. *Cicero's* Topica. Oxford.

Reinhold, M. 1970. *History of Purple as a Status Symbol in Antiquity*. Brussels.

Reynolds, L. D., ed. 1983. *Texts and Transmission: A Survey of the Latin Classics*. Oxford.

Richardson, J. S. 1983. 'The *Tabula Contrebiensis*: Roman Law in Spain in the Early First Century B.C.', *Journal of Roman Studies*, 73: 33–41.

—— 1986. *Hispaniae: Spain and the Development of Roman Imperialism*. Cambridge.

—— 1987. 'The Purpose of the Lex Calpurnia de Repetundis', *Journal of Roman Studies*, 77: 1–12.

Richardson, L., jr. 1992. *A New Topographical Dictionary of Ancient Rome*. Baltimore and London.

Rickman, G. 1980. *The Corn Supply of Ancient Rome*. Oxford.

Riedweg, C. 1997. '"Pythagoras hinterliess keine einzige Schrift"—ein Irrtum?' *Museum Helveticum*, 54: 65–92.

Riggsby, A. M. 1997. '"Public" and "Private" in Roman Culture: The Case of the *Cubiculum*', *Journal of Roman Archaeology*, 10: 36–56.

—— 1999*a*. *Crime and Community in Ciceronian Rome*. Austin, Tex.

—— 1999*b*. 'Iulius Victor on Cicero's Defenses *de Repetundis*', *Rheinisches Museum*, 142: 427–9.

—— 2006. *Caesar in Gaul and Rome: War in Words*. Austin, Tex.

Riginos, A. S. 1976. *Platonica: The Anecdotes Concerning the Life and Writings of Plato*. Leiden.

Rilinger, R. 1976. *Der Einfluss des Wahlleiters bei den römischen Konsulwahlen von 366 bis 60 v. Chr.* Munich.

Risselada, R. 1996. 'And Now for Something Completely Different? Temporal Discourse Markers: Latin *Nunc* and English *Now*', in R. Risselada, J. R. De Jong, and A. M. Bolkestein (eds.), *On Latin: Linguistic and Literary Studies in Honour of Harm Pinkster*. Amsterdam, 105–25.

Rivet, A. L. F. 1988. *Gallia Narbonensis: Southern France in Roman Times*. London.

Robinson, O. F. 1973. 'Blasphemy and Sacrilege in Roman Law', *Irish Jurist*, 8: 356–71.

—— 1981. 'Slaves and the Criminal Law', *Zeitschrift der Savigny-Stiftung für Rechtsgeschichte*, 98: 213–54.

—— 1995. *The Criminal Law of Ancient Rome*. London.

Rollinger, C. 2009. *Solvendi sunt nummi: Die Schuldenkultur der späten römischen Republik im Spiegel der Schriften Ciceros*. Berlin.

Roloff, H. 1938. *Maiores bei Cicero*. Diss. Göttingen.

Rosenstein, N. 1986. '*Imperatores Victi*: The Case of C. Hostilius Mancinus', *Classical Antiquity*, 5: 230–52.

Rotondi, G. 1912. *Leges publicae populi Romani*. Milan.

Rowland, R. J., Jr. 2001. *The Periphery in the Center: Sardinia in the Ancient and Medieval Worlds*. Oxford.

Ruebel, J. S. 1975. 'When Did Cicero Learn about the Conference at Luca?', *Historia*, 24: 622–4.

Rüpke, J. 2007. *Römische Priester in der Antike*. Stuttgart.

—— 2008. *Fasti Sacerdotum*, tr. D. M. B. Richardson. Oxford.

Ryan, F. X. 1996. 'The Quaestorships of Hirtuleius and M. Fonteius', *Hermes*, 124: 250–3.

—— 1998. *Rank and Participation in the Republican Senate*. Stuttgart.

de Ste Croix, G. E. M. 1956. 'Greek and Roman Accounting', in A. C. Littleton and B. S. Yamey, eds., *Studies in the History of Accounting*. Homewood, Ill., 14–74.

Salmon, E. T. 1969. *Roman Colonization under the Republic*. London.

Sanders, H. A. 1932. 'The So-Called First Triumvirate', *Memoirs of the American Academy in Rome*, 10: 55–68.

Scheidel, W., I. Morris, and R. Saller, eds. 2007. *The Cambridge Economic History of the Greco-Roman World*. Cambridge.

Schmitz, D. 1985. *Zeugen des Prozeßgegners in Gerichtsreden Ciceros*. Prismata, 1. Frankfurt a.M.

Schneider, A. R. 1876. *Quaestionum in Ciceronis pro M. Fonteio orationem capita quattuor*. Diss. Leipzig.

Schönberger, H. 1911. *Beispiele aus der Geschichte: Ein rhetorisches Kunstmittel in Ciceros Reden*. Augsburg.

Schulze, W. 1904. *Zur Geschichte lateinischer Eigennamen*. Abh. d. königl. Gesellschaft der Wissenschaften zu Göttingen, philol.-hist. Kl., N.F. 5/5. Berlin.

Scullard, H. H. 1981. *Festivals and Ceremonies of the Roman Republic*. London.

Seager, R. 1972. 'Cicero and the Word *Popularis*', *Classical Quarterly*, 22: 328–38.

——2002. *Pompey the Great: A Political Biography*. 2nd edn. Oxford.

Shackleton Bailey, D. R. 1970. 'The Prosecution of Roman Magistrates-Elect', *Phoenix*, 24: 162–5.

——1975. Review of Gruen 1974, *American Journal of Philology*, 96: 436–43.

——ed. and tr. 1986 *Cicero, Philippics*. Chapel Hill, NC, and London.

Shatzman, I. 1975. *Senatorial Wealth and Roman Politics*. Brussels.

Siani-Davies, M., tr. and comm. 2001. *Cicero's Speech Pro Rabirio Postumo*. Oxford.

Sinkovich, K. A. 1974. 'Cicero Historicus', *Rivista di Studi Classici*, 22: 164–75.

Sherwin-White, A. N. 1973. *The Roman Citizenship*.[2] Oxford.

Skutsch, O., ed. and comm. 1985. *The Annales of Q. Ennius*. Oxford.

Smallwood, E. M. 1967. *Documents Illustrating the Principates of Gaius, Claudius and Nero*. Cambridge.

Spielvogel, J. 1993. *Amicitia und res publica: Ciceros Maxime während der innenpolitischen Auseinandersetzungen der Jahre 59–50 v. Chr.* Stuttgart.

——1997. 'P. Clodius Pulcher: Eine politische Ausnahme-Erscheinung der späten Republik?', *Hermes*, 125: 56–74.

Spina, L. 1989. 'Cleombroto, la fortuna di un suicidio', *Vichiana*, 18: 12–39.

Stockton, D. 1979. *The Gracchi*. Oxford.

Stroh, W. 1975. *Taxis und Taktik*. Stuttgart.

——2008. *Cicero: Redner Staatsmann, Philosoph*. Munich.

Suerbaum, W., ed. 2002. *Die archaische Literatur von den Anfängen bis Sullas Tod. Handbuch der lateinischen Literatur der Antike*, ed. R. Herzog and P. L. Schmidt, 1. Munich.

Sumner, G. V. 1976. 'Scaurus and the Mamilian Inquisition', *Phoenix*, 30: 73–5.

Suolahti, J. 1955. *The Junior Officers of the Roman Army in the Republican Period*. Helsinki.

——1972. 'Princeps Senatus', *Arctos*, 7: 207–18.

Swain, S. 2007. 'Polemon's *Physiognomy*', in S. Swain (ed.), *Seeing the Face, Seeing the Soul: Polemon's* Physiognomy *from Classical Antiquity to Medieval Islam*. Oxford, 125–201.

Talbert, R. J. A. 2000. *Barrington Atlas of the Greek and Roman World*. Princeton and Oxford.

Tatum, W. J. 1999. *The Patrician Tribune Publius Clodius Pulcher*. Chapel Hill, NC, and London.

Taylor, L. R. 1942. 'Caesar's Colleagues in the Pontifical College', *American Journal of Philology*, 63: 385–412.

—— 1960. *The Voting Districts of the Roman Republic*. Rome.

Tchernia, A. 1983. 'Italian Wine in Gaul at the End of the Republic', in P. Garnsey, K. Hopkins and C. R. Whittaker (eds.), *Trade in the Ancient Economy*. Berkeley and Los Angeles, 87–104.

—— 1986. *Le Vin de l'Italie romaine*. Rome.

Thilo, R. M. 1980. *Der Codex accepti et expensi im römischen Recht. Ein Beitrag zur Lehre von der Litteralobligation*. Göttingen.

Thomasson, B. E. 1991. *Legatus. Beiträge zur römischen Verwaltungsgeschichte*. Stockholm.

Toynbee, J. M. C. 1971. *Death and Burial in the Roman World*. London.

Treggiari, S. 1969. *Roman Freedmen during the Late Republic*. Oxford.

—— 1999. 'The Upper-Class House as Symbol and Focus of Emotion in Cicero', *Journal of Roman Archaeology*, 12: 33–56.

—— 2007. *Terentia, Tullia and Publilia: The Women of Cicero's Family*. London and New York.

Untermann, J. 2000. *Wörterbuch des Oskisch-Umbrischen*. Heidelberg.

van der Blom, H. 2010. *Cicero's Role Models*. Oxford.

van Dommelen, P. 1998. 'Punic Persistence: Colonialism and Cultural Identities in Roman Sardinia', in R. Laurence and J. Berry (eds.), *Cultural Identity in the Roman Empire*. London and New York, 25–48.

Vasaly, A. 1993. *Representations: Images of the World in Ciceronian Oratory*. Berkeley-Los Angeles and Oxford.

Ventura, A., and L. Moretti, 1966. *Dizionario biografico degli italiani*, viii, s.v. Bembo, Giovanni. Rome.

Venturini, C. 1979. *Studi sul 'crimen repetundarum' nell' età repubblicana*. Milan.

Versnel, H. S. 1970. *Triumphus: An Inquiry into the Origin, Development and Meaning of the Roman Triumph*. Leiden.

Walbank, F. W. 1957–79. *A Historical Commentary on Polybius*. 3 vols. Oxford.

Walser, G. 1956. *Caesar und die Germanen: Studien zur politischen Tendenz römischer Feldzugsberichte*. Historia Einzelschriften, 1. Wiesbaden.

Ward, A. M. 1968. 'Cicero's Support of Pompey in the Trials of M. Fonteius and P. Oppius', *Latomus*, 27: 802–9.

—— 1970. 'Cicero and Pompey in 75 and 70 B.C.', *Latomus*, 29: 58–71.

—— 1977. *Marcus Crassus and the Late Roman Republic*. Columbia, Ohio, and London.

Watts, N. H., ed. and tr. 1931. Cicero, *The Speeches: Pro T. Annio Milone, In L. Calpurnium Pisonem, Pro M. Aemilio Scauro, Pro M. Fonteio, Pro C. Rabirio Postumo, Pro M. Marcello, Pro Q. Ligario, Pro rege Deiotaro*. London and New York.

Weinrib, E. J. 1971. 'The Prosecution of Magistrates-Designate', *Phoenix*, 25: 145–50.

Wiedemann, T. 1981. *Greek and Roman Slavery*. London and New York.

Wildfang, R. L. 2006. *Rome's Vestal Virgins: A Study of Rome's Vestal Priestesses in the Late Republic and Empire*. London and New York.

Williams, C. 2008. 'Friends of the Roman People: Some Remarks on the Language of *Amicitia*', in A. Coskun (ed.), *Freundschaft und Gefolgschaft in den auswärtigen Beziehungen der Römer*. Frankfurt am Main, 29–44.

Williams, G. D. 1995. 'Cleombrotus of Ambracia', *Classical Quarterly*, 89: 154–69.

Williams, J. H. C. 2001. *Beyond the Rubicon: Romans and Gauls in Republican Italy*. Oxford.

Wills, J. 1996. *Repetition in Latin Poetry: Figures of Allusion*. Oxford.

Winkler, L. 1995. *Salus vom Staatskult zur politischen Idee*. Heidelberg.

Winterbottom, M. 2004. 'Perorations' in J. G. F. Powell and J. Paterson (eds.), *Cicero the Advocate*. Oxford, 215–30.

Wirszubski, C. (1961). '*Audaces*: A Study in Political Phraseology', *Journal of Roman Studies*, 51: 12–22.

Wiseman, T. P. 1964. 'Some Republican Senators and their Tribes', *Classical Quarterly* 58: 122–33.

—— 1970. 'Roman Republican Road-Building', *Papers of the British School at Rome*, 38: 122–52.

—— 1971. *New Men in the Roman Senate 139 BC–AD 14*. Oxford.

—— 1987. *Roman Studies, Literary and Historical*. Liverpool.

Wissowa, G. 1912. *Religion und Kultus der Römer*. 2nd edn. Munich.

Woolf, G. 1998. *Becoming Roman: The Origins of Provincial Civilization in Gaul*. Cambridge.

Yavetz, Z. 1970. 'Fluctuations monétaires et condition de la plèbe à la fin de la république', in *Recherches sur les structures sociales dans l'antiquité classique*. Paris, 133–57.

Zetzel, J. E. G., tr. 2009. Marcus Tullius Cicero, *Ten Speeches*. Indianopolis and Cambridge.

Index[1]

[1] Homonyms are distinguished by the highest datable office held, family relation, or number of entry in the *RE*.